Life in a Blue Suit

A Sailor's Tales of Grit, Humor,
Loyalty, and Leadership
in the Royal Navy

Life in a Blue Suit

A Sailor's Tales of Grit, Humor,
Loyalty, and Leadership
in the Royal Navy

Barry "Jack" Frost

Thank you for an amazing journey Jon. Your leadership and grace helped me tremendously

Barry "Jack" Frost

Bell Bottom
Press

ISBN 978-0-578-68362-1

Bell Bottom Press
Loveland, Colorado

Cover design by Robin Locke Monda

DEDICATION

I would like to dedicate this book to two naval personnel who were instrumental in launching my career and making it possible for me to succeed. There were many other significant senior rates and officers, but these two stand out:

- Peter "Cactus" Plant was a leading hand on HMS Bulwark who mentored, tutored, and befriended me. His encouragement and strength kept my nose clean and my hopes high, for which I am eternally grateful.

- Bernie Kossar, whose last name I may remember incorrectly, was my chief on a guided weapons system on HMS Blake. He pushed me to take an exam two years earlier than expected. Without his enthusiasm, cajoling, and tutoring, I would not have been promoted so quickly. Again, I am eternally grateful for his efforts.

ACKNOWLEDGMENTS

I would like to thank the following:

- My editor, Cheryl Miller Thurston, who went beyond the fringes to dig in the weeds and ground clutter to make this book presentable for publishing. As a first time author, I probably made the task more difficult than is usual. Cheryl's work and intuition have been exemplary.

- Mark Wayne McGinnis, author, for his insights and honest comments, along with his wisdom and kindness.

- Jayme Parker for his patient computer tutoring and Photoshop help.

- David Page for permission to use the "Ganges Mast" photo from his website (www.navyphotos.co.uk) and Terry "Stacks" Heaps, who shot the original photo of the "Ganges Mast."

- My wife Laraine who has given me unparalleled support throughout this process and encouraged me every step of the way.

INTRODUCTION

Life in a Blue Suit is not intended to be a story about the Royal Navy. It is about my own personal journey through the Royal Navy.

While most names in the book are fictitious, they do portray actual people, most of whom will know who they are if they read this book. Two names, however, are real. Peter "Cactus" Plant had such a significant impact on my life, and I will be eternally grateful for his guidance in my early days as a *sprog* on my first ship. I'm also grateful to my chief, Bernie, who coached me for the *leading hand* exam. Without passing that test, my promotions would have been much slower and my whole life changed.

Military life can be crude and nasty in some respects, and I have endeavored to skirt around that aspect of my journey. But while there are difficulties, Navy life can also be challenging, joyous, and even a lot of fun. For every story and event I have written about, there are, oh, so many untold!

Sit back, relax, and enjoy an escape into the world of "Jack Frost."

THE FIRST STEP

On careers day in my final year of high school, the district careers officer and my headmaster sat across from me, intimidating me with their stern faces and slick city suits. I felt the warm trickle of sweat beads running inside my now damp shirt, and the old brown desk didn't seem like a big enough buffer for my protection. The headmaster, a bomber pilot in World War II, was as tough as frozen leather. "You've only put down two choices for occupation, boy," he boomed. He demanded a third choice as strands of my hair, the ones not bristling on the back of my neck, settled back down on my head.

To my surprise, "Royal Navy," gushed from my lips. Where those words came from, I have no idea.

The headmaster filled in the slot, and the career man took over, trying to narrow down my strengths and weaknesses. Twenty minutes later, with a dry throat and wet armpits, I quickly left the office to safety and freedom.

The library was my next stop. I grabbed multiple career books, but for some reason I concentrated on only the ones about the Royal Navy. Why this sudden interest in the Navy? I didn't know, but I just couldn't stop gobbling up information on the topic.

I had not mentioned my new interest at home yet, but at dinner one evening, I revealed my intention to join the Royal Navy. After oxygen-clearing gasps from Mum and Dad, the instant response of, "No, you're not!" came across the table." The ensuing back and forth ended with the first walk away from the *table* that I had ever done. I yelled the classic, "It's my life!" as I stormed off to my bedroom.

Minutes went by before dad came up the stairs and asked me to return to the table and talk. I agreed, but things were frosty, to say the least. Dad, an ex-serviceman who fought in WWII, started revealing all the pitfalls of military life. I didn't care; we were not at war now. Dad then asked which branch I was considering, and I said, "Chef."

"You mean cook," he said. Despite more arguing, I did see his side of the argument. The Navy brochure showed all these fancy banquets and a lavishly laid-out table with a pig's head on a plate with an apple in its mouth, glistening garnish, and so on. "Do you realize who peels the vegetables and washes the cooking dishes and scrubs the floors or decks?" Dad asked. He suggested the mechanical engineering or electrical branches as more advantageous for a future career.

I remembered his advice later when the recruiting office tests opened the way for me to choose any branch I wanted. I checked the slot for electrician.

"Okay, lad," said the recruiter. "Here are your directions and times for your physical in Portsmouth."

"Portsmouth?" I said. "But that's sixty miles away."

"You'll be going further than that after you join, son," was his reply.

Later, during the physical, there was blood pulling, muscle testing, and eyesight and hearing tests, all of which seemed normal. But then things got more personal. They wanted me in a room just wearing my underpants. After a short period of what could be construed as molestation, one of the two examiners said, "Okay, take off your knicks and march up and down the room." Thinking back, I wonder if they were just making fun of me or testing how malleable I would be to taking orders without question. Either way, in this day and age they would probably be locked up. However, I did as they asked as they watched, looking at my butt cheeks and a toggle and two.

Two weeks later I received a letter of acceptance into Her Majesty's Navy.

A NEW LIFE

September 6, 1965, was my own personal "D Day." Standing in the hallway by the front door next to a small brown suitcase Dad was issued when discharged from the army after WWII, heart racing just a tad, my head was totally devoid of thought. My mother was very quiet and, I'm sure, had a tear in her eye. Dad? I will never know what he was thinking. He had been in my situation himself as a young man leaving to go to war. I wasn't going to war but leaving home, at age 16, to join the Royal Navy. I didn't know it at the time, but at 5'3" and weighing 103 pounds soaking wet, nobody gave me a chance of being successful. They thought I would be home before the end of basic training.

Dad and I arrived at the train station with an eternity to wait—or at least that's what it felt like. I had a one-way ticket from my home town of Lewes to Plymouth, my first stop on the way to what? I had no idea.

We waited on the platform, both of us looking down the empty track, in silence. Soon enough, I could feel the ground rumble, hear the squealing on the bend of the rails, and then the chugging of the engine. There it was, smoke belching from its stack, brakes screeching. The train hissed to a stop. Dad walked me to the door and opened it. We didn't hug or shake hands. That wasn't the way we were in those days. He said, "Good luck, son," and turned away. I found out years later that he was in tears at seeing me go and didn't want me to know. I leaned out of the window and waved at the disappearing form of Dad.

London greeted me briefly as we bullied our way into Victoria station. It wasn't long before I had transitioned across the underground to Paddington Station and boarded the train to the land of Sir Francis Drake, Plymouth. It was a long 200 miles for me to wonder what the next chapter of my life would furnish. I had no idea of what to expect in the following weeks, let alone the years after that. Nine years was the minimum time to sign up for from the age of eighteen. I was just sixteen, which meant roughly eleven years of service.

The final screeching of complaining brakes told me we had arrived in the Plymouth railway station. Now what? Where should I go? How would I know who to meet and what do I do?

"Over 'ere son, what's yer name?" I heard.

"Frost, but how did you know I was for the Navy?"

The petty officer or chief or whatever he was rolled his eyes and smiled. "Maybe the really short haircut and the small suitcase and scared innocent look gave it away. On the bus then, Popeye," he said. So up the steps I trotted to a dozen pairs of eyes staring at me with equal fear in them.

Other people from various trains slowly joined us, all looking about the same. A short while later the engine burst into life, the doors closed and we were captured with nowhere to go but where we were told—a situation we were soon to be very familiar with. We trundled down the road as some of the older lads started singing songs I had never heard with words I was not used to hearing. I chatted with my seat companion, who seemed to be about the same age as me. We were, it was established, in the same boat. "Punny" how that worked out.

I was sure we were on our way to HMS Raleigh, but the bus pulled into a place posted HMS Fisguard. The doors slid open and the driver said, "Raleigh stay on the bus. Fisguard get off here."

I yelled out, "Raleigh didn't make it today," and everybody burst out laughing, some, maybe, because it relieved the tension and some because they thought it funny. The chief may not have, as he told me to sit my wise butt down and cool it. That was my first of many wise cracks that continually peppered my naval career from that point on.

Fifteen minutes later we rolled into my new home for the next six weeks, HMS Raleigh. The concertina doors mashed to one side, and we all stepped out into a new world. We were told to "form three lines, one behind the other, twice." What the heck did that mean? After shuffling around forever, the petty officer got us sorted out, and we were told to quick march. That was a joke. Everybody's idea of quick was different, and despite the shouting of, "Left, right, left, right, left, right," we also had different ideas on that message. When we ended up outside a wooden hut, I said, "Maybe this is where they keep the gardening tools." Laughter ensued, and the PO yelled, "Keep silence!"

"Oops, better engage brain and shut mouth," I thought.

These were to be our living quarters for the next six days. It was where we would lose our civilian clothes into that suitcase we were told to bring, forever. Picking a bed and a locker was relatively easy as everybody rushed in to claim their lot. I was slower and chose one of the three left.

"Everybody follow me," was the next order from the man we were to call "Sir," even though he had not been knighted. Oh, well. Off we trotted to a room further up the passageway that was common to several huts that we were now to call *messes* or *mess decks*. There were several tables with piles of uniforms on them, all with a name in front of them. I quickly found mine and stood in front of my new wardrobe.

An ink pad and name stamp soon went into action after we were told, piece by piece, where to mark each item, even the pairs of hippo underwear that a granddad might wear. There were also strips of white, one-inch-wide cloth to be stamped. They were our name badges that we had to sew on our shirts. The name of the establishment was on a black ribbon in gold lace and was to be placed around the rim of the hat. Now this was a challenge as it was to be tied tightly in a very precise manner with fluffed out wings. These were done over and over again later that day. The whole process took forever and as each item was dealt with, it was placed into a kit bag that was at least four feet tall. It required superman strength to hoist it upon my shoulder and carry it to my bed space. Some of the older lads laughed at us puny ones and took off like mountain men on a hike.

Now was the time to remove our civilian clothes and get into our work clothes, which were comprised of the granddad underwear, a light blue shirt, dark navy blue trousers, navy blue woolen socks, and black leather shoes. At first, standing naked in front of all those people seemed a little weird, to say the least. But that was an experience I got used to in time.

Was I a sailor yet? That was a big "No."

Learning more basics. We were led by PO Jarvis, commonly known as "Sir," to the dining hall, also known as the mess. One couldn't sleep there, so that was confusing. It was very echoic with hundreds of people clashing metal plates with metal knife, fork and spoon. Everybody spoke at once, ever escalating to be heard over everybody else. There was a line that was like Space Mountain at Disney World. It quickly moved along, though, as food was splashed into our trays from real sailors serving the food. Our class sat more or less together, each person watching for when the others finished so we could all be lost together, not knowing what to do next. We thought it was fortunate that the PO showed up to take us to the mess deck again but, of course, it was no accident.

There was a lot of talking that night among the older lads, but us youngsters just wanted to sleep. That didn't happen as it should have for us. Suddenly there was banging and yelling for us to get up. I wondered why we were getting up thirty minutes after finally going to sleep. Turns out it was seven o'clock and we were rolling again.

PO Jarvis was cajoling us to pick up the pace, get washed and dressed, and form up "one behind the other twice," or three deep, which we now understood, and marched us to breakfast. I say "marched," but that was, at this point, a misnomer.

I have to say they fed us well. It was noisy and chaotic to us, but there was plenty to fill our teenage hunger pangs.

We went back to the mess deck and were off to the barber shop. I wasn't sure why because I had got my hair cut just three days before. Anyway, we all lined up and were shorn. The Navy doesn't buzz cut you, so we all looked decent at least.

Next stop was the sick bay. Nobody was sick, so we assumed it was inoculation time. We became pin cushions in a matter of minutes, or so it seemed. No disease in the world was going to get us now. Maybe we would die from all the holes in our arm, or maybe all the drugs, but not any disease.

We were allowed the rest of the morning off. By now I had befriended a couple of boys my own age who I felt were as scared as me, so we could sink or swim together. The older ones had done the same, so there were little cliques of companions in the twenty-six member class. One of my friends lived in a suburb of Plymouth and one was of Pakistani descent. I had found a comfort level and now felt I was on the trip of a lifetime–still scared but maybe more excited.

Afternoon activities started at 1300 hours. I didn't know there were that many hours in a day. At this juncture in my naval history, it was still one o'clock. We were marched to the parade ground where the gunnery instructors, commonly known as GIs, were waiting for us. After being handed over to these scary monsters, our nursemaid left us to their mercy, although as we soon realized, no mercy was ever shown. The GIs were of the seaman branch, which was far more disciplined than other branches of the service, especially the electrical and engineering departments, as I later found out. They screamed out instructions for how to do all the necessary movements in order to march with some decorum. They reminded me of the brakes on the steam trains that brought me to my future. After striking the fear of God into us young ones, we saw, with some relief in sight, our savior, PO Jarvis. Surely this must mean the end of our marching session on the parade ground.

It was. We were marched back to a classroom, where we learned about various aspects of our first week. The rest of the day was spent on finishing off the chore of fitting our kit into the small locker by our bed. A shoe horn would have been helpful, but that was not furnished. The older men with some life experience enjoyed proving how worldly they all were with tales of drinking and sexual exploits. Each man tried to tell a better story than the other. This I later found out was called *blackcatting*. That got too boring after the initial few stories. A few of us got together and told of who we were and where we came from.

The rest of our first week was spent with PO Jarvis preening and chipping the barnacles of youthful civilian life off of us to prep us for the real world of the next five weeks of boot camp. He was firm but kind and didn't want us to get scared and run before we officially signed on the dotted line for, in my case, eleven years of service in the Royal Navy.

Was I a real sailor now? No.

Getting paid. The day of reckoning was on day four. We all got in line alphabetically to take a deep breath and put pen to paper for that moment in time that stood still until you signed your name. Okay, that was it then. I did it.

We were given this booklet that was our pay book. It had all of our info in it as to our tax number and all that kind of thing. It also had a slot, which we signed or not, to say whether we smoked or not. I was going to say "no" when "Sir" stepped up, knowing I didn't smoke. He told me to say "yes" in a way that I really had no choice. As fragile as I still was to my new situation, I said "yes." He explained that all smokers were given three stamps a month, just like postage stamps, that would allow me to buy one hundred cigarettes per stamp, duty free. That was about two shillings and six pence per hundred. This made them very cheap by any standard. They were made for the Navy and had a blue line down them on the white paper. It was also explained how it was illegal to give them to anybody else. "However," the PO said, "Nobody will ever know, and they are a useful bargaining chip." I felt like a crook and was worried for a long time about this lie. I don't think I'd ever lied before.

After basic electrical training and on board my first ship, I just gave the stamps away to friends and people who deserved them in any given month. This was common among any decent shipmates, though not all. There were always the few who would want something in return, maybe somebody's tot of rum for example. This continued throughout my naval career.

Soon it was promotion day as far as we were concerned. We got to move to our new digs in the main part of the camp. We thought we weren't new entries anymore. It's funny how the mind works. As we were marched to our new mess deck, the other classes before us were outside their huts jeering and catcalling and pointing in ridicule like they were real sailors now that they had a week or two under their belt.

WHAT'S IT ALL ABOUT?

Our next petty officer was waiting for us, and we were handed over rather like a package from the post office. Petty Officer Davis was his name, which still didn't really matter because his actual name, to us, was Sir. Strange how both POs had the same first name. He barked out our next move, which was to unpack our kit into our new lockers, and he would inspect each one to see how neat and tidy it was. There was a time limit placed on the procedure, which we thought was tight but, of course, nobody complained. We scurried into the building, claimed a space and started unpacking. After the inspection, which we all failed, probably no matter how well anybody did, we were shown again the washroom for clothes and toilets and showers. There was also a drying room. This was comprised of an enclosed room with hot water pipes all around and lots of wooden slatted shelves where you draped your clothes to dry after washing them. We were told the rest of the day was free and to make sure we got a good-night's sleep because tomorrow was going to be busy.

Once again the objective of a good sleep was not met. We young pups needed rest, but it seems the older ones did not. We were also raided by the senior class members, who were heading out to their various departmental training the next morning.

This mess had double stacked bunks; I was on a top bunk, which I liked for some reason, maybe because it was different. The first morning, though, it would have done me a great service to have remembered this fact. There was a large metal trash can, polished, in the mess at one end which was crashed and banged savagely by our new Sir at seven in the morning. I leaped out of bed and unceremoniously landed hard on the floor in a big snotty mess; this, naturally, to the extreme delight of all. The instructions, which I thought at first were coming from a nearby foghorn, were to get washed and dressed and down to breakfast. Anybody who thought they would skip breakfast was told, "Think again. You are going to need it."

I was thinking, "Oh boy, sounds like a busy morning." Once again this new phrase, which became commonplace, came into play: "Be ready to fall in one behind the other twice outside at 0800 or four bells. Do *not* (a louder emphasis on the word not) be late." It sounded like a definite hint that death could be imminent if this order was not carried out. We all made it, thus saving some lives, I'm sure.

We were marched down the fairly steep hill to the dreaded parade ground. This was to be the scourge of our next few weeks, for sure. The rest of the trainees were there in their classes, all aligned along the edge of the parade ground, which had lots of white dots on it. Each class, at the given signal of a bugle, was to double out to a predetermined dot for their class. Our PO guided us through this procedure and came out with us to our spot, as did all the other class POs. The camp commander addressed us from a podium. Then a chaplain read a quote from the bible, said a prayer and stepped aside. A royal marine band blasted into action, and we were to march past the podium with an "eyes right" to look at the commander and then go off to a classroom.

The other classes looked pretty good marching. They were in step and in a nice straight line as they passed by the commander. By comparison, we must have looked like a frenzied lynch mob walking to take on the town sheriff. They let this slide for a couple of days until we had received some more parade ground training. We knew this free passage had ended when the PO was given a slip of paper by a runner from the podium, hereby known as the dais, to turn left instead of right to march off the parade ground. We were to march past the dais again because we were not good enough to satisfy the commander. If that wasn't good enough, it would be extra drill training in the evening. Trust me; that would not be friendly.

Lots of learning. Over the next few days Sir taught us how to wash our clothes by hand. This involved, preferably, standing naked in front of a large porcelain sink and scrubbing your clothes, with your knuckles, in soapy water. He explained that the more bashful of us could place a towel around our waist. Once again, the more manly lads were naked right away. I ended up not so shy after a couple of days with a too wet towel after washing.

Clothing became the most consuming part of our free time. Items were required to be more and more perfect as time marched on. We were taught how to iron and fold each item exactly how they wanted it for inspection. At the end of this second week, there was what they called a kit muster. This consisted of laying out your clothing in a very particular order on your bed. The items were to be ironed and folded exactly as taught during the week. They were then inspected harshly by God, I mean PO Davis. These kit musters were an end-of-the-week thing every week. They gradually got harder and harder at each session, and were being inspected by a higher and higher rank each time.

A lot more other training was also the order of the day during that week. Parade ground drilling by the ogres was the worst. Learning how to tie twelve knots was okay because I already knew some of them from my scouting days that seemed an eternity away but were actually just a few weeks earlier. We learned the names of parts of a ship and how the compartments were identified. This was especially needed on larger ships, as I later found out.

Another beating of the ever-present trash can one particular morning was a little different. PO Davis had a rolled up
towel under his arm. After breakfast, he boomed with a smile,
"We are going to the pool for your swimming test." Although I
could swim, I wasn't that good. "What do they mean by test?"
I wondered.

As we stood by the pool in silence, I almost jumped in the
water when a high-pitched whistle screeched across the rafters
and echoed for a good minute or so. The physical trainer had
arrived to torment the class. His strutting gait and bulging biceps
encouraged my throat into a hard swallow. He explained what
we needed to do to pass the test: swim two lengths of the pool
and float for five minutes at the deep end. This would be followed by leaping off the diving slab, which was fifteen feet high.
Did I mention we were wearing one-piece, full-length boiler
suits? Along with several others, I failed the test. We were told
we would be tested at our next training establishment or while
on our first ship.

The parade ground antics got worse, even though I thought
they couldn't. We were now given rifles to nest on our shoulders
while marching. At least it could be called marching to most
novice onlookers. The rifle sort of bounced as I strode along,
the stock banging on my collar bone. At the end of a session,
the bone was very sore. I took to putting some padding under
my shirt, but that eventually would either make no difference
or slip down. When we were not performing to the level the
drill instructors wanted or we made a mistake, we were encouraged to double around the parade ground until the baying grizzly
bear felt satiated. This doubling around hurt my collar bone even
more and even drew blood. I was not alone in this matter, but I
am sure the instructors knew this. That's why they did it.

On the last night of that second week, some older chaps
burst into our mess deck. They were wearing white gaiters and

belts and were very official looking. They ordered us to form up outside, and when we had done that told us to double round the block. We did this, but when we returned to the same spot we became the laughing stock of the whole division as they were just the honor guard of the next outgoing class. Oh well, they all had a good time at our expense. This tradition went on every week with the new class, so we got our turn to laugh every week thenceforth.

The following weekend one of my friends who lived somewhat locally asked if I wanted to go home with him as were granted time to be able to leave the camp. This involved getting dressed up in our number one uniform and getting inspected at the main gate. This we did, and off we went. John's parents were wonderful. They didn't know we were coming and greeted us, especially John, with great gusto. They were pleased he had found a special pal. They were of humble means and lived in a mobile home. I had never seen or even known of such things from my personal background, so I learned how lucky I was right off the bat. They fed us well and we had plenty of stories to tell.

After our visit, we were inspected again on the way back into the camp. We were back into the business of becoming sailors.

Apart from the daily parade and march-past, there was the passing out parade every Sunday for the classes moving on to the next stage of their career training. This is where the best class of that group was the honor guard and wore the white webbing. The other classes wore green webbing and looked more ordinary. It was something to aim for, I suppose.

Tear gas and damage control. Life rolled on with more learning about ships and the Navy. One day we marched to a brick building with our gas masks. I was thinking maybe we hadn't done well enough and were too bad to put back into society.

Thankfully, it was a test of our masks, and they wanted us to get a whiff of tear gas so we knew what it was like. We all filed in with our masks on, and PO Davis cracked open a gas grenade. One by one, we had to take off our mask and say our full name, rank and service number before exiting the brick room. We then ran around outside to help shake off the gas clinging to our clothes. This didn't, however, stop us from coughing and spluttering and choking with tears streaming down our faces. So that's why it's called tear gas.

The next day we were to learn about damage control onboard a ship. They had a mock section of a ship with pipes and all kinds of duct work and motors. After much instruction and film watching on how to do this, we quickly learned we had better have being paying attention. In groups of five at a time, we were locked into this air and watertight room with the material needed to repair holes and leaks. Then it started. First water started pouring in through a broken pipe. Then another hole spurted water, then another. The water was soon up to our ankles and more was coming in. We blocked two leaks, and then they opened up a big hole for gobs of water to cascade in all of a sudden. With water now at our thighs and rising fast, we started to get worried, as the instructors had told us the door would not be opened; it would be up to us to stop the flow.

We got some sheets and blankets and some wood and jammed the biggest hole with these, a board and a two-by- four stick of wood. We slowed the water, but the room was still filling up faster than we wanted. Seven different leaks were now still filling the quickly disappearing air gap between our heads and the deck head commonly known before as the ceiling.

Was I a sailor yet? No.

As we finally went under water, with our last breath the water stopped pouring in and huge pumps made quick work of sucking out the liquid that was about to take our lives. The door swung open, and our instructors laid into us for doing so poorly. I still believe the instructors had this situation for every class and picked people who they thought could handle it to go first. We were the first group in, so I, unfortunately, happened to be one of the chosen few. We went back to the classroom where everybody paid much more attention. Later we all, in groups of five, had to go through the room of hell again. This time things went much more smoothly, although there was still plenty of room for improvement.

Payday—oh, yes, we did get paid for doing this—came along. This is when I started to get the idea that nothing was simple in the Navy. There was a desk on the roadway with an orderly and two officers standing by it. We were to line up in alphabetical order, exactly. As we slowly stepped forward and our name was called we were to step up to the desk, smartly salute, and shout out our rank and last name, followed by our service number. Oh god, what was my number again? At the same time, we were to hold out that pay book, with the cigarette signature page open in the left hand. The right hand was busy saluting. The thumb needed to be on the top with the rest of the hand underneath. Did I mention the wind was blowing? The two weeks of pay were thrust under my thumb, the amount read out by said orderly, a sharp right turn and off I marched. If this wasn't done to the satisfaction of the officer, the money wasn't given and you had to go around again after placing yourself at the end of the line. This, I was soon to learn, was carried out in the open, come rain, hail or shine.

Payday was every two weeks, and I received exactly five pounds. That was only two pounds and ten shillings per week, but back then that was more than ample to do what I needed. This included buying boot polish and other required items to keep up my kit and myself, hygiene-wise.

The assault course. Now a few weeks in, we were all experienced and familiar with the routine. We were next corralled down at the assault course. We were walked around the course and taught about all the obstacles and how to handle and process them. We could earn points and lose points depending on how well we tackled each project. I knew I would do well, mainly because of my fitness and scouting.

I was really tackling all the units with great strength and gusto and going for the record. That's when it all unraveled. My last obstacle was to cross a ravine on a rope pulled taught between the banks. "No problem," I thought. That was until the strap on my rifle, slung diagonally over my shoulder, broke and fell into the muddy water fifteen feet below. I hung there for a couple of seconds not knowing what to do. My hesitancy didn't last long before plunging into the abyss shortly after hearing, "What are you waiting for, boy? Get in after it. Go! Go! Go!" There were actually a lot more words involved, which I assumed came from a special Navy swear word dictionary. He must have used up most of the words in the book. They came flooding out of his cavernous, echo sounding chamber that reverberated, I am sure, across the English Channel. I believe it was the shock waves that made me let go of the rope and splatter myself into the mire. After fumbling around for what seemed an eternity, I located my fire arm in the now swirling mud-activated water and clambered up the steep, slippery bank to the finish line. My record-breaking attempt was vanquished and dissolved into thin air. PO Davis was really pleased, though, and congratulated me on a good effort. That was a first for me in getting personal recognition. It felt good, oh, so good.

Getting into mischief. Life in boot camp soldiered on, or should I say *sailored* on, with a few close calls on getting beaten up by the big boys. One time the loudest mouth came back to the mess having had one too many beers, and I was a little too cheeky making fun of him. He chased me around and around and would have half killed me had he caught me. Thank goodness for my agility and swiftness. He was mad and half crazed. The other bigger guys grabbed him and calmed him down as he promised me that he would kill me next time. Next time was good, so long as it wasn't this time.

My best buddy got into some trouble with the lads in the class. They felt he had let them down at various tasks and was bringing down the class, giving us less chance to get honor guard. For this, they decide to give him the kit bag treatment. The building consisted of a long passageway with three steps at intervals where a mess deck went off at right angles. There were eight mess decks, each with a different class in them. The steps were there because we were on a hill. They took him to the top end, stripped him naked, put the clothing in the kit bag, and used boot polish to *blackball* him. The bag was tied up, and he was dragged all the way to the bottom at speed. I can hear him crying out for mercy to this day, fifty three years later. This was a common practice in classes throughout our stay. I helped a couple of other more compassionate classmates get him out, and we consoled him the best we could. I felt terrible; he was my friend.

Because this was a really old Navy establishment, there were many ghost stories bandied about. Now at this time in my life, I was still very wary of these phenomena and would scare easily. One night, after a few ghost stories, I was a little frazzled. Eventually we turned in and the lights went out. Of course the loud mouths started whispering about hearing something in the connecting passageway, and then the door to said passageway slowly crept open. The door creaked badly anyway, so the sound was eerie. Then somebody said, "I see it, I see it!" My brain was in overdrive, and I was worried.

Then in the middle of the night, it happened again. I needed to use the bathroom up the hallway but was so scared I was putting it off. Finally, I had to break down and make a run for it. As I quickly turned back into my mess deck in the dark, I ran into a huge body and yelled out in horror. The lights went on and I was the laughingstock of everybody. Somebody had tied a string to the door from both sides, and two of the lads were able to swing the door to and fro. While I was gone, one of the biggest lads stood just inside the door for me to run into him. Very funny, ha, ha. I had to take it in stride, or I would have been toast for the remainder of training. I was thankful I had already used the bathroom.

Learning, painfully, to row. At 0700 hours, we all did the morning routine before being, by now properly, marched down to the pier. Here we donned life jackets and were divided into two groups and placed in two huge row boats called *three-in-one whalers*. They had a motor to propel them along or could be sailed or rowed. "Oh, good," I thought to myself. "This'll be a doddle, a ride out on the river." For a moment there I thought I was in Hyde Park on the Serpentine on a Sunday afternoon. Afternoon tea and crumpets anyone?

That lasted long enough for me to only say, "Oh." At this point the sailor in charge of our boat told us to pick up the oars and hold them upright. That was easier said than done. With two of us to each oar, the pairs of us struggled like crazy to hoist these redwood tree trunks into the air, and our fun day on the river was falling away quickly. After the seasoned sailor pulled away from the jetty, he cut the engine and told us to lower the forest of pine. Lowering was not on our agenda. The oars crashed into the water like a belly flopping whale. After being chastised for being weak and wimpy, we had to get the oars back in the rowlocks. The minutes that followed, which seemed like an hour, were chaos as we tried to coordinate ourselves. Eventually things got better, and the Viking galleon eased forward, albeit at a slow pace. After a while the fun began to fade again as our arms felt like cooked spaghetti. The oars were now hitting the water more from us dropping them than anything else.

Then, as we approached the jetty, the coxswain barked out the dreaded order, "Oars." This meant for us to lift them perpendicular again. We could barely do this when we started; now we were to do it with limp noodles for arms? My muscles screamed for help as my heart pounded the inside of my chest, willing the rest of my body to join in. Every muscle, sinew, ligament and tendon strived to achieve this aim and, by the smallest of margins, prevailed. "Thank god for that," I thought until I realized we now had to lower the oars inside the boat. The word "lower" in this case wasn't really in play. Most of us managed to restrict the oars only enough to stop them from going through the bottom of the whaler. Despite all this, we did enjoy the morning because it got us out of the classroom—a break that was always welcome. Dinner was a two plater, and I got the best night's sleep I'd had since arriving at the stalag.

Tests and more tests. Our last week of boot camp was upon us. We were the cock-of-the-hoop and knew it. We put the new class through its rite of passage. We marched like champions and had plenty of swagger. We knew the routine and nothing really bothered us. Wow! What had they done to us? After five weeks of training, they had given us strength of mind, confidence, and forthrightness. I did feel nervous about all the final written tests we were about to take, but the top of the list was the final kit muster. This was to be inspected by the camp commander, and commanders were, by all accounts, notoriously difficult.

The written tests were all taken and passed, and we had just the kit muster and passing out parade to go. I thought I should be good with the kit because many of my peers came to me for help with theirs. Mine had always been one of the better ones throughout the weeks before.

The whole class had their kits laid out, the final tweaking complete. The commander walked toward my sweating body. Springing to attention, I sputtered out my name and rank while crisply snapping off my best salute. He stared for a while at my layout and then moved in for the kill. He started pulling various items apart and poking items I had carefully prepared. By the time he had finished, my kit muster looked like a ploughed field. "Re-scrub," he said.

My heart sank. I was one of the best in the room. Didn't he like my face? Why was he was so cruel to me? Everybody was shocked, including PO Davis, who gave me a glance and a shrug that said it all. I was almost in tears. The lads after me were all worried about themselves now. They were not as good as me. However, they all passed. A re-scrub was not a fail. That would have meant being back-classed one week. I would have to do it all again, along with four other unfortunates. Nobody could believe it, but nothing could be done.

What happened next was a wonderful lesson in teamwork. Just about everybody put themselves out to help to make sure all five of us got everything perfect for the next inspection. To our surprise, the re-inspection was carried out by our divisional officer. He was a good person who, on thinking back, knew of our injustice. He gave what I thought was a cursory inspection and passed us all. What a relief.

The passing out parade was a non-event for me. Mum and Dad couldn't come all that way. It was a two day trip by car and a difficult journey to boot. John's parents came and included me in their joy for the both of us.

The rest of the day was spent getting all packed up for Monday, the day we would leave. I had collected several good friends over our six week stint, but most of them were now going on to other establishments and I might never see them again. Some, though, were going to be electricians like myself, so at least I wouldn't be alone in my new digs. What surprised me a little was that PO Davis seemed to be a little sad. I realized that he must go through this with every class, though I'd learn later that wasn't quite the case. We were loaded onto buses and roared out of HMS Raleigh to raucous cheers and great frivolity.

Was I a sailor yet? No!

The railway station slid under our feet, and I was off to another chapter on my way through life.

ELECTRICITY FOR DUMMIES

The clickety-clacking of carriage wheels on the tracks soon became very muffled and disappeared into the ether. As we sped through the countryside, my eyelids became like closed drapes to the world. My three pieces of luggage were somewhere on the train in a cargo storage carriage. There was my bone-crushing kit bag, my new green suitcase issued by the Navy, and my dad's weary suitcase that had my civilian clothes inside. Juggling those through Plymouth railway station and onto the train was no easy task.

Fortunately we had a direct train to Portsmouth, so we didn't have to lug our gear from platform to platform. That was a relief. When the engine hissed into Portsmouth with the obligatory complaining of wheels and brakes a few hours later, we rocked forward as the carriage bumped into the one in front and, crunch, we were there.

To my dismay and all those with me, this was not our final destination. HMS Collingwood, the electrical training school, was actually in Fareham. This was across the other side of the River Solent. A suburb of Portsmouth, it was fifteen miles around the land. We lugged our luggage down a large number of steps under the tracks and back up the other side. An age later, the Fareham train pulled in and off we went again.

This time a couple of Royal Navy senior rates awaited us at the terminal. There, they loaded us onto a military truck or *lorry*, and we entered the gates of our new home.

Was I a sailor yet? No.

Jumping out of the back, we were told to form up in the customary way, one behind the other twice. They did say three deep sometimes; after all that's what they meant. Standing at ease, we were called to attention because the chief of our division was now present. He called out our names, and we answered, "Yes sir." Each time somebody answered in this manner, he became more and more frustrated. "Do not call me sir, I work for a living," he would bark. The first two times we laughed. Then it wasn't so funny anymore. Apparently senior ranks are only called *sir* in boot camp.

He also called us six week wonders. We learned that if you joined before the age of sixteen, a one year training school was in store for you. What the heck would they teach them for a whole year? We found out later in the week.

Living quarters. This was Faraday Division and most of the huts were in this drop off area. However, my hut—or should I say *our* hut—was number thirty-nine. This was across the other side of the parade ground. Now I'm not exaggerating when I say this was a large parade ground. One day, in an emergency, a small aircraft landed on it with room to spare. Needless to say, by the time we got our kit over to hut thirty-nine, our arms and legs were cooked. Where did that truck go anyway?

The row of huts was just like our old one, joined by a long passageway with showers and drying rooms open to all units. There were ten double bunks, sixteen single beds, and a corner area that seemed special. It had a much larger area with carpet and a regular wooden wardrobe, along with the normal locker. I quickly discovered this wasn't reserved for me. This is where the *killick* bedded down. A killick was a rank or *rate*, as we called it, one below petty officer. Officially, the rate was a *leading hand*. He could also be called *hookey* or *hooks* along with the *killick*. He was in charge of this hut, and what he said went.

It wasn't a position any killick wanted, looking after a bunch of low life newbies who knew nothing. Consequently, killicks were always grumpy and mean. Ours seemed to be especially so, but all the huts probably thought that. Several people in this hut were from various classes at different stages of training, so some had an air of superiority and lauded their seniority over us. This changed as we ourselves found our niche in the grand scheme of things.

These particular huts were the oldest in the camp, and it showed. The hut was about two feet off the ground, and you could see a lot of the ground between the cracks. Two panes behind my top bunk were missing. The heating was marginal from the old boiler. The linoleum on the passageway floor to the bathrooms was cracked and torn. The window outside of the passage door was half missing. We were to be the last occupants of these huts. I found out later that the class that came in behind us went into a brand spanking new building that was pristine with four beds to each little area. It had great heating and air conditioning and wonderful bathroom facilities with about sixteen people to each bathroom group. We had about two hundred to ours. Maybe I should have been back-classed at HMS Raleigh.

The dining room was, of course, on the other side of the parade ground. When on the parade ground, all junior rates were to move on the double. This was a little treacherous in the winter, as we soon found out. It was already the middle of October.

Learning routines. We were schooled on our approaching school routine, which was similar to our previous one. Our class would form outside the hut and march to the parade ground edge. At the signal of a bugle, we doubled onto the parade ground to our pre-designated spot. This was done with approximately three thousand other students. There were 4500 being trained at any one time. At least that is what I was told. The petty officers and above could walk to class independently along with specialty training trainees.

After prayers and comments from the commander, we marched in columns to our classroom. This was mainly done as a swift and efficiently organized way of getting everybody to class on time. We were given a map and our class leader got us, eventually, to the right room. Two hours later, we had a fifteen minute break, and then two hours later we marched off to lunch. The afternoon was the same way until we marched back to our own mess deck/hut. During the breaks, food and drink were available to buy from tea shops spread throughout the training area. The Navy Army Air Force Institute (NAFFI) ran these watering holes.

Throughout the next six months we were not allowed to wear civilian clothing, not even to go ashore. It was considered to be going ashore when you left the base, even though we were already on shore. On the second weekend of training, we were told we could go home for the weekend if we put in a request form and were not scheduled for duty watch. I was not scheduled, so I was going home.

My first visit home. As ever, on leaving the camp, we were inspected at the main gate and then let loose on society. Once my ticket to Lewes was bought, I needed to get to Portsmouth before getting the connection to Brighton. Once in Brighton, it was just an eight mile train ride to Lewes. My parents didn't have a phone, so I walked the last couple of miles home. I knocked on the locked front door. Nobody opened it. "That's strange," I thought. I knocked again, but to no avail. It was around eight o'clock in the evening, so I just stood by the front porch and waited. A car from the end of the cul-de-sac went by, and the driver waived excitedly to me. I waved back and smiled. It was dark but the street lighting was enough for our two way recognition.

About ten minutes later, there was a squealing of tires and a growling engine coming round the bend. It was Dad. He jumped out of the car and came rushing up the steps, grabbing me and just about knocking me over. I assumed that he was glad to see me. While asking a zillion questions on the way to the car, he bundled me in and took off. He explained that he and my mother had gone to the local pub for a drink with friends. This was unusual for my mother, as she didn't normally drink alcohol. The neighbor who waved had seen Dad's car in the parking lot of the local and pulled in to tell of my arrival.

Dad was so happy to see me and so proud. He pretty much barged into the pub, dragging me along behind him. Mother was waiting by the door, and she was just as happy. No hugging or holding though; we were British, you know.

"Do you want a Coca-Cola?" Dad asked, since I was only sixteen.

The landlord looked at him and said, "Peter, I think he can have a beer. He's a sailor now." Everybody cheered and laughed.

So, now was I a sailor? Still not, according to my peers, but I was to my locals.

Although, technically, it was against the law, the landlord had no problem serving me up the suds. I didn't have time to answer one question before five more were asked. It was all rather overwhelming, but I sure felt good.

The rest of the weekend was full of tales from my first two months in the "mob," as it was sometimes called. I was somewhat nervous all weekend about making sure I got back to base on time. This spoiled it a bit for me but not for my friends and family. I looked up the train times and made my plans, which I stuck to. My uniform donned, off I went. Man, did I feel special, traveling back in my Navy blues.

Back at work. Back in the saddle at Collingwood, we all were roused Monday morning. "Here we go again, back to school,"

I thought. Because all the material was alien to me, I struggled quite a lot. The exams, which came up about every two weeks, always had me on edge. One could only get back-classed twice, and then it was a choice of civilian life or becoming a seaman branch candidate. No thanks. Even at this early stage of my Navy career, I knew that wasn't for me. Painting, scrubbing decks and general dogsbody work was not my idea of a trade, though some people would like that and that's okay. "Horses for courses," as they say.

Anyway, I did manage to scrape through by the skin of my teeth. John, my boot camp friend, also hopscotched through the course and came out the other end unscathed. The course lasted about six months with a dozen or more exams. They comprised of titles like *AC Theory, DC Theory, Motor Theory, Trouble-Shooting Theory with Math*, and *Electronic Theory* thrown in for good measure.

I haven't yet mentioned that dispersed with the course was the matter of *duty watch*, an ominous task we were assigned every four days. When on duty, one could be assigned chores that were to do with the general running of a camp. One of the main jobs was security patrol. This entailed spending four hours at the guard shack with seasoned Navy personnel. At regular intervals, we were to accompany them on patrol around the instructional area. This area was massive, four thousand plus students learning everything from the mundane to top secret missile systems and beyond. Some buildings, as you can imagine, were highly protected.

Our protective equipment to fend off any espionage efforts from highly trained James Bond types consisted of a flashlight and a short wooden baton. They did not train us on how to deflect a bullet with the baton. That would have, at the very least, been a little helpful. These patrols went on throughout the night. This meant we could get a session from 1600 hours to 0800 hours the following morning. When I got the midnight shift, it was scary. There was sparse lighting in the instruction area that was out-of-bounds to all persons after class was finished. The leading patrolman would send me off around an area on my own to meet him at another point. This was troublesome at times because I didn't know the route and guesswork was involved. I was too nervous to say I didn't understand. These sailors were gruff and tough and impatient with us underlings. Getting back to the guard shack was always a relief. It also brought a snack and a cup of coffee.

Many other jobs were assigned when on duty, which I didn't like either. Cleaning the galley after the dinner session was yucky to say the least. I never did hear any oink, oink sounds but wouldn't have been surprised if I had. Scouting the accommodation area for litter was another activity that was okay for two hours, except in the rain and freezing cold. Sometimes I got to be the office runner for the evening. That was the best; inside in a comfortable chair, answering the phone, sipping coffee and watching television. I could also study my books, which was a great help. The day after duty watch, class would start on time after the daily parade. It, apparently, wasn't obligatory to be conscious or have your eyes open the following day after patrol.

Many evenings were spent either in a recreational area or playing cards. There were many favorite card games, but we never played for money. One night turned a little nasty for me. An older recruit came into the mess deck a little the worse for drink. He got into it with my friend John, and I stepped in to help. At this point, Loudmouth head-butted me viciously and laid me out unconscious. After I regained consciousness but still very out of it, I was uneasy. I was being carried by four of the lads, including my assailant, outside the mess. They were taking me to the sick bay. Blood was running across my face, and I wanted to throw up.

While being attended to, I could see that George, my attacker, was very worried. I knew he didn't mean me that much harm. He was probably standing closer to me than he thought. When I was asked how this happened, I told them I tripped and fell onto a bedpost. This was very plausible, as they were metal. They bought my story, fixed me up, and sent us all on our way. George was telling me how sorry he was all the way back to the mess. He was actually quite a good person, which is why I covered for him. As is often the case in situations like this, George and I became closer friends. It's good to have friends and work as a team. My place in the pecking order was somewhat elevated.

Another highlight in the mess was when Brian came back from weekend leave. It was very late on Sunday night, around 0200 hours. Nevertheless, his whispering to his bunkmate was loud, and eventually a bunch of us were awake. Then all of us were awake. This was because his news was juicy and spicy. His eyes were wide open, and his face really serious. His loud deep voice added to the decibels. When he whispered, it was like a sea lion calling the zookeeper for his food.

Anyway, the news was that he was going to have a shotgun wedding, literally. The father of his girlfriend came round to his house and told him he had a choice. He could either be strangled by said father or marry his daughter. Yep, she was pregnant. Brian was only sixteen and his whole life was changed in a jiff. I'll never forget the look on his face—scared and panicked. As soon as we awoke the next morning that was all we talked about.

Getting my first ship assignment. Gradually our mess deck was filled with fewer people as the lads who came before us were excitedly leaving for their first ship. Everybody wanted to be drafted to a small ship, maybe a mine sweeper or frigate. Even a destroyer wouldn't be too bad. The thought of a cruiser or an aircraft carrier was the worst, though, because it was widely thought that discipline would be much greater on larger ships. This seemed logical to me.

Rumor had it that an aircraft carrier was crewing up. Sure enough, all but a couple of us were summoned by HMS Bulwark, an aircraft carrier that was now a Commando carrier. I later found out that it carried only helicopters, but that made no difference as it was still the size of an aircraft carrier. The excitement of our first draft was squashed, even though it was still really good to be joining the real Navy.

Was I a sailor yet? Not really. But "not really" was an improvement over "no."

A couple of weeks later, we were packing our bags and journeying off to our new adventures. Another piece of luggage was added to our load. Mustering at an unfamiliar building, we all filed inside and stood alongside lengthy trestle-type tables. This reminded me of when we were first given our kit at boot camp. This time, however, there before us was a large metal toolbox full of tools. This was our very own tool kit to be looked after like Fort Knox and locked with the supplied padlock. It was explained that if we lost any tool on board ship we would have to pay to replace it. If we broke one, t it would be replaced for free.

Then we picked up the tool box, which was easier said than done, and struggled back to our mess deck. Thank goodness we didn't have far to march because it weighed a ton. In order to board HMS Bulwark, we would need to travel back to Plymouth. But how were we ever going to lug a suit case, a very heavy kit bag, and a toolbox that weighed a ton across the South coast a couple of hundred miles?

Eventually the day arrived to depart for my first ship. The bus pulled up near our mess deck and after loading our treasures, we all piled on. Nervous excitement abounded. Again I thought, "What am I doing? What have I done? Where am I going?" I still couldn't see the horizon.

It seemed an age went by before great concrete pillars dashed past our window and we trundled through the gates of the dockyard. There, way down the road was the top of the mast of HMS Bulwark. It was peeking over the top of some seemingly tall buildings. There she was, our home in all her glory.

Looking out of the window of the bus, I could see a large expanse of grey metal. A patchwork of grey, with lines of rivets just like a quilt, faced us. We were in shadow, as the sun was blocked by this juggernaut of steel. When I emerged from the bus, the enormity of the situation really hit me. I was a 108 pound, 5'3" inch man/boy, standing next to a twenty-seven thousand ton statue. Now I knew what it was to be an ant in New York City or London.

We unloaded our wares onto the jetty, and the transport sped off. There was shouting, banging, hissing, scraping, the sloshing of waves, and general, unrelenting noise. We were, for sure, in absolute awe of the situation. Again I thought, "Where am I? What have I done? Where am I going?" The excitement, adrenaline rush, and anticipation of adventure was hotter than ever, and I was ready to get aboard and get started.

The quartermaster, who is in charge of all gangway activities, sent a runner down the gangway, a gangway so long and huge that it reminded me of the Firth-of-Forth bridge of Edinburgh fame. The quartermaster told one of us to go up and speak to him, and one of the older lads went up. He wasn't as spritely as the first runner, I might add. Those gangways took some getting used to.

Our instructions were to take one piece of gear at a time and follow a designated sailor to our mess deck. I decided to take the kit bag first as that was the more cumbersome and heaviest. Getting onto the gangway, there was a very high step, a job unto itself. The awkwardness of the bag along with the weight was as much as I could handle. Two minutes later—or was it an hour?— I stepped upon a warship. What an incredible feeling of power!

THE REAL NAVY AT LAST

Standing on the *brow*, as I later found it to be called, I saluted. This was customary whenever boarding a ship. You are saluting the flag, the Union Jack. I scaled the drop down to the deck, four steps, and waited for all of us to assemble. The seaman guiding us led us straight down a hatch and fourteen steps to the deck below. Although we were now in a small passageway below decks, I could still feel the enormous size of the ship. After quickly turning right into what I learned was the main drag, we headed forward. (See how quickly I jumped into sailor jargon? I was so pleased with myself.)

The sections of a ship, the spaces between watertight doors, are lettered from fore to aft. We entered the main drag at (N) November section and proceeded to (K) Kilo section before turning left or to port. There was a large, empty, mess deck. Passing through that and a smaller opening with a door, we stepped over a combing. That's what the rubber on the door presses onto to make it watertight. There was a ladder going back up to three deck, but to the right was a regular door with a regular handle. There, finally, were our new digs. This was really exciting only for about the one and a half seconds it took before we saw the grizzly bear, a man with a scowl on his face that was mostly buried by curly ginger hair and a large beard. "Put your gear down and go get the rest. Don't take all night." It was 2200 hours, yep, 10.00 o'clock at night.

We scurried back the way we came, trying to remember the left turn to make for the ladder to three deck. After a little back and forth up we went. I seem to remember there were about twenty of us all in this side mess called 4K4. (That's four deck; section K, two compartments to port. The odd numbers go to starboard.)

The grizzly told us to go into the larger mess and wait, where there were large rectangular, tubular frames laid out on the deck. Next to each one was a folded canvas with brass eyelets going all around, also some rope. Once assembled, this was to be the base for our bunk. The order was to lace the canvas to the frame with said rope. Now, one might think that was easy enough. It was not. To balance tightness with not scrunching it up and having enough rope at the end to tie a knot was tricky. Consequently, it was at least an hour before most of us were finished. We then affixed these frames to the metal poles lining the mess deck. Some bays were along the side of the ship, some in the middle of the mess. I got one along the side and by a scuttle. Civilians would call it a *port hole*. Our mess was one deck above the waterline.

Then we were each given a body bag that had a zipper going two thirds around, as well as bedding that consisted of a pillow and two blankets as fluffy as coarse sandpaper. They had at least removed the horse from the hair for the pillow, although I think two teeth were left in mine. "Grizz" then showed us the toilets and the bathrooms, which were one deck below, down a ladder right outside the mess door. There were also small lockers for each of us for our toiletries. Further down the same passage was a room with our main kit lockers awaited us. This would be dealt with the next day.

It was now gone midnight and we were exhausted, but "call to hands" was at 0700 hours. Brian Towers, the grumpy leading hand in charge of us, Grizz, was ready and waiting. The speaker system throughout the ship soon burst into life; its request for us to wake up and get up was not too subtle. For us new sailors, it wasn't very effective either. That's where Grizz comes into play. He was already up, washed and dressed. Surely he had been relishing this moment in time. While we stirred slowly into life, I was standing by my bunk with eyelids that seemed to have padlocks on them, or— at the very least—lead weights. Grizz bellowed for us to get moving. The words flew across the mess, carried by waves of spittle and saliva.

This is where I got my first big lesson on board a ship of Her Majesty's Navy. I mumbled something I don't remember, maybe because of the next blinding action. Grizz spun me around and clocked me one across the jaw. I dropped like a lead weight in a vacuum. I awoke lying on the floor in the bathroom below. Apparently a few of my peers had carried me there. Grizz was kneeling over me with a worried look on his face, the part that was visible through the brush anyway. After wiping the blood away and sitting me up slowly, things returned to normal. He said he was sorry; he hadn't meant to catch me so hard. I said okay.

After washing, brushing and dressing, someone led us down to the dining halls. I say *halls* because there were two of them side by side and taking up two sections of the ship. 4E and 4F were behind 4D, which was a whole section taken up by the galley full of cooks. We all ate a lot of food; we were starving. Hey, we were still teenage boys. Walking back to our mess we were given two hours to unpack our kit into our lockers. Then muster and collect, in the mess.

One deck above our mess and a section forward was a boat deck, one on each side of the ship. We mustered on the port side boat deck and waited for the chief electrician, who ran the electrical office in 5P2. Each boat deck had a sea boat on winches and quite a large open space. Hence, this was handy for large gatherings for meetings.

The chief and a couple of lieutenants with two gold bands

around their uniform wrists arrived. We were called to attention and then stood at ease during a lot of welcoming small talk.

We were told which watch we were in, just like in our training bases. I was given *second port*. This meant that every morning I was to muster at the port side boat deck with the *first port* watch by 0800 hours. The two starboard watches naturally mustered at the starboard boat deck. We also were assigned to our daily work workshops.

LEARNING THE STRINGS

I learned that the *light workshop*, whatever that meant, was my assignment. They told me where it was by the ships code system, and off I went to find it. I entered the shop to the reception of several raised heads and some smiles. I have to say that they all treated me kindly and with open arms. They went around the room telling me their names and I offered up mine. A petty officer came to my side and told me to go and find Chief Johnson in a particular compartment.

It was tricky to find as it was a really small sub compartment within a compartment. I creaked open a door and saw the chief. Phew! I had made it. He had a very large door open to a control panel with lots of relays, contactors and dashpots. After the niceties and intros he asked me to just hold a torch (flashlight) for him. As he kept moving position I kept moving position to keep the light where his hands were. This went on for maybe an hour. As we wrapped up the job, the chief said to me, "Well done, son. You did a good job."

I didn't understand. "All I did was hold a torch," I said.

He explained to me that the lighting was poor and it was important for him to see what he was doing, especially as there was live 220V DC involved. He then told me that most people wouldn't be paying attention to what he was doing and wouldn't follow with the light.

You may be wondering why I am mentioning this. Well, it made me feel really good, and it was something I hung on to the rest for the rest of my naval career. I learned that whatever you are doing, you should pay attention, no matter how small the task. Everything is important in different and unusual ways. In other words, "Do your job." It was break time and the chief even bought me a Coke and a candy bar.

The rest of the day was spent with a seasoned electrician who, although kind enough, I think felt encumbered with me. It was tricky trying to work on a defect and explaining all of his moves to me. I had so many questions. I don't believe I'd ever before been so voracious for knowledge.

At lunch time in 4K4 I encountered Brian, the Grizz, again. There was a loud silence in the air. The other juniors trickling in were quiet and watching the situation. Brian spoke first and said that he appreciated me not going to the office. He also let me know my place and to watch my mouth. Looking at the rest of the lads, he made sure they knew this applied to them also. We all knew that they were lucky that I got my face clocked before one of them did. So the line in the sand had been set, and I have to say Brian had a certain respect for me because I didn't report him to my divisional officer. This was a mutual respect because I learned a lot that day.

The rest of the electrical ratings, all one hundred and ten of them, lived in one mess. This was situated below the after dining room, which was 5K0. The zero meant the compartment stretched all the way across the ship and took up a whole section. I learned that this is where Brian used to be. He was then told he would be living with and in charge of us babies. His disgruntlement over this explained much of his attitude. I believe he was thirty-four years old and been up and down with his promotions and demotions a few times. This was probably the least popular job he had ever been assigned. At least this explained a lot of his anger and misery.

Daily life. My daily work and life, while still stressful, seemed to be smoothing out. Then one of my workmates asked me to go to one of the electrical store rooms for a weight that was a weird shape and size. He told me to go to the store, which was run by an electrical petty officer, and ask him for a long weight. "He'll know what you mean," he said.

So off I trotted to the store. The PO was sitting at his desk going through some paperwork so I just stood by his desk. He didn't even look up but said, "Hang on. I'll be with you in a minute." He took forever, but I was too scared to say anything. When he finally asked what I wanted, I told him and he started looking in books— no computers in those days. After the fourth book, he said, "You know what? I don't think I have it in this store. Go to 2P2 store and ask there. If nobody is there just wait. He'll be there soon."

The 2P2 was five decks up and almost at the other end of the ship. I stood and waited for quite a while and worried because it had been so long since the chief had asked me to do something. Just then the chief happened to come by. "What the hell are you doing up here? I thought I told you to go to 4G5 and meet up with George."

I told him he did but I was asked to go for a long weight.

"You idiot," he blurted angrily. "How long have you been after this long weight?"

"About an hour," I said.

"They are kidding you, you numbskull. They sent you for a long *wait* not a long *weight*." I insisted that the electrician was sincere, but he asked, "Who sent you?"

I told him Pete Socum and chuckled, but he was not amused. I left to work on my original task, a little embarrassed. When I arrived back at the workshop Pete, the prankster, was waiting for me. He was a big chap really and stood towering over me like the Leaning Tower of Pisa. "Why did you give the chief my name? He just roasted me for wasting his time, and I have to work an hour extra tonight."

I said I was sorry and let him know I didn't go to the chief. After explaining how it all went down, Pete was okay and put it down to bad luck. The rest of the shop workers got a big kick out of me and the fact that Pete got caught.

Off to Portland and then home. A couple of weeks after joining the ship we went to Portland for a work-up. There we practiced dealing with any situation the ship might encounter as part of its duties. This included fire, flood, any type of warfare attack, shore side support for hurricane relief, and on and on. This went on for six weeks. At my level of expertise, which on a scale of one to ten was a minus five, I pretty much just tagged along. It was hard work, and I did exactly as I was told. Sometimes that involved just keeping myself out of the way.

After we sailed back to Plymouth, everybody was granted leave in preparation for our trip. I say *trip* like it was a vacation. It wasn't. But it would be an adventure. We were going to the Far East!

Was I a sailor yet? No. But at least I was working at it.

At home, my tales of service were passed around among my friends, family and the pub's loyal members. My proud dad encouraged me at every opportunity. For me, though, what was most important was thoughts of my next major life-changing adventure. Going to China and all ports east was a formidable trip to try and digest.

The final day of my two week leave came fairly quickly, but I had enough time to relax from the fervor of life on board Bulwark. I was excited, scared, exhilarated and joyful all at the same time.

I wanted my parents to see my keenness and verve, not my concern and stress. I think it worked out okay. Their pride and love also fooled me into not seeing the same from them, I'm sure. After all, I was leaving for up to two years to go to the other side of the world—all 110 pounds and 5'4" of me. Yes, I was getting heavier and taller.

Mother came to the rail station this time. That was nice, but it made parting a little harder. Mum and Dad's blackening shapes disappeared into the swirling steam and soot of the sooty tunnel, and I was on my way.

LOOK OUT WORLD,
HERE I COME

I arrived at the bottom of the gangway amidst a flurry of tremendous activity. There were bodies going in all directions, naval personnel, dockyard mateys and vendors. Cranes were swinging pallets full of supplies onto the flight deck and swinging back to the jetty with a pile of empty ones. The constant stream of bodies on the gangway was like a line of marching ants getting ready for winter. I made my way to the brow, saluted and was back in the groove. That brow is like a magic doorway into mystery. There is a definite consciousness change from the moment you salute and step forward onto the old grey mare.

My first morning back was sure better than my first morning on board. In the workshop everybody greeted me and I felt different, more accepted. I still had to keep my place as an *OD*, a term used for a young, inexperienced whippersnapper. I was still a junior electrical mechanic second class. The only item on the planet lower than that was a slug, maybe a worm at best.

This was brought home, very sharply, after my next significant life lesson. I stood in the workshop one morning next to a sound-powered phone. These are those phones you see in old war movies during a battle. They wind a handle and there is a "whoop, whoop" noise at the other end. There is a wire running between the two phones, and there is a network of these phones throughout the ship that can be linked via any station.

The one next to me whooped. I didn't like talking on these phones because the sound is very poor. Worse, if you don't readily understand the naval jargon along with the work jargon, it can be tough. I sort of slinked away as unobtrusively as I could. That didn't work. "Pick up the phone, skin," was bellowed from a fog horn across the shop. Skin is another endearing term for a young fresh-faced sailor. I reluctantly picked up the phone, my heart racing. Oh, great. It was the chief.

"What was that, Chief? The what? Say again?" I didn't understand, and the chief was getting more and more agitated on the other end.

After more garbled words, he finally yelled in frustration, "Is there an idiot on the line?"

I instantly said, "Not at this end!" Arghhhhh! Oh, god, what had I gone and done? At this point, a terror like that of a large, molten piece of iron plummeted into my stomach.

Fortunately for me, the chief laughed and calmed down a bit. This slowed him down, and I was able to at least make out enough to relay the message. My joy was short-lived, however. About half an hour later, I happened upon the chief in the main four deck passageway. I smiled at him, but it wasn't reciprocal.

He seemed angry and irritated. This was confirmed by my inability to walk. He had me up against the bulkhead with both hands clutching my shirt, my feet dangling about four inches off of the deck. He tore me a new one and yelled about insubordination and respect for the badge and many other things, but at this point my mind had gone off with fear into la-la land. My memory banks were on overload and had shut down. What I did understand was that I had learned a lesson. After my frantic, shaking apology, the chief completely changed his whole modus operandi and said, "Come with me I need your help." It was over.

Every day I was learning the truth of an old expression: *You get out of work whatever you put into it.* My lack of knowledge was overridden by my hard work and enthusiasm; I was really trying to do my best, and that was noted by a leading hand in my section/workshop. His name, Peter Plant, will be honored by me to my grave. He started to volunteer to take me on tasks. I don't think the chief was behind this, but who knows for sure. Anyway, he seemed happy to have me along. I tell you this because we started forming a friendship of sorts, which was unusual between a *sprog* and a ranking sailor. (*Sprog* is a term for a youngster or for a baby. When one of the lads' wives was having a baby, someone would ask if she has dropped her sprog yet.)

There was still so much to learn. Was I a sailor yet? No.

ALL AT SEA

The next step of my life adventure was about to take place—our journey to the Far East. We climbed into our number two uniforms and mustered on the flight deck. We lined the perimeter of the deck and watched the jetty fill with families of many onboard. Even though they looked so small down there, you could see they were crying. They waved incessantly, and suddenly there was the unmistakable blast of the fog horn. The releasing of the *hawsers* (ropes) and a slight rocking of the ship signaled we were on our way.

It took forever to clear the safety of the harbor and break into the English Channel. Once in the Channel, though, we picked up speed and sailed into the wild blue yonder. The speed was more of a lumber, but at fifteen knots the cool sea breeze was a joy to the lungs. I stayed on the flight deck for quite a while watching England disappear. The horizon, now a straight line, was empty where it met the sky. I felt very alone, and it was a poignant moment. The wind picked up as the ship changed course, and I went below decks.

I wanted to be alone for a while so found a small compartment in the bowels of the ship and folded into myself. I was quiet that evening as were everybody else. The ship itself seemed to be in a different state of consciousness. It must have known the sadness of the husbands and fathers it was holding captive.

The next morning everything was abuzz again, and the workshop didn't miss a beat. There was work to be done and machinery to fix and maintain. By now, I realized that a large part of our work was to maintain the equipment before it broke down. So inspections at various levels and depth were performed every day. The ship was mainly DC, direct current, which meant equipment was much larger and heavier and required more maintenance than a more modern AC ship. This was another downside to this particular draft for me, but more on that later.

Sailing and working. The seas were good to us for the first portion of our tour. We rocked and rolled and plunged but not with any ferocity. I was having the time of my life while working hard and still keeping as low a profile as my personality would allow. I had not yet realized who my true self was, but I knew I was growing and changing fast. In which direction would I go? This was not going to be determined by me alone, although I didn't know this yet. Peter Plant would end up being the leading edge of the rest of my life, although neither of us would know that for a long time.

A few days later, the mouth of the Mediterranean Sea gobbled us up and we docked in Gibraltar. Since this was my first port of call with the Royal Navy outside of Blighty, I was excited out of my gourd. I wanted to get ashore and let everybody know how I felt and what I was about.

Before all this excitement could take place, the ship had to be secured alongside. Lighting needed to be put on gangways, one down aft for the officers and then the main one for the also-rans. Ropes and wires were looped over bollards, and bunches of people came aboard for who knows what. I learned all about the intricacies of Navy protocol and niceties as my experiences continued and my horizons widened.

Going ashore in Gibraltar. Finally I went ashore with a trio of lads from my mess. Not one of us knew what to do or where to go, so we wandered aimlessly through the streets. Looking at a multitude of different sights and scenes was kind of fun, and everybody there spoke English. In the end we fell into a bar and bought a beer. Three or four beers later we swayed back on board and put our heads down until morning. We were not used to drinking, especially me, because I was just seventeen and my journey thus far had not involved such habits. I'd had beer before but not that many at a time. My drinking future would remedy that scenario for sure.

Peter was the first to see me in the workshop and enquired about my lethargy and spaciness. He then said for me to go with him on a job assignment, and we disappeared into the network of passageways. I knew he was protecting me from the wrath of the chief and was grateful for that.

Some new members had joined us in our mess deck before leaving England. Because they were newer than us, they thought of us as at least slightly seasoned. This couldn't have been further from the truth, but we were saltier than them. They were engine room mechanics, commonly known as stokers because their job used to be, literally, stoking the boilers. Intelligence-wise, they were a step lower than us electricians but better than all the other branches. Naturally, we were the best and brightest.

They were accompanied by their own branch-leading hand who was an old salty sea dog like Brian. This made Brian a little happier as he now had a drinking buddy. Now and again they would have a bunch of older sailors come by and they would party. I should mention here that at the age of eighteen you could purchase two cans of beer a day at sea and four cans a day in harbor. This was tightly controlled, and any violations that were caught were harshly dealt with, resulting in anything from the loss of beer for a determined amount of time up to being demoted to your previous rank.

I tell you this because one night at sea, these reprobates were having a party with beer they had collected over a period of time. Word came down that they were going to be raided in a couple of minutes by the regulating staff, naval police. As I said before, we had a scuttle or two in the mess, so we opened them and tossed about twelve cases of beer into the *oggin*, common slang for the sea, much to the chagrin of all concerned. We youngsters were thrilled to bits because they would have been drinking into the night and getting obstreperous and rowdy. Of course we could not share our joy. This would have involved capital punishment from said parties.

Seconds later the door burst open, and their stood the patrol, all dressed up with nowhere to go. They still searched the mess but went away empty-handed. The enquiry was now on as to who had ratted them out.

On toward the Suez Canal. After four days of Gib, as Gibraltar was affectionately known, we sailed east toward the Suez Canal. Wow, the thrills just kept coming. There was a twenty-four hour stop anchored off Malta on the way, and then Port Said was upon us. We anchored off of Malta to top off our fuel tanks before a larger segment of our journey.

We anchored near Port Said, waiting for a planned convoy of ships to form. This included ships from all parts of the world carrying everything known to man. A team of Arabian pilots came aboard along with some trusted, I assume, vendors and entertainers, and we were ready to get into position to go through the lock and into the canal. A white pin light was placed on the bow for the pilot to line up with a white pin light on the stern of the ship in front. Then there was a pin light on our stern and so on through the convoy.

We slowly got under way and proceeded forth. I seem to remember it took at least a full day to transit the canal. Halfway through, the convoy waited in the Great Bitter Lake to wait for the convoy coming from the south so that we could pass each other. The canal was only just wide enough for one ship, especially an aircraft carrier or a super tanker, and there was no margin for error. That's why we needed the very skilled pilots.

The vendors had all kinds of solid gold jewelry, leather goods out the kazoo, and all kinds of beautiful jade. Then there were the magicians and illusionists, who were quite remarkable. The one that comes to mind kept pulling little yellow chicks from every part of his body. He must have had at least a hundred or more that he kept producing. Peter was with me during this market place on the flight deck, and we had a lot of fun that day and evening.

Have I mentioned the heat? It was so blistering hot that one could literally fry an egg on the deck. As we entered the Red Sea at the south end of the Suez, I distinctly remember saying to myself, "There is no way I am going to make it for two years in this unbearable heat." This was not a *fleeting* moment (Excuse the pun). I was deadly serious. Fun time was over. What had I done? Where was I going? What was I doing? Was I a sailor yet? I was getting there.

Peter, who had been to the Far East before, assured me it wasn't as bad in Singapore and the like. It would be more humid, still hot, mostly, but not like this.

HEAT AND SAND

The real reason for taking this route to the Far East was to go to Aden to assist in the withdrawal of British troops and their equipment. This was, unbeknownst to me at the time, the end of our presence in this country. We anchored off the port, mainly for security reasons. This meant barges had to bring all the trucks, jeeps, tanks and all other types of equipment out to us. On the side of the ship was a large crane that hoisted everything to the flight deck. We worked at this for, if I remember correctly, about four days.

At intervals, I was assigned to assist Chief Towers. This entailed unhooking the strops on the equipment and being his *gofer*—you know, "Go for this. Go for that." This was mainly to get drinks and snacks and convey messages to various involved personnel. Chief Towers was a very large barrel-chested man with a very hairy body. Why do I tell you this? Mentioning him reminded of a later incident on the trip to Singapore. The chief was sunbathing on the flight deck one day, and I happened by with Peter. We stopped to say hello, Peter more than myself as I would have been too intimidated. He stood up, and I saw him without a shirt for the first time. "Wow," I said. "You look like the abominable snowman." Of course I shouldn't have said that out loud, just like I shouldn't have said what I'd said earlier to Chief Johnson.

Chief Towers yelled, calling me a cheeky young whipper-snapper, along with many other expletives I won't repeat. I'm pretty sure he even came up with some I had never heard before.

At the same time, he charged me like a raging rhino. I spun around and ran for my life, leaping down the nearest ladder and disappearing into the maze of passage ways. Peter caught up with me a little later and suggested that after a while I should brave it out and go and apologize.

A day or so later I slinked into the chief's office and weakly said I was sorry. He stood up and grabbed my shirt. "Look you little punk. You need to engage your brain before opening your mouth in the future. I've heard good things about you so don't let your mouth get in the way." As I left his domain, I heard a soft voice say, "It *was* kind of funny." I didn't turn around but smiled to myself as I scurried off to work. Maybe my hard work and dedicated attitude were not only being recognized but getting me out of trouble.

Going ashore in Aden. I did go ashore in Aden. We needed to go with a group of at least three but no more than five. Hostilities abounded, and we needed to be aware of our surroundings at all times. Just before we were going to return onboard, the ship's siren sounded, which meant we were to get to the jetty right away as an incident had taken place. We got the intel later that some of our crew, who were in a café, had a grenade thrown among them. Three of them received shrapnel wounds, and an Arabian man had been killed. He, actually, may have been the target as he was sympathetic toward the Brits.

The red sea and Aden came and went as we made our way to Singas, the common name for Singapore, with our payload of equipment and soldiers, along with Marines. By now I had learned that I could take the rough seas without being sick.

You might be forgiven for thinking that an aircraft carrier doesn't move that much. You'd be wrong. Once she gets rolling in the open sea during a prolonged storm, there is no stopping her from her arrogant posture through the waves.

I did enjoy my free time on the upper deck, especially the flight deck. We could sunbathe, play volleyball, football or deck hockey most days. The volleyball was placed in a net type bag and tied with a long piece of light but strong string to the center of the net. The hockey pucks were circles of rope wrapped in the ever faithful masking or duct tape. If they went overboard, oh well; we had plenty of pre-made pucks. Reading and playing chess plus a host of other board games was also a choice.

All this activity, of course, was only possible when there was no activity with the helicopter training maneuvers. In my spare time, watching the action on the flight deck was fascinating to me. Peter and I would go onto the bridge wing or the deck above the bridge and watch the spectacle. When the choppers landed there was a flurry of activity to immediately secure them to the deck with chains and eyelets that folded down into a dip when not in use. People ran with fuel hoses from a trough that ran all along the port side like a dry river bed to refuel or defuel the aircraft. The trough contained fire hoses and anything required for flight operations. It also contained the control panels for lowering the landing craft. The landing craft were for assault charges on the beaches for the Royal Marine detachment.

LEARNING DAILY LIFE

Part of the duty watch responsibilities was to go around the upper deck at night when "Hands to flying stations" was paged. The official call was, "Darken ship." This meant to turn all the white lighting off and turn on designated red lighting. As you might imagine, this was quite a monumental job on such a large ship. Two people would go down the port side and two down the starboard. We were given cards with locations of all the switches. For speed, though, which was required, it was a tough task. Peter always assisted me, as I did him, which made life much easier.

Part of the journey was to go across the catwalks. Imagine a wire grate hanging from a gantry eighty feet in the air. On the sides are two rails, the top one being just above waist height and you are dangling directly above the open water. The first couple of times are scary and slow, but when you get used to it you just fly along. These catwalks also included going up and down ladders under the flight deck where the ships sides sloped under the bow end.

One day in harbor when a new officer on board by the name of Lieutenant Gash was officer of the day, he was called to the gangway by the quartermaster. The quartermaster is a seaman leading hand who runs the comings and goings of the gangway. I should also explain that *gash* is also the naval term for trash that is thrown overboard when at sea.

So the page went, "Lieutenant Gash, gangway." Moments later a furious Lieutenant Gash was yelling at the quartermaster, letting him know the name was pronounced *Gaysh* not *gash*.

What's wrong with that one might think? Well, later that week we were at sea again and about to go to flying stations. During flying procedures, no gash can be ditched, i.e. thrown overboard, for obvious reasons. The quartermaster came across the broadcast system and announced, "Hands to flying stations, *gaysh* may not be ditched." I swear that the ship jumped a good foot out of the water with laughter. Everybody knew of the previous dialogue.

The next day, said quartermaster was put on a charge of insubordination. Everybody thought it a little harsh, but that's life in a blue suit. He took it on the chin like a trooper. I'm sure he thought it was worth it.

An SOS at sea. One day when sailing through some really tough weather of force eight winds and better in the Indian Ocean, we received an SOS. A merchant ship in trouble had been tossed up on the rocks of an atoll reef. We charged toward the distressed vessel as fast as possible, but we were getting beaten up. When going at maximum speed in rough weather, a ship really gets pounded, but the ship's action is really enhanced. It took nearly a day to get there, and the storm was beginning to recede in strength. Thank goodness, because the helicopters were needed to rescue the beleaguered crew. The large ship was well and truly up on the reef with no chance of being pulled off.

We stayed a day or two offloading some of the important cargo and assessing the situation. I was still a young no-nothing, so I was really in the dark as to the final decisions and settlements. The crew was informed that there was a salvage reward, by international law, to first responders. We all cheered and thought we were going to be rich. Later we found out that the captain gets the hogs' share, followed by the commander and then through the officers and on downwards. I think I ended up with ten shillings and sixpence, which was the equivalent of about two dollars in the 1960s. Drink up me hearties, and rub-a-dub-dub.

On the passage to Singas, I needed to go to the boiler room to look at a defective light fixture. To get into the boiler room, one had to pass through an air lock. To prevent both doors being opened at the same time there was a small round window in each of the watertight doors. When a lever handle was pulled up to open the door, it turned on a light in the lock.

It wasn't working. There was a stoker named Tiny on board who was probably 6'2" and three hundred pounds, bald with tattoos on each side of his neck. I had never had any contact with him but he looked fearsome, and I had never seen him smile. I was thinking he ate junior ratings for lunch; who knows? So I lifted the lever to open the door, step inside, lock the door, and turn around.

I literally cried out in shock. I was facing Lurch in a boiler suit, my nose at about belly button height; it was Tiny. He laughed so hard it probably hurt him, but he reopened the door I had just closed and in a really soft voice apologized for scaring me. He then smiled again, put his hand on my shoulder, turned and strode away. I often wondered if his father wanted to name him *Sasquatch* but ruled it out for the lack of hair.

A NEW HOME FROM HOME

We traversed the Straits of Malacca, one of the busiest shipping channels in the world, and ended up in Singapore. We were going to be there for several weeks and a shore rest. After the now customary two gangways, shore power, telephone lines, and ropes were installed, the old grey mare seemed to sigh and relax.

I could hardly believe the hustle and bustle of activity on the jetty. Hundreds of people met us with great fanfare. I later realized that a large ship coming in like ours with supporting flotilla meant a lot of work and money for the local population.

All kinds of dockyard workers poured onboard. Then the vendors with their wares scrambled up the gangway. These men were funny. They wanted our business over their competitors, especially the ones with dry cleaning companies. One, called Peanuts, was a huge Chinaman, not Singaporese or Malaysian. He had a completely bald head, hence the name Peanut, and a fantastic smile. Although very loud, he was extremely friendly. His big cry when entering each mess deck was, "Free dry clean, free dry clean. Free today, pay payday."

Most other vendors sold clothing and toys that were mostly clockwork and battery driven. Everybody bought these toys. The married men sent them home to their kids, and the rest of us—well, boys will be boys, and so will most of men.

The next day I experienced for the first time the huge task of keeping the ship supplied with all the basic necessities. Store ship was a monumental task. Teams of men were requisitioned from each department to carry goods from the jetty or the flight deck to the store rooms. Some items were passed along a chain of men and some needed to be individually carried to their destination. Imagine fifteen hundred sailors on board, and let's say they each have two eggs per day. Then think of how many eggs would be needed for baking the bread and cooking the meals. I'm guessing that maybe five thousand eggs were used every day. That's just eggs. I'll let you think about the rest of the food.

On top of the food was all the fuel and spare parts for repairs and maintenance. The worst, for me, was carrying the five gallon barrels of beer for the senior rates messes. They were metal barrels and very heavy. Just stepping up onto the gangway with one of these on your shoulder was tough. Stepping down at the top bounced the barrel on my collar bone, and then having to go up and down ladders killed me. There was not a straight shot to any senior rates messes. When I finished with one barrel, there were only two hundred and ninety nine to go. There were ten of us on this detail, but ouch, I was raw at the end of it. When we were done and still groaning, it was, "Okay, lads. Over here. Get these boxes aboard." I decided I was either going to become a big boy or dead by the end of this deployment.

Was I a sailor yet? No. But I was so much closer.

Going ashore for the first time was mind boggling. Peter was familiar with the terrain and went with me. We walked for what seemed an eternity to the main gate of the dockyard. I thought that was it, but that just got us to the outer area of the naval base proper. Another mile down the road and through another policed gate, and we were free. The heat was bearable but the humidity was outrageous. The first stop across the road was for a long cool drink.

The village of Sembawang. To my surprise, we were not in Singapore City itself; we were in a fairly small village about sixteen miles away. It was called Sembawang and was basically a long line of stores and bars. It was all dirt and raised wooden walkways. A deep monsoon ditch made of concrete ran parallel to these between the road and the stores with many crossing at short intervals.

Sembawang village was a fascinating place. The smells, the sounds, the activity—it was all happening. The restaurant workers were very attentive; they want our business and it showed. They knew new ships were in town and first impressions counted. Peter said, "Let's go," and off we went. The stores were a wonder to peruse and chat with the locals. Little kids ran, laughed and played. The storekeepers offered us a free drink and attended to us with great respect. Peter started teaching me the art of bartering for everything available. Although nervy and intimidating at first, it would eventually be fun and enjoyable. We stopped by a man on his haunches tending a wok over an open fire and bought a plate of delicious food for only pennies. We enjoyed the spicy meat and vegetables even though we weren't sure what was going down the hatch. I did learn much later in my travels that rat tastes like venison— just sayin.'

Later into the day and rolling into the evening we sank a couple of Tiger beers and headed back on board. Tiger beer was a chemical beer and took some getting used to. I never really did, though. Being a junior rate, my shore leave ended at 2100 hours except weekends, Friday and Saturday which were extended to 2200 hours Peter always made sure I got on board by then, especially later in my runs ashore when I got the worse for wear. He was my champion on so many occasions it would be impossible to tell. I know for sure later that he saved and built my naval career, giving me a solid base to spring from.

Swimming test. Remember my failed swimming test? I still needed to pass that. There was a swimming pool in the dockyard which was used by all military personnel from the shore base and their families. It was very large with food and drink available during peak usage.

Early each morning, myself and all the other non-swimmers, as we were called, were to muster at the pool for swimming instructions from the physical training instructors commonly known as PTIs. I could swim but failed the test, so just needed to have more strength. The boiler suit worn for the test weighed heavy during the long floating part of said test.

Peter came with me and encouraged me during these sessions, and it wasn't long before I passed. The nausea of getting up early for these swims was an incentive. I also did a lot of swimming at Aggie Westerns. This was another family facility just outside the first dockyard gate. It was run by a religious organization that had places all over the world and also served as a hotel and restaurant. On weekends I could stay at this hotel Friday and Saturday night, which meant no curfew. I did this with Peter on several occasions throughout the many return visits to Singas. During the day we would swim, sunbathe and eat. The evenings and some afternoons we spent in Sembawang village or Singapore city.

Sembawang had bars frequented by some really nice girls who paid a lot of loving attention to us military folk. To keep them at your table, all you had to do was buy them expensive drinks. These were called *sticky greens* by us dupes. We were charged for a supposed alcoholic drink, which was actually some cheap non-alcoholic concoction. At any time they would encourage us to go walk with them for extracurricular activity. Fortunately, at this time in my career, these girls were way too much money for what I could afford. Also, Peter kept a watchful eye on me. One could get more than he bargained for, followed by a trip to the sick bay.

The rides into Singapore were always interesting. There were two taxi fares, one by a legitimate taxi cab company and one by the pirates. The fare for a legit ride was about sixteen Singapore dollars. It was only five to eight dollars for a pirate. The sixteen dollars took us straight to the city while the pirate picked up and dropped off people all the way along, even going way off the road into many small villages, of which there were many. It took two to three times longer this way. We often went by pirate to the city and got a direct ride coming back. The slow route coming back during the night was not a good move. You might not even make it back.

Some taxis could go through the first gate up to, but outside, the dockyard gate. Others unloaded us at the village gate. It was a toss-up in the city which taxi you could get. If we were early enough at Sembawang, we would catch a banjo to scarf down before returning on board. A *banjo* is a submarine-like sandwich. We would buy these at places that were, shall we say, local–sort of behind a hut or business down by the ditch that ran behind the buildings. There were log seats and old upright deck chair seats and the like. It was fun because you got to chat with the locals and laugh. Sometimes, though, I had too much Tiger in me, and we were not so enjoyable. They still served us because they wanted our business but left us alone until we departed.

On the other side of the ditch was the rubber plantation, so jungle type noises were rampant all through the evening. Other activities were also prevalent in the plantation. There was a network of men with signaling flashlights. They were lookouts for the cops, a rare commodity in Sembawang. Camouflaged huts abounded with movies and girls available at a given price. Again, Peter kept me honest, but so did my small wallet.

A SECOND HOME FROM HOME

A few weeks went by, and we sailed for Hong Kong. The soldiers, marines, and all their supplies were safely in there quarters in Singas. We always kept a detachment of marines with us, but the main parties stayed behind.

This leg was longer than I had anticipated. Firstly, there were sea-going exercises with other R.N. ships along with other nation's ships. Then the distance between the two countries was greater than I thought—I think around twelve hundred miles.

Eventually, Hong Kong crept over the horizon and made itself toward us very quietly. First the skyscrapers poked above the waves, followed by all and sundry. From a distance all was peaceful and quiet; it was a beautiful scene with added serenity. At the bow, even from the flight deck, you could hear the shush of the waves follow a sort of boompfing sound as we slowly eased forward. As we neared the jetty, the tug boats, as usual, nudged us to our resting place and connected us to the noise, hustle and bustle of a vibrant Island. This place was alive and throbbing from the moment of contact.

Everybody on the planet should be made to visit Hong Kong. It is the most diversified island of any place on earth. The sounds and smells, the large shopping stores, the small family stalls in the narrow streets, messages of all things you need to have and do whilst in port, people of all races and creeds. Naturally, the bars and night clubs and all the niceties that go along with those peppered the region. Neon lighting advertised its stuff during the day and night. Every building was shrouded in neon; it was quite a sight to see. About a half mile from the RN dockyard gate was the China Fleet Club. This was a club for all military persons. It contained a bowling alley, several massive bars, game rooms and a restaurant upstairs. I say *massive* bars, and I mean it.

To show you how massive they were, let me tell you what happened at Christmas that year. The senior leading hand of electricians organized a run ashore for the whole department. He collected five Hong Kong dollars from everybody to cover the first four pints of San Miguel beer. At least a hundred of us mustered on the jetty and fell in three deep–you know by now, the old one behind the other twice. We were going to march out of the dockyard and down the street to the China Fleet Club. When the officer of the day asked what the heck was going on, the quartermaster said, "It's the greenies, sir. They're going on a run ashore together for a Christmas bash." His reply was, "Oh, my God." (A *greenie* was an electrician. An electrical officer had a green stripe between the gold stripes on his uniform arms.)

Off we went marching, in step, to the club. Everybody we passed on the way stood and stared, wondering what the heck was happening. We all filed into the club and got seats while our leader ordered over two hundred pints of beer. He figured that by the time the first round was finished the recipients of the early pints would be finished and ready for the second. That shows you the size of the bars.

They handled the orders without batting an eye. After the fourth pint and some words from our leader about the commission, the department, and being away, we were on our own to buy drinks and stay or go. Naturally, the customary songs of the Navy were sung after enough lubrication had oiled the larynx.

Peter and I sauntered back on board together, where he helped me navigate the gangway and its staff. He was good at this after much too many practices by far. He has always been my hero. I slept off the rest of the day.

Another story involves the trip to Kowloon. Kowloon is the area across from the island of Hong Kong on the mainland but still under the British flag. It also carries all the trappings of the island itself. The engaging part then was getting to and from Kowloon on the "Star" ferry. If you can imagine ten people in a British phone booth, then you can imagine how compacted we were on the boat. It only cost ten cents and was purported to be the cheapest ferry in the world. I could only think to myself, "Don't fall over or they'll be scraping you off the deck like chewing gum."

The junks were a site to see. The notable thing about those was that sampans would swing a hook onto them to get towed along at greater speed. Then the junk crew would spot them and unhook the sampan, much to the dismay of Mister Sampan. A lot of shouting also ensued, using a Chinese version of the special naval dictionary I'm sure.

A typhoon heads our way. The weather made a turn for the worse, and we were informed that we needed to sail for the open sea. A typhoon was headed our way, and it was safer for the ship to be at sea because a storm of that magnitude could keep thrusting us against the jetty. At 27,000 tons a pop, that would hurt both the jetty and the ship. So it was batten down the hatches and head for the hills—well, the South China Sea anyway.

I had no idea how much work this would entail. Everything, I mean everything, had to be stored away in drawers and lockers. Items, even of a larger nature, had to be tied down and drawer handles looped with rope and tied up. I just did as I was asked and kept out of trouble.

We pulled away from the jetty and set off from the shelter of the island into the open sea. Immediately the rusty "B," as she was affectionately known, started to roll. This action was not unusual, of course, but this time it seemed different. Maybe it was anticipation of greater things to come. Maybe it was the dark unlit sky that had pulled the blinds down on the sun. The wind was starting to complain to all who would listen, and larger waves started to slap and beat our flanks.

The rolling was then joined by the rise and fall of the bow. A whoomphing followed by a heavy shushing of the descending spray could even be heard below decks. A more severe test of my sea legs and stomach resilience was looming on the horizon. For the first time of my short naval experience, I needed to check my gait and hold on to the nearest available whatever to remain upright.

The typhoon was just warming up. The upper deck was becoming treacherous at the lower levels and was deemed out-of-bounds. All kinds of small items came out of their hiding places. The cable deck at the bow and the third deck down from the flight deck was soon underwater at each downward plunge. This area contained the two capstans that raised and lowered the anchors, plus each capstan's motor generator set and all kinds of other electrical equipment.

The pitching and rolling eventually reached an enormous level. I even had to hold on while trying to sleep in my bunk. As a wave of tremendous size, speed, and power smashed into the bow, the bow was forced up. Now, don't forget, we were 27,000 tons, so could resist at least a little. With the speed of the ship and its mass, the ship continued to rise as a trough came along. Before the bow dipped into the trough, another wave hit us, and the bow went up again to another level. This happened seven times, each time lifting the bow higher and higher. Then the amount of the ship out of the water got grabbed by gravity and started to plunge and nosedive toward Davy Jones' locker. The downward drive seemed to last forever until the density of the sea equalized with the weight of the ship and we started a seven-wave stint again. We rose out of the waves like a cormorant taking flight. As we sank below the waves, the spiteful blue monsters crashed and rolled over the flight deck. They then flew to the stern, where they took off back to their home. I watched this seemingly unending movie for quite a while from the bridge, where I was sent to repair the window wipers. (These are different from conventional wipers. They are spinning discs within the glass that whisk the water away.) I changed the carbon brushes in the small motor and all was well.

As we eventually passed through the storm, I learned another seagoing lesson. An aircraft carrier doesn't stop rolling for a couple of days or more. Don't forget, the seas don't just suddenly become calm either. The nasty seas and weather continued for several days, and finally we returned to normal and terra firma.

Now the work really started. All the damage had to be inspected and repaired. This was a daunting task and it was all hands to the pump. All the equipment on the cable deck had to be stripped down, dried out and maintained. The motor generator sets took the longest to overhaul and get working again. Then there was the complete replacement of all the lighting fixtures and wiring, the inspection of all the junction boxes and switches and other smaller motors, not forgetting all communication systems that included all the microphones and loud speakers. That's just one area and one department, but you can get the idea of the enormity of the work for the whole ship.

Naturally, almost everything needed to be painted. The dockyard workers were ecstatic because it gave them reams and reams of work to do with plenty of overtime. I was happy for them because my experiences with them were wonderful. Most of them spoke at least some English, which made communication fairly easy. I just loved the Chinese people; in fact, I loved all the Far Eastern people and places. I often wonder if I had spent past lives there. The connection to the consciousness was definitely at a high level, so something was going on there for sure.

On one of my runs ashore with Peter, we went to the top of the highest peak in Hong Kong. There was a cog railway going up the steep climb, so we could literally lie back and enjoy the view. At the top were the usual trappings for tourists and the like, which we took advantage of. The panoramic scenery all around was stunning, enhanced by the silence. The hubbub of the city was way below and out of reach; it was pleasantly exhilarating. The cool breeze in your face, the fresh air in your nostrils and the peaceful experience beckoned you to stay forever.

The meat market was our next stop, and we had heard so much about how large and interesting it was. Yes, it was massive. There were, it seemed, miles and miles of hanging meats at all different stages of being carved. That was okay. What wasn't okay was the stench of intolerable strength and the five trillion flies whose buzzing sound transcended all the other noises. The market was all open air with no air conditioning and no sanitary application of any kind anywhere. I was concerned that I wouldn't eat another slice of meat of any kind ever again. Talk about *Lord of the Flies*. Wow.

From there we ate at a mom and pop stall where we polished off some local cuisine. I'm not sure what I enjoyed, but it was very tasty and different, which is why we liked to frequent little places. We also ate at established restaurants, but it was never as much fun. A couple of beers at the China Fleet Club and back on board completed our day.

MOVING ON UP

Life onboard was about to change dramatically. My life in the small 4K4 mess deck was coming to an end. This group of youngsters seemed to be looked upon as just that, a young bunch of also-rans. I felt I rose above that status. For instance, one night when I was on watch in the main switchboard with another electrician, a chief came in. It was just after midnight, and we were to be there until 0400. The set up was that a more senior junior rate ran the actual switchboard of hundreds of switches and perused the generator loads and took phone calls. We were there to go to any situation that might come up electrically during our watch of four hours. The chief saw me and said, "Oh, thank goodness you are on watch. I have an important job for you throughout the night." It was to baby a fan, which was going on the fritz, until morning. He didn't want to replace it until later that day. It was arcing badly and needed a cleaning of the armature every half hour or so. He knew I was good at this and also reliable enough to do it carefully. I had never worked with this particular chief, which meant that he knew about me from conversation among the electrical hierarchy. I took that as a plus and a vote of confidence for someone with such a young skin.

Peter, unbeknownst to me, had been waiting for a chance to move me to the large 5/0 mess deck. He knew one of the electricians was going home early, for reasons I do not know. He went to the office and suggested I could be moved into his bunk space. The office agreed, and I upped and went. It happened that I was below Peter on a three bunk high tier. He actually had the top and me the bottom bunk. He certainly was taking me under his wing. I was very grateful for this move.

Most in my section of the big mess were okay, but some of the salty sea dogs didn't approve of this young punk joining their space. I learned later that they didn't like that I was doing so well, and another major issue was tot time at 1200 hours. One had to be 21 to receive the one-third pint of grog every day. I was nowhere near that, so I couldn't even be in the mess when it was being dished out and drunk. Some of the elders drank more than they should, and one day Pete Socum, commonly known as Gigs because he fancied himself with the women, got a little frisky and declared he'd like to strip me. He then wanted to cover me in Swafega, a slimy degreasing agent for the hands, and chase me around the ship. Naturally, everybody laughed and thought it a great idea. They were just joshing, of course, but I knew to suck it up and roll with the punches. I smiled a sheepish grin and left the area.

I had to learn to live life on the razor's edge and figure out how to blend in and gradually be accepted. This also helped on my next main ship, big time. My hard work and dedication to the job was paying off and helping me be accepted in the general population.

It's time for a funnier story. By now I was transferred to another workshop. This was done to all personnel every few months to give everybody varied job experiences. I was then in the ventilation workshop; this entailed looking after all of the D.C. fans on the ship, an arduous task as they needed constant maintenance. I was given fifty fans to keep going by myself. If the larger fans needed to be removed and brought to the workshop, then all the help I needed was given. "Just talk to the chief, and he'll set it up," I was told.

One afternoon I was asked to help others remove a huge axial flow fan. These fans were massive and were in flow with the trunking. They needed blocks and tackles and maneuvering through the passageways above the deck and up through the hatches. The job went on way into the night and the chief, at around 2300 hours, told me to go and get my head down; he needed me in the morning. I told him I wanted to stay and finish the job. He said, "Okay, but I still need you in the morning."

We finished at about 0400 hours, and all eight of us were very pleased with ourselves. This is where it gets funny. The chief disappeared for a moment and came back with some neat 120 proof rum. That is what senior rates get every day and because it is neat can be saved. It isn't legal to do that, but who was looking. He doled it out to all of us and everybody looked at me. He said, "Down the hatch," and we all glugged it down in one shot. I just about choked to death on the strength of the neat rum, went bright red, couldn't speak, and could hardly breathe. The chief deliberately asked me a question, knowing I was incapable of answering. They were waiting for this and laughed their heads off, cheered, and slapped me on the back.

Was I a sailor yet? Maybe. I believe that at this moment in time, I had arrived.

The next morning I arrived in the workshop on time and was greeted with a great deal of thanks. Oh, yes, and my red faced choking story was repeated to all who weren't there at the time. The chief said I could take the afternoon off to get my head down. I knew that I wanted to work on a particular fan that was in bad shape. So after lunch I went back to work to fix it. The chief saw me after a while and told me to leave the shop and take the rest of the afternoon in my bed. I did.

A couple of the old sea dogs accused me of groveling to the chief, but I didn't care. I was building my career, not theirs. I continued to work hard and built a pretty good reputation for myself. Eventually I became more accepted in the mess, and I settled in for the duration.

Earning more trust. A few weeks later one of the more senior killicks asked for my help on a really large fan. He trusted me to be helpful and conscientious. It was late at night and nobody was around. We had dismantled the fan at its location and removed the huge armature. Colin and I decided to carry it back to the workshop between us. It was extremely heavy, and he took the heavier end and walked backwards. He was a very strong individual and could handle it, that is until his heel caught the coping as he stepped through one of the watertight doorways on four deck. As he crashed to the deck, he dragged the armature and me toward him. His head whacked the deck, and the heavy armature landed on his chest. Now you would think this would be a serious moment in time, and indeed it was. However, for some inexplicable reason, I just started laughing, so much so that I could hardly stand or breathe. Colin was a trifle upset at this, but I couldn't help it. I also couldn't lift the armature from his chest.

I felt awful but still couldn't stop laughing. Poor Colin was in pain. I told him not to move, that was a given, and ran for help. When we had extricated him from his dilemma I apologized profusely and he saw the funny side of it. If this had happened months earlier, I would have been in deep doo-doo. (I learned later that he had actually broken a couple of ribs.)

The following day a senior chief, Derick, along with three others, got the huge armature onto a massive lathe. What happened with a lathe was that as the armature spun, an extremely sharp and strong cutting tool was slowly moved across the armature and skimmed some of the copper off the copper segments. These segments were about a quarter inch wide and were separated by an equal width of insulating mica.

After the cutting, somebody (Guess who?) had to slice between each copper segment to create a valley to stop the mica from spreading across the copper when the carbon brushes rushed over them.

The chief sternly warned me not to scratch the newly cut copper while cutting the mica. I was as nervous as a lobster in a restaurant water tank. The gang all watched me as I started around the armature of around eighty segments. Sure enough, after a few successful cuts, I scratched the copper. My heart thumped in my chest like a bent piston in an engine. The chief went ballistic and said we had to start all over again. I was bright red with eyes bulging out of my sockets, apologies spewing forth from my vibrating teeth. They all burst out laughing while slapping me on the back. The chief told me how to fix the problem by spinning the armature and pressing some fine sandpaper onto it. He did, however, say, "Be as careful as possible, but we are going to leave you alone now." They had known exactly what they were doing and forced me into a nervous mistake. Life in a blue suit was obviously going to involve a lot of teasing and camaraderie. I was going to have to take it on the chin now and again, but it did mean I was accepted as one of the crew, I think.

THE WORLD DOWN UNDER

The next leg of our journey took us back to Singapore, where we stored ship, as was the norm on docking, and prepared to go on a major multinational seaborne exercise off the coast of Australia. This entailed a drive by of the Great Barrier Reef and a visit to Brisbane.

Once we had docked alongside the jetty and the gangway was lowered the usual events happened. Dockyard workers scurried aboard, we tied up more proficiently, and welcoming parties greeted the captain and major officers. Then a scruffy, skinny and disheveled long-haired individual slowly plodded his way to the brow and stepped on board. The weird thing was, he asked for his station card. The quartermaster asked what he meant, as nobody could possibly have gone ashore yet. Mr. Scruff answered, "I went ashore four years ago and went absent without leave.".

Wow, he had jumped ship, as we call it in the RN, four years ago and I'm guessing didn't make the grade. He apparently was jobless, homeless, and down on his luck. After the big stir was over, he was taken below, cleaned up, fed a good meal and placed in the brig. I really don't know what happened to him, but I assume he was flown home, did time in a Navy jail, was court martialed, and then spent time in a civilian jail.

Welcome home, Jack, me hearty, and God Save the Queen. Navy jail is not the nicest of rest homes. He probably spent the maximum of three months there in misery. The bed in Navy jail was wooden, along with the pillow. He would be up early in the morning to eat his gruel before doubling around the quadrant with a rifle on his shoulder, seven days a week. The inmates were permitted one letter per month in and out, along with one book to read, God bless their little cotton socks. The fine he would also receive when court martialed would include the air-fare from Brisbane to London. I do hope he recovered his life and wish him all the very best.

Moving on, Peter and I had the good fortune to be taken ashore by a resident of Brisbane and his family for a day. They were absolutely wonderful and took us on a tour of the city, took us ten pin bowling, and brought us to their home, where they cooked a slap up dinner and entertained us. It was a terrific day for us, and we were truly grateful for a civilian change of pace.

Accidents occur. The exercises were underway with shore land-ings of the commando groups we took on board in Singapore. One of our helicopters took off from ashore with thirty comman-dos, and at about thirty feet in the air, the main rotor blades flew off. The Wessex Five copter plummeted. Fortunately, nobody was seriously hurt. A couple of men had broken bones and that was about all.

Another incident occurred after more than twenty inches of rain fell in two days while in Brisbane. Apart from the obvious flooding, the river was in full flow, and an anomaly was that the river was completely chockers with blue jelly fish. They were about a foot wide with three to four foot tentacles. This was all well and good, but as I was looking down from the flight deck, a young sailor fell overboard from three deck. His screams were heard above the roar of the ship; I'm sure he was anticipating the jelly fish. As soon as he surfaced, he struck out for the con-crete steps that, fortunately, were close by. He did get stung but survived the ordeal. Personally, I think I would have had a heart attack on the way down.

Brisbane was also one of several places where we escaped from the clutches of the grim reaper. Peter and I had complimentary tickets to Dr. Zhivago, which was playing in the city for the first time and was all the rage. However, we couldn't make it due to urgent repair requirements on board that needed fixing before we sailed the following day. During the performance, the balcony collapsed and many were badly injured. Our disappointment about not going was eradicated on the spot.

A trip to the hospital. Back to Singas it was, and a rest up was due. On the way back one night, I could not sleep at all. I had this tremendous pain in my right side by my kidney. No matter what position I got into, I couldn't relieve the ache. I even tried to sleep in an arm chair to no avail. That morning I went to the sick bay when it opened at 0800 hours. There were at least ten people in line, and the chief medic had not opened the door yet. When the chief opened the door he looked down the line and walked passed some individuals, hypochondriacs, I'm guessing. When he got to me, I was bent over in pain and clutching my midriff. He immediately shouted, albeit calmly, for a young medic to join him. They took me straight to the examination room.

After many questions and much probing, they told me I had pneumonia. They handed me a set of pajamas and told me to get into bed. An aircraft carrier has a full blown hospital on board with operation rooms and all and sundry. A medical officer confirmed everything and said I would be getting three penicillin shots a day for seven days. This was included with the total bed rest. I haven't worn any clothes to bed since the age of ten, so jammies seemed strange to me.

Now comes the fun part, my first injection of penicillin. The orderly told me to roll over and drop my pants. Unfortunately, I saw the at least 6" long needle that was going to go into my backside. He then asked which cheek I wanted to have speared, after warning me that it would be painful afterward. He then slapped me hard and literally threw the needle in. He said it was the best way. The horror then struck me. I was going to go through this three times a day for seven days? Oh, boy. I'm also pretty sure they tossed a coin or something to see who would view my lily white cushions and fire the next round.

I was in serious pain for a couple of days, and then it was just the pain of the needles and medication. My butt really did ache, but I chose the left side for twenty shots and on the last shot chose the right side. They asked me why I kept choosing the same side, and I told them it was so I could have one side I could sleep on without it hurting. In the end, I just couldn't take it anymore and switched to the right for my final stab.

I stayed another three days in the brig. Peter and John from basic training did visit with me and we played some games. This helped break the monotony. Pneumonia though really took all my strength out of me and I slept a whole bunch of the time. Finally, I was let loose on society again.

Back on the job. One day I needed to work on a small fan that was placed on two bars across a narrow passageway. The passage was about sixteen feet high, and the fan was near the deck head (ceiling). I took a couple of tools and left my tool bag on the deck as I climbed up to attend to the fan. For the last step up, I grabbed the top of the fan and heaved my body upward. This is where it got hairy; the previous person had left the top off of the connection box. I had fully grasped the 220V DC power and, as I was in midflight, couldn't let go until I had secured a foothold. I almost dropped the sixteen feet to the deck. This shocking experience was something I didn't need.

While I was up there maintaining the fan a sailor walked by and saw my tool bag. He looked up and down the passageway and bent down to steal my torch. I said, in as deep a voice as

I could, "Leave the torch alone." He freaked out while, again, looking up and down the passage. Seeing nobody around, he took off like a gazelle. There were many ghost stories on this old wartime ship and that, sometimes, came in handy.

THE WEDDING TRIP

Much later one of the killicks in my portion of the mess, Chris Jabbs, was getting married to a Malaysian girl. He had met her in Manchester, England. Anyway, they were having the ceremony in Ipoh, the third largest city in Malaysia and halfway between Kuala Lumper and Penang. To my surprise I was one of the twelve people, along with Peter, that he invited.

He had rented two Volkswagen buses to drive us there. Now, let me tell you, this was quite a trip. We all got the legal leave requirements, and a week or so later we were on our way. The sights and sounds we encountered on the road were too many to mention, that is except for one. We were driving down a really steep hill and entering a small village in the middle of the jungle. The mud road was a little slick from the misting, almost constant rain we had encountered. You're probably getting the idea already: at the bottom of the hill, unbeknownst to us at the time, was a sharp right hand bend. Well, we didn't make it and brushed a small car parked on the curve. We, of course, stopped.

We soon learned that although stopping was the right moral move, it wasn't the wisest. Within 0.3 seconds we were surrounded by what seemed to be hundreds of angry villagers. They looked a trifle upset at these white invaders and were shouting profusely. That wasn't too bad, but then they started rocking the bus more and more. Just as things were about to go south from there, a parting started to appear in the throng. This arrowhead of space slowly crept toward us, and finally a very small uniformed officer stood at our window.

Thankfully he spoke English. We explained all that had taken place and the minimal damage, which we would gladly pay for. We figured our lives were worth something, as they were hanging in the balance. He turned to the mob in front of us, pulled out a short baton from his light brown uniform, and waved it from side to side. The throng parted like the Red Sea with a low murmur. The smallest man with the greatest power said, "Get moving quickly. I can't hold them for long." We thanked him and sped off at the safest speed we could. Another bullet dodged and another lifeline used. How many did I have?

We arrived in Ipoh without further incident and came to a stop outside the best hotel in town. Surprisingly, it was called The Hong Kong Hotel. This entire trip was paid for by the bride's family. We figured Chris must be marrying into money.

The wedding was the next day, and we were up, not so bright, but early. The ceremony was absolutely beautiful and went off letter perfectly. The lavish reception later that day was even better. There were so many tables of ten I lost count. On each table were all the required real silverware, fine whiskey and fine brandy. No other alcohol was available, strangely enough. The twelve course meal was out of this world—yes, twelve courses. They were served on a very large platter in the middle of each round table. One took the food from this platter and placed it in the finest delicate china bowl, hand painted in bright, beautiful designs. We were seated with Malaysian friends of the family. Thank goodness because, not only did they speak English, but they educated us through the meal.

We recovered somewhat from the all-day affair and eventually bundled back into the Volkswagens and hightailed it back to Singapore. In case you're wondering, yes, we traversed the dreaded village again but came through unscathed.

This excursion took place during a three month stint in Singapore as the ship was doing what they termed a *mini mainreq*, short for *main requirements*. Periodically the ship needed to do planned maintenance and catch up on larger defects of equipment that couldn't be shut down during operational times and had to be nursed along. For this huge task, we were moved into barracks in HMS Terror, the Navy shore base inside the main military base. This is a massive area, like a whole town really, that includes two huge bars, one above the other, a restaurant and a soccer/rugby/field hockey field with bleachers that held thousands of people. The apartment-like building we lived in had no air conditioning, just ceiling fans, and no door and no windows, just cut-out window shaped holes. We could step out onto a covered balcony.

I remember coming back from ashore with Peter one late afternoon on a weekend when we had been down the *vill*, as it was known, of Sembawang. A couple of Tiger beers had joined us on the trip before heading back to HMS Terror. It was monsoon season and the descending rain was indescribable. The buildings next to the road had those really deep and really wide monsoon ditches running by them. They had bridges every so often, but not often enough during a monsoon downpour. A monsoon downpour in these parts is different than the average westerner's idea of monsoon rain. You can barely see three feet in front of you, and those ditches fill up real fast. We got a taxi that could go into Terror and paid him off right near our building, which we could barely see through the rain. A shortcut could be achieved by jumping the monsoon ditch.

Or could it? Why we did our next most stupid move ever was totally due to that Tiger. It made us attempt that jump over the ditch, which immediately devoured us and nigh on drowned us. We would have made it, but it seemed to grow while we were in the air. We did manage to grab some grasses and, come to think of it, our asses, and scrambled out. You know, why we did that is beyond me. One second in the rain and you're drenched anyway. Why bother trying to get to our building any quicker? That darn Tiger, that's who made us. Yeah, that darn Tiger. On relaying our experience to our roomies and next door companions, we all had a good laugh. It's a good thing our shots were up to date.

TYING ONE ON IN THAILAND

Our next foray into the wide blue yonder was to Thailand and Bangkok. After some of the exercises were complete, we took a break, anchoring off the coast close to Bangkok.

For personnel who put their names on a list, the ship arranged for a three day stay in the city. This involved a flight in on a Wessex 5 helicopter and a two-night stay in the Ambassador Hotel. The rate for the room was exceptionally low, so am not sure if it was subsidized or not. Peter and I decided to go and room together. That was part of the deal, two to a room.

That was my first ride in a helicopter. What a rush! I seem to remember twenty-five people at a time were flown in to an open field. We were then bused in to the hotel from there. We had to get all geared up with the flight helmet and suit, so I felt like a real military man now, for sure. We trotted for the chopper while ducking down, hopped on board, and sat in those string-like seats—all very movie like and professional. This was an exhilarating experience and felt like magic.

We had a fabulous time and saw a great deal of extremely colorful sights and sounds, such as some Thai boxing. The boxers sparred to rhythmic music by a live band. The kicking was brutal, with spit, sweat and blood flying in all directions. The massive crowd in the huge stadium was baying for more and more action. Bahts—the Thai currency—were flying from hand to hand like floating confetti at a wedding. The noise was ear pounding, and it was easy to get caught up in the frenzy of activity, which we did. We were cheering on the combatants as much as anyone else. Well, maybe it was a little less because we had no money riding on the outcome.

When we left that venue we wandered in town and nestled into a bar. After a beer or so, we ordered some Thai whiskey, probably because we had been warned not to try it because it was bad juju news. I believe it is seventy percent paraffin, but who's counting? We sucked it down anyway and had many regrets the next morning. The splitting headaches were bad enough to make us believe our heads were squeezed in a vice. Eventually, after removing the axe from my skull, we recovered enough to saunter outside and eat some of the local specialties. The eggs and toast I recognized, but the rest, I wasn't so sure about. It tasted real good, so all was well.

It was soon back to the field by bus and back to the ship on the chopper. Landing on the ship was very different from taking off. Were we really going to land on that coin below us? Also, the short drop of the last foot was unexpected as we slammed to the final resting place, spot seven. On arrival at the edge of the flight deck next to the *island*, the common name for the superstructure, I removed my helmet and life jacket. I noticed that my whole body was atingle with adrenaline rushes and god knows what. The whole few days had been a blast; I was pumped.

Beach landings. Soon it was back to the open sea and more exercises. One exercise in particular stands out. It's funny now but it wasn't so humorous at the time, at least for the commandos. The idea was to practice beach landings on an island in the Indian Ocean. The commandos boarded the four landing craft and headed for a landing beach quite a distance away. Before the landing craft could get anywhere near the beach, they came under fire from the cliff tops. This was not part of the exercise; they were real bullets. The boats did a quick spin around and headed back to the ship.

The ensuing inquest revealed that there was a miscommunication with the locals. They had not been informed of our sortie. A local policeman was riding along the cliff path and saw warships off shore with landing craft heading his way. "We're being invaded, we're being invaded," he yelled as he ran into the small garrison detachment. The guardians of the island rallied and rushed to the cliff tops to let loose with all their might, all seven of them at once. They probably felt proud of repelling the mighty British Empire all by themselves.

After meetings with said parties and many a jovial conversation, the exercises were conducted as planned. I believe we gave the people on the island gifts of high octane booze as a parting gift of thanks.

It was about this time that the cookery officer changed an unwritten rule. We, in 5/0 mess deck, could no longer walk through the dining halls during meal times in just a towel. This had been common practice as our bathroom was a couple of sections aft and back down a deck. The new rule meant going to the showers dressed, getting undressed, showering, getting dressed and so forth.

Matt Bream, a very large killick and Scotsman, decided he could get around this new rule. He didn't wear a towel whilst walking through the dining room. In fact he didn't wear anything. Yep, stark buck naked was the dress of the day. The cookery officer, who was in the dining room at the time, went into an immediate conniption fit. Matt explained that he was following the new rule. He was put on a charge of insubordination, but matters were made worse for the poor officer as the whole packed dining room was in major uproar with laughter.

Matt got a bit of a slap on the wrist when confronting the commander at his punishment table. However, he won the day because the new rule was rescinded and we got back to normal. We all hailed Matt as our hero.

RUN, RABBIT, RUN

I was about due for another lesson on engaging brain before opening mouth. We were back in Hong Kong, and Matt—this old salt and rough and ready Scotsman— was to be my teacher. It was a peaceful morning in the mess, and people were getting up and ready for the work day. I was about to ruin this quiet start to the day, even though I wasn't aware of it at the time. How quickly things can change.

Matt had come off shore the previous night having been involved in a fight. He was a big guy and knew it. However, this particular night he met somebody bigger than him. Short story is, he had this great big fat bottom lip and, unbeknownst to me, was hung over and still angry this next morning. Well, I was about four rungs up the ladder going to wash up and clean my teeth in the bathroom when Matt stepped on the ladder to come down. I looked up, saw his bottom lip, and said, "Wow, look at Donald Duck."

Now, I need you to realize that Matt could have squeezed me up in his huge hands and placed me in his trouser pocket. He yelled, "Whhhhaaaaattttttt? You little punk!" along with a fusillade of words from that very special naval dictionary. I leaped from the ladder and ran for my very future existence. He pounded down the ladder and was racing through the mess, hot on my heels. On the other side of the mess was another ladder that went up, and I was making a beeline for it. I could hear cheering as I jumped the first two steps and was flying northward. I felt his hand clip my ankle, but I kept going at full bore.

I bolted down four deck passageway, as if shot from a bow. Then I sensed he was no longer in chase. I was right, and my heart, banging on the inside of my chest to get out, started to slow down to a gallop. I slinked back to the bathroom and got ready for work.

Later that day I was walking along four deck passageway and saw Matt several sections away. Luckily, he didn't see me before I whipped up a ladder to three deck, walked along, and dropped down behind him back to four deck. I got a hold of Peter to find a way out of this predicament without having my throat ripped out. He suggested I buy a case of beer and have him give it to Matt. Then I could approach Matt with some hope of physical survival.

I did all of the above and went to his area of the mess to apologize. He told me that at this point he had calmed down and thought it was actually quite funny. I'm sure the beer gift had something to do with that. Anyway, he gave me a couple of cans from his stash and all was well. The thing is, if an older jack tar had said that to him it would have been all right. I was still a whippersnapper and had not quite arrived yet. Maybe all would fall into place on my next ship.

I didn't think about this at the time, but incidents like that were setting me up for a great career. Ducking and weaving were all part of the growing process, and Rome wasn't built in a day. Peter talked to me about watching what I say and keeping my head down a little more when in the company of seasoned mess members.

Working hard. My working life was going very well. I had a good of deal respect from the senior rates in my workshop, and I was careful about not letting that go to my head. They trusted me, and I kept my fifty fans running with great success. This was due to hard work and consistently working on my own time. I only later found out that the chiefs knew of my dedication. I also helped others with their group of fans without any fanfare. (Pun intended.)

As before, I was rotated to another workshop requiring different skills and knowledge. This was the heavy flight deck workshop. This workshop was responsible for all of the fuel pumps around the flight deck, the crane, all winches and hoisting motors, the two lift wells that brought the aircraft to the deck from the hangar below, two decks down. These lift wells had multiple motor generator sets and control systems along with lighting and safety cut off switching and lots more. We also maintained the four winches for the landing craft. The magnetic ring communication system also came under us along with flight deck lighting. The magnetic ring was how the chopper personnel communicated without pulling along reams of cable to their headsets. The magnetic headsets picked up the magnetic variations emanating from a large cable running around the deck.

The chief, Sam Collins, was a really good person who would listen and teach. He was always cool, calm and collected, and I learned from him. The petty officer under the chief, Toby Cranden, was the exact opposite. I didn't like him at all, and neither did anybody else. I suspected that the chief didn't either, but after the next incident, I was sure of it.

I had been on this section for quite a while and knew most of the ropes to a certain degree. Colin, only a slightly more experienced electrician than me, and I were given a task. It was to do planned maintenance on a landing craft winch controller. It's a huge panel with about sixty nuts and bolts holding on the front plate. We were to remove this plate and inspect all of the many contacts inside and do general touch up husbandry. There were several maintenance cards to tell us what needed to be done. These cards were to be signed off for each task we completed. The controllers were in the well that ran along the entire length of the flight deck on the port side. This well contained all of the equipment needed to assist in all kinds of flight activity. This included firefighting equipment and fuel pumps with their hoses and so on.

Colin and I spent a good three hours on this task and were really pleased with our work by the end of the day. The next morning on arrival at the work shop, the petty officer was standing there with legs akimbo and hands on his hips. We could tell he was about to explode. He did, and when he had finished, we both had two new orifices by which to excrete waist matter from our bodies. He asked us where the planned maintenance cards were. We couldn't find them. So after the screaming had stopped and he'd lowered his voice to a bellow, he suggested that we had left them in the equipment. Off we trotted with our tails between our legs and undertook the monumental task of removing the front panel again. The larger task here, though, is making sure it is watertight again afterwards.

The cards weren't there, and on returning back to the workshop, there was the petty officer waving the cards in his hand. He had them all along and then blasted us again. Apparently we had left them on the flight deck the day before. This, obviously, is very dangerous, as they could have been sucked into the intake valves of an aircraft. Fortunately, there were no flying stations during this time frame. The "airy fairies" had found the cards and taken them to the workshop. Airy fairies are what we called the Fleet Air Arm, the flight department of the Navy.

The chief had arrived during this time and sized up what had gone on, then sent us off on a short errand. We figured he wasn't happy with the way the PO had handled it. We were extremely busy at this juncture in time, and we had spent a good three hours on that fool's errand. With this in mind, we hung out within earshot of the workshop and were glad we did. The chief gave the same second waste management ejection stimulus to the PO that he had given us. Naturally, that made for an even grouchier pain-in-the-neck petty officer.

On another occasion when we were in Hong Kong, we went through an awful time. Our workshop was literally right under the flight deck. The deck head (ceiling) was the underneath of the flight deck itself. Why am I telling you this? Well, the powers that be had arranged for the flight deck to be stripped and re-layered and painted. So what? There were at least fifty, and that's a conservative guess, pneumatic hammers drilling away on the deck at the same time, chipping away the very hard landing surface. They were commonly called windy hammers and were so, so noisy. This went on for ten days and, as I said, our workshop was right below the deck in question. Even when ashore far from the ship, you could hear the hammers thundering away. It was just so awful I had to give this a mention.

REST AND RELAXATION

Life was good, and we were settling into a relaxed routine in Singapore. George knew of a neat place to go in Malaysia with a popular picnic and swimming hole. He could drive and invited Peter and me along for the trip. Although, technically, this entailed going into another country, there were no restrictions or papers required at the border. Also, the money was the same. Singapore dollars and Malaysian dollars were worth the same, and both were used freely on opposite sides of each border.

We crossed the causeway over the river to Johore Baru, checked in with the border guards, and were on our way to Kota Tinggi. It was about an hour drive with mainly jungle to look at, but it was a pleasant drive. On arrival we joined all kinds of families enjoying the park. The main attraction for us was the swimming. There was a fairly large swimming area at the base of a small river that came pouring down a hillside surrounded by trees and brush. We decided to climb up the sides of the river bed to explore the head of where the river came from with its multiple small cascading waterfalls. To our wonder and joy, quite a way upstream there was a sort of Adonis pool about forty feet in diameter. This fed the cascading small river and itself was fed by a larger waterfall that fell about twenty feet. We were far enough away from the crowd that all we could hear were the birds and the waterfall. The scenery was beautiful.

As nobody was anywhere near this area and we could see down the way, we decided to go skinny dipping. The water was cool until you got used to it, and the sun was hot. Life was good.

After a while, we joined the throng below, got a drink, and bought some food from the vendors. One thing I will never forget was a man across the road from the parking. He had a small stand on the edge of a pineapple field. He had fresh-cut pineapple sitting on ice. We bought some of his wares and, holy sweet Jesus, it was the most fantastic sweet, dripping juicy, tasty pineapple I have ever eaten. I have not had anything even close to it since. I can taste it just writing about it. I can feel the juices running down the sides of my mouth. This was a wonderful day in the life.

Something else I had got into was dingy sailing on the river. The ship had several boats, and I joined the sailing club and learned how to sail. I spent many a day on the river and got involved with racing and such. I never did win a race, but for me that wasn't the point. I did get close a couple of times and came in second. Racing downwind with the spinnaker up was my favorite thing to do. The wind zooming me along and the waves splashing my face was unadulterated fun, just plain exhilarating. Of course, then there was the dousing down of the dingy to remove all the salt and then storing it in the sheds. It was all worth the effort, even with the two mile trek back on board. Another good night's sleep always followed these days.

Our workshop was up five steps from the deck on a raised section. So it was five steps up, walk six or seven steps, and then five steps down. On the forward side was a huge spud locker, on the aft side a large open area. One day a stoker in the well up by the flight deck opened a fuel valve to fill a small bucket. When no fuel came out, he opened it some more. Realizing the pump must be turned off; he went to turn it on. The pump was two decks down. Of course, when he turned the pump on, fuel came spewing out of the valve and pouring down onto the deck by our workshop. By the time the valve was turned off, the deck was about three inches deep in fuel. Colin and I stood there in awe as a dockyard worker came ambling by, wading through the fuel, smoking a cigarette. "No! No!" we yelled. "Put out the cigarette!" He did, by throwing it into the aircraft high octane gasoline. Colin dove into the workshop as I dove wildly into the spud locker while covering my head. Fortunately, the cigarette just went out and didn't ignite the fuel. That was a certainly an underwear changing episode.

THE ROARING PAPER TIGER

When things are going hunky dory, it's best to glance over your shoulder and watch the terrain. We received word that the Chinese Red Guards had flooded into Hong Kong, and there were riots and organized demonstrations. This was in the days of Chairman Mao. Yep, ol' Mao Tse Tung was flexing his muscles. Before I knew it, actually I felt it, we were sailing at full speed ahead for the Island. I say I felt it because we had three days of frantically storing ship, fully fueling, and loading up fifteen hundred marines with all their equipment. This was no easy task and a test of my stamina, resilience and strength. I was gaining height, weight, and muscle by the minute.

I learned that when a ship is at full throttle even small waves send you into rising and falling more that you want. The commandoes trained daily on the week long trip, for riot control. This was done on the flight deck, which had multiple rows of jeeps, trucks and infantry mobile weaponry. When we sailed into the harbor and came alongside, it was done with great pageantry and fanfare. We wanted to make our presence known. The Red Star Hong Kong newspaper, a Chinese publication in Chinese and English, had a headline that read *We are not afraid of your British Paper Tiger.* "Well, then," I thought to myself, "why did you run and hide as soon as we came in?"

All day and night we had sentries walking up and down on the jetty with rifles, as well as sentries with rifles at various stages along the outboard side of the ship. On the second night in port, I was on duty watch and became one of those sentries on the jetty for four hours. I had the middle watch, 2400 hours to 0400 hours After they gave us our instructions, they handed us our rifles. I was looking at the Master at Arms waiting for my magazine or magazines when he asked, "What are you looking at?" I said that I had not been given any ammunition. He said, "That's right and you're not getting any." Apparently we weren't considered trained and experienced enough to be trusted with live rounds. I was thinking, "Well, you trust me enough to get my defenseless self-killed." This time I did manage to engage brain before opening my big mouth and said nothing. I didn't even have a walkie talkie to report anything I saw. I guessed all this was for show, but what if they did attack? I felt like that bird in the miners' cage. If I dropped dead, then something was wrong. I did make it alive through my watch and went to bed.

The commandoes were busy for the three weeks we were in port and cleaned out the Red Guards. This was a bad move by China because we found their entire secret hiding rooms. They were behind secret walls in hotel hallways, with some even having medical operating rooms. They were highly organized but the constant raids helped by information from the Hong Kong people were precise and in depth.

The people of Hong Kong knew which side their bread was buttered on. They didn't want to go back under Chairman Mao. The only real reason the riots were successful was that the Red Guards paid the really poor people to be part of them. The guards then threatened them if they didn't perform.

All's well that ends well. The peace restored, we sailed back to Singapore. Once there we continued catching up on all the planned maintenance schedules and really made a dent in the repairs to all kinds of equipment, including ourselves.

THIS STORY IS A STRETCH

One day in Singapore, my neck sort of hurt a little. As the day progressed it got worse. That night I was in great pain any time I moved my neck. When I say pain I mean pain. Excruciating pain. I only had to move a micro-inch and, ouch, it hurt. The next morning at the sick bay the chief told me to report to the hospital. I didn't know what was going to happen. When I got there at 1400 hours as required, there was the chief, a surgeon and two rather large male nurses.

Everybody helped me onto the operating table as they stretched me out. I was then positioned like a horizontal Jesus on the cross and told this was going to be very painful. I looked around a bit and didn't see any nails. Maybe things wouldn't be so bad after all. Their faces told me they were serious. My heart was pumping and seemed like an alien trying to escape the chest cavity as my eyes popped out of their sockets.

The two large nurses were pinning my torso and legs down as the surgeon pulled my neck out toward him as far as he could. "Not too bad at this juncture," I thought. Then he twisted it hard to one side and back again as my body reacted to what seemed like a ten thousand volt shock.

He asked me if I was okay. Stupid me said yes. "Okay then let's try two more of those to the same side," he said. The sweat must have drained my body of all natural fluid as I braced myself for the next jolt. After two more twists and yet two more twists to the other side he said that was enough for this session. He was speaking like a trained torturer from a Russian Gulag.

"Next session?" I thought. "Next session?"

I did go back the next day more prepared for the neck stretcher dude and once again survived the torture. After that session, although somewhat sore, my neck slowly returned to normal without further treatment. Nobody knew what caused the anomaly, or at least I wasn't told. Those were different times, and being a junior also-ran probably had something to do with my being kept in the dark.

Not long after that, I was on duty sitting in the mess with Peter, playing cards. Over the *Tannoy* or loud speaker system came the message, "Sunset is in five minutes time at 2117 hours." When you are the lead ship in port, all the other ships follow your lead for turning on and off the navigation lights. If they are late, they send a bad message from the lead ship that somebody is in trouble.

I didn't know exactly what that message would be if the lead ship was late, and I didn't want to find out. I was on five deck, and the navigation switches were on zero three deck next to the bridge. That's eight decks to climb and several sections to go horizontally in five minutes. Peter and I looked at each other and made a wild dash for the ladder. I was flying up the ladders two steps at a time and dodging around people in the passageways with Peter hot on my heels.

As we bolted the last few feet to the bridge we heard the quartermaster page, "Standby, standby, now. The time is 2117 hours." This was as I snatched down one bank of switches as Peter snatched down the other. Whew, we made it with zero seconds to spare. We laughed between gasps and gulps of air as we slid down the bulkheads to the deck. That was too close for comfort. Of course, we then had to walk around all the navigation light positions to check they were all on and change any bulbs that were defective. That could be done in slow time.

Shore leave excursion. We were well into our stint in the Far East by now, and the crew were offered a week's shore leave if they chose to exercise it. Peter and I decided to take a trip back to Ipoh and the Hong Kong Hotel.

This time though we went by train. On buying the tickets we were told there were three classes of carriages. We thought third class would be people, chickens, ducks and geese. First class was pricey for our budget and so we decided on second class. This was to be a sleeper train through the night with a stop in Kuala Lumpa to change to the regular day train.

That evening on boarding the train we were a trifle dismayed at our quarters. The carriage had a walkway down the middle. Then on each side were ten two tier bunks with a curtain to pull across the bunk-type bed for privacy. There was no air conditioning unless you counted the window by the top bunk, which could be opened. Of course, this allowed free travel for the hordes of mosquitoes all the way to our destination. This gave our assailants free snacks and breakfast. We smiled and joked and accepted our new adventure, but it did make us wonder what third class was like. Maybe standing room only with the aforementioned farm yard menagerie?

As the narrow gauge train trundled through the night, we did manage to get some shut eye. Next thing you know, we were rolling into Kuala Lumpa and disembarking for the next stage of our journey. We had time to look around the city for a short while before the next train. This we did and had ourselves a hearty breakfast that included some local cuisine. We topped that off with liquids and were well satiated. The fresh pineapple juice was almost as good as at Kota Tinggi.

It was time to return to the rail station and we boarded without delay. There was enough room on the seats, but they were made of plain wooden slats. No cushioning, that's right, no cushioning, except for that on our tushes. The trip, which was meant to be two hours, took four hours. One hold up was cows on the track. Another was a wheel of the engine coming off the track. A crane was brought in for the latter and we carried on our merry way. Apparently this was not so unusual. All in a day's travel, I suppose.

On our eventual safe arrival in Ipoh, we hailed a taxi and bailed out at the hotel. We were welcomed with open arms and great ceremony and shown our rooms on the third floor. Outside of the rooms was a small dining area for each floor where the free breakfast would be served. This was quite different and enjoyable. There was also a little office where a key boy, who looked after the rooms and the breakfast orders, was stationed.

After a couple of days we realized we were the only white people in town, which made us a bit of a novelty. We enjoyed the wonderful people and the way we were treated, especially in the restaurants.

Adventure in Penang. On day four we took a train to Penang, which turned out to be an experience of a lifetime—or at least up to that point in my life. Penang proper is an island. This meant a boat ride from the mainland on what Peter and I described as the *African Queen*. The only thing missing was Humphrey Bogart and Katherine Hepburn. The sides seem to be held together with glue, string, and a few nails. There wasn't a sign of any paint left on the woodwork, and once we got under way the clanking and the chunking sounds coming from the engine room were ominous. The belching thick, black smoke was the final touch to this scary picture. We made the crossing without sinking, which was not only a blessing but a minor miracle. The other million or so people aboard were used to this breath-holding trip, it seemed, as they didn't seem to be fazed at all.

This was only a day trip, so we made as much haste as possible to see the sights. The ancient temples of worship were fascinating, and the two guides, whom we hired, were extremely knowledgeable and helpful. In one temple we were a little surprised because an illegal gambling game was going on. It was a card trick where the shyster laid out three cards and, after placing a bet, the player picks out the queen. Of course, he shuffled the cards at amazing speed and mostly won the money. Moving on, we enjoyed the city and its sights along with the friendly locals. I always enjoy the bartering for souvenirs and trying the street vendor goodies from the small carts.

The day went quickly and we traversed the waterway back to the mainland via Puffing Billy, also known to us as the African Queen. The train ride was uneventful, and on arrival in Ipoh, we supped a couple of beers in the hotel bar and sank into our beds.

We explored the city the next day and enjoyed some beautiful gardens and later that evening took in the fun at a fair. On one stall with rifles we had to hit five, finger-like digits sticking up to win a prize. After a couple of failed attempts, I figured out if I aimed slightly to the left I would hit the target. I collected several coupons to win one of the larger teddy bears, which I gave to a young boy with his grateful parents. When I went to fire again, the proprietor wouldn't let me continue. That was okay. We went on our merry way and had a whole lot of kid stuff fun.

After the obligatory couple of beers, we rested our weary bodies. This is where things got hairy. Between our two beds was a bedside table and a lamp. Suddenly in the middle of the night, I sprung my eyes open to the sound of a sharp clunk. It seemed to come from the bottom of my bed. I was lying on my stomach and looked over at Peter's bed, thinking he might have gotten up. He was fast asleep.

You know how you get the sense that someone or something is there? I had that feeling. I braced myself for a leap out of bed. Then I sprang, at the same time whipping my covers to one side. There before me stood a man, my wallet with six hundred dollars in it in one hand, my trousers in the other. I yelled at Peter, who was closest to the door, as said man tried to dash out. Peter reacted really quickly for somebody asleep and pinned the man between the door and door frame. He managed to wriggle free and fly for the stairwell. I was in hot pursuit, clad only in a skimpy pair of brief underwear. Pounding down the three flights of stairs, the man flew across the foyer and made it to the street. That's where I halted my enthusiastically blind, reckless chase. He may have had buddies waiting, and I was also not prepared to continue outside almost buck naked.

This is where it got even weirder. Although it was still dark outside, it was later in the morning than I thought. As I turned to go back upstairs I noticed quite a lot of people at the checkout desk, as well as a few porters and other characters. Naturally, they were all staring at this near naked white boy's body. In true British fashion, with my chin slightly raised, I slowly started to ascend the stairs, turned to the gaping persons, and said, "Good morning, everyone." Nobody said a word, and I returned to our room. Stiff upper lip and all that, y' know, ol' chap.

Peter was waiting on the third floor for me, having witnessed the scene from over the balcony. We chuckled to ourselves and went back to bed. We did inspect our belongings and everything was present including my money-filled wallet. Out of the ordeal, we did gain a pair of flip flops that fell off the burglar as he fled. We didn't keep them.

Later we spoke to management and the police. They indicated that they wouldn't be able to catch this perpetrator, which we understood. The manager did place two sliding bolts on the inside of our door the same day. He said he did this to all the rooms, but I'll bet he didn't. We decided the boy in the little kiosk on our floor must have handed the thief the key, as no break-in marks were evident. Also, we didn't see the same person there again. As we were the only white folk in town, they must have thought we were well off financially. This was partially true, as we both had around the same six hundred Malay dollars—quite a haul to street people, especially fifty years ago.

Scary times. The journey back was just as harrowing and interesting, and we landed back on board to the safety of familiarity. A short while later I was sitting in the mess, all quiet and serene. That didn't last long. One of the senior killicks, Bruce Crandon, came bursting in, yelling and screaming at me. He was a monster jerk at the best of times, but I had no idea what he was blabbering about this time. He was waving his arms at me and asking how the hell a punk junior rate could get a VG/SUP on his first report. "This is ridiculous. You don't know anything, you groveling snot!" he said. Other disturbing special dictionary words were thrown in for effect, but I lost count. I had no idea what he was going on and on about, spitting out of his lame mouth. I just stood there and took it as Peter tried to go between us. Peter did slow him down and got a hold of the situation. Everybody in the vicinity did know what he was freaking out about, but I still did not.

After Bruce stormed off, Peter sat me down and went through the excited message with me. Apparently, every year we got a report on our behavior and working abilities. The VG means "very good" for conduct. That was the top mark, which almost all crew members got. One had to be a fairly consistent offender, like often late off shore for instance, to be marked down in that category.

The SUP stood for superior. This was also the top grade mark for your working life. There were ten sub-categories under this umbrella each with a mark out of ten. These were given by the chiefs I had worked for. I was given high enough marks to be ranked superior overall. Knowing Bruce, he didn't score very well in some areas. His electrical knowledge was really good as far as I knew, but his attitude and work ethic were something to be desired. He more than likely rubbed people the wrong way. Who knows his family life and background, though? It is so dangerous to judge a fellow man until you have walked a mile in his footsteps. Everybody else congratulated me including the killick in charge over all, even over other killicks.

Much to the chagrin of my latest chief, I was transferred to the domestic workshop. This entailed looking after all the lighting on board, refrigeration, the sound reproduction equipment, and anything of a domestic nature. The *SRE*, as it was referred to, is a radio system that goes to speakers in all of the mess decks. It does go to some other places but primarily mess decks. There is a studio and volunteer DJs. Some of the chiefs grumbled because they wanted me on more sophisticated work, i.e. their section.

A dangerous repair? One day I was asked to go to the shaft passageway near the stern to repair the lighting. "Sure, no problem," I said. Hah, it was not so easy. I needed to go to the bridge and get a *Leave open* sign for the hatch in order to go down to the shaft passage, port side. The entry hatch was on four deck beyond the wardroom area, which was the officer's mess. I opened the hatch and looked down the 2' X 2' shaft that went to nine deck. Halfway down there was a net with a hole in it to squeeze through. This wasn't the problem. The problem was that it was pitch black at the bottom, which is why I was there.

I was still somewhat scared of being alone in the dark. Under the net I went, clutching my tool bag. The noise of the shaft that turned the port screw was deafening. If I shouted out that I was in trouble, nobody would hear me, and I was also in a part of the ship where nobody goes. Wonderful. Ghost stories abounded for this area, and there I was trapping myself with nowhere to escape.

The part where my legs went below the cross passage was scary. This was because I couldn't see if anything was there until I got my full body in the shaft passage itself. What if something touched my leg? Would I survive the shock? Would I burn the ladder as I buzzed my way up at breakneck speed? I had a flashlight, but what if that failed me or I dropped it and broke the bulb? What if, what if, what if? Aaaaarrrggghhhhhhh, panic.

The churning of the shaft was eye-popping on its own; the staleness of the air was awful. There was hardly any decent oxygen and no help in sight. Fixing the light fixture itself was difficult under the circumstances. It had a safety shield around it that needed a special key, which I had, to unlock it and turn the cage. This, of course, was rusted tight. My hammer loosened it enough for me to continue. Once one light bulb was changed, I could see properly and all was calm again. I was in an oval, small hallway well below the waves with this massive shaft churning away inches from my leg. It took some getting used to. The rest of the fixtures were then easier to deal with.

On ascending the ladder, I felt uneasiness until I got the other side of that web-like net I told you about. Just as I was reaching over the combing of the hatch, my arm was grabbed to help me up. I just about freaked and almost fell into that net. I had to swallow hard to push my heart back down my throat. Peter had come down to check on me as he had done this task himself and knew how hard it was. This was really nice of him, but he just about gave me a heart attack. We laughed so hard, but that's life in a blue suit.

GETTING A THUMBS UP

Another thing Peter introduced me to was showing movies. He and another crew member had the knowledge to use the old Bell and Howell projectors with the two reels, one reel to feed into the projector and one to roll it onto. Peter taught me to set up the whole system in the lowered aircraft lift. The movies were shown in the lift well itself. He taught me on how to thread the film through a multitude of spinning wheels and sprockets and run a show. I quickly learned that when it was time to change reels you had better be quick and correct. The film goers who had paid a modest fee were always anxious to get on with the plot.

Once, when Peter couldn't be there, I was doing a special showing on my own in the wardroom with officers in attendance. The film was going along nicely and was nearing the end of the first reel when, to my horror, I noticed that the take-up spool was pinched a trifle. It was just enough to stop the film feeding into the center and building to the outside. Consequently, the film was stacking up on the outside of the spool and was about to topple. I was already nerve wracked from being in the wardroom with all those officers, including the electrical commander and his henchmen. I stopped the film, turned on the light, and explained my dilemma. I was so embarrassed and as red as a beetroot. To my amazement, one of them said, "Okay, let's take a break for drinks and let the young man get sorted out." Then two or three others helped me carefully unravel the film up and down the deck all the way out. I was shocked at getting so much help, and relieved. To me, as a junior rate, officers were gods and to be worshiped. This changed everything as I saw they were human. We got underway again and finished the session. A couple of the officers even came to me afterwards and congratulated me on how I handled the situation.

Wow, by Jove, maybe I was a sailor now! I could talk to officers without my heart beating like a drum and my stomach roiling. Thanks to Peter for giving me so much knowledge and information.

Another incident involving movies happened during a fairly rough sea. The film had ended, and Peter and I were rewinding the reels on a special gadget. Because the ship was rolling quite heavily, I was guiding the back spool with my hand to stop it tipping over. When one spool is getting full and the other empty, the lesser spool will spin very fast. Suddenly, the ship jerked, and my thumb went into the holes of the spool. My thumb was shredded from top to bottom, and blood was everywhere.

It was late, midnight or so, and a young and inexperienced orderly was at the sickbay. He took out some iodine, then soaked some cotton wool with the iodine and wrapped it around my thumb. As the iodine struck my nervous system, I folded like a deck of cards. I don't know who the biggest idiot was—the orderly for doing it or me for letting him do it.

I came around, lying on the deck, to the sight of the sick bay chief running smelling salts under my nose. The chief took care of me then, and when Peter and I left, we could hear him chastising the poor orderly all the way down the passageway. I was to check with the chief in the morning, which I did. He put his arm around my shoulder and said, "Sorry about last night," and smiled. I thought that was really classy, and I felt respected.

I was now a "junior electrical mechanic first class." This was a promotion given by age, not by taking a test, so no big deal. I still felt good about it, though, because it took me off the ground onto the first step. I was now above the worms, at least. There is safety in height, as I would find out later.

Dry dock in Singapore. When we were in dry dock earlier in Singapore and boarding off of the ship, we could see the whole ship and nothing but the ship. The shape of the bow was not what I expected; the cut away under the top deck went further back before going down to the keel. I did get a pass, along with Peter, to go down to the bottom of the dock. (A pass was required so that they know how many are down there in case of accidents. At the end of each day all tickets have to be returned to a check point.) When we went around to the stern, there was the biggest surprise of all. The size of the screws was mind boggling. They were absolutely gigantonockerous. I could now connect those screws to the shaft size I encountered during my foray into the shaft passage.

Workers were everywhere, some chipping and painting, some welding. A major job was the stern glands being changed. That's where the shaft protrudes through the stern to the actual screws themselves. The vastness of the whole operation and depth of the dock was stunning. We felt like micro ants, not just regular ants, looking up at the flight deck worlds away. The noise was something else; no wonder we were issued ear plugs. We also wore hard hats, even though a missile falling from so high would probably finish anybody off anyway. It was a little spooky for a few minutes, but we got used to it quickly. The climb up the steps back from the bowels of the earth was breath sapping; we were thankful to have made it safe and sound to live another day.

PROMOTIONAL STUDIES

During some of the evenings at sea, Peter and I would go to a quiet workshop or office, where he would start asking me questions from a preparatory book for promotion to LEM, or leading electrical mechanic. This was very premature, as I was just a junior first class. To become a killick or LEM, I needed to go through being an electrical mechanic first class. This required taking an oral test, so brushing up with this prep book would certainly put me in good standing. This training was very difficult for me with my limited experience, but Peter kept pushing me. We plugged away at this book relentlessly, and I learned a lot.

Before leaving the Bulwark, I asked if I could take the electrical mechanic first class exam. This was several months before I was eligible to be promoted to that level. I'm guessing the powers that be considered me smart enough or thought I deserved a shot at it because I had worked so hard, so they agreed. The day of the exam arrived, and I got all dressed up to look my best. I walked into the room and freaked out. There before me sat the electrical commander, two lieutenant commanders and two lieutenants. This exam didn't warrant this much high power. Were they trying to intimidate me?

Peter had prepped me well; the questions came flying in from all angles. They covered many electrical divisions and angles, some easy, some tricky. I know I didn't do well on all the questions but felt good overall. I was sweating and my heart was in overdrive. I didn't want to disappoint Peter and I didn't want to go through that grilling again.

I was asked to step outside the room, and just a couple of minutes later I was called back in. Was the quickness good news or bad news? I figured if I had failed they would have gone back and forth longer. I was right; I had passed, and they said for such a young man they were impressed. That's was the first time in my life I had been called a man. The ordeal over, I rushed to tell Peter the good news.

Some of the lads in my previous junior mess were glad for me, but some were jealous. A couple of the older juniors who were almost eligible had not even thought about going for it. They were just coasting, and I was going full throttle, mainly due to Peter.

The chiefs were all happy for me and when I came upon them by chance, they all slapped me on the back. I think that made me the happiest. The petty officers were the same way. I was euphoric.

Time was closing down for me on the Bulwark. Apparently the ship was staying in the Far East, and the crew that had been aboard over two years was being replaced. We were being flown home.

MOVING DAYS

Three months earlier, we had filled out drafting preference forms. The forms asked where we would like to be shore based and which type of ship we would like. This didn't mean we would get our choice, but we might.

When my next station draft came through, my head exploded. Submarines. That was the last thing I wanted. That, of course, was what I got. To be fair, the last thing I had wanted before was an aircraft carrier, but that was the best thing that happened for me because I got so much diversified experience, not only in work but life. Were the karma angels at it again? They seemed to know what I needed more than I did.

Before going to submarine school, I had to have a physical. With my unseen angel on my shoulder, I reported to sick bay. There, to my surprise, a commander did my testing. After finding me fully fit, he asked if I wanted submarine service. I told him, "No," and he asked me why not. I explained that promotion on submarines was very slow, and I wanted to move up the ladder more quickly.

To my amazement he said, "Look, I can report that your ears are not good enough for submarine service. You have eleven weeks shore leave before reporting to base. If you are not drafted differently before the end of your leave, you must report to the submarine school. There you will be retested and will pass. That's the best I can do for you, okay?" I couldn't believe he would do that for me. I thanked him profusely and went on my merry way. Surely a new draft chit would arrive before the end of the rest of my time on Bulwark and my eleven weeks of shore leave.

My final days in Singapore were coming to an end. I shopped down the vill for the last time to get gifts for home. I also said goodbye to some of the shop keepers Peter and I had become friendly with. They wished us well and shook our hands.

The day before our departure, we all packed our kit bags and prepared for the flight home. The Navy had chartered a DC10 for us, and we headed out. I watched my recent home disappear as we rounded the first corner in the dockyard. There was a hollow feeling in my stomach; I felt quite nostalgic. The airport soon loomed ahead, and we were one step closer to departure. I had never flown before, so this was another new experience to notch on my belt. The flight was going to be interrupted for refueling in Bombay and Istanbul, two countries I had not visited on my world tour, courtesy of Mother England.

George Sands, the Fleet Air Arm friend I had gone to Kota Tinggi with, was onboard and sat next to me. I was nervous about flying, and he made fun of me a bit. Still, he took care of me and even buckled me in for take-off.

On landing in Bombay we were told there was to be a three hour delay. I remember going to the restaurant in the terminal and asking for a coffee. The waiter asked if I wanted milk, and I said yes and poured some in the cup. I just about threw up; floating on top of my coffee was a multitude of curdled globs bobbing up and down. That got left, and I ordered Coca-Cola.

Back in the plane, we took off and then touched base in Istanbul. The next stop was Brize Norton, a Royal Air Force base in the West of England. The old sea dogs on the trip had prepped me for customs. I had bought a Rolex watch and a Pentax camera in Sembawang. It had taken me three days of bartering to purchase the watch, but I had fun doing it. Anyway, I'd been told the custom officers were very good to returning sailors. They might look at a Rolex and tell you that it's a fake, a knock-off. I knew to just go along with it and curse my luck. I would not have to be paying taxes on it. I declared everything I should have and, as predicted, the customs officer laughed at my fake knock-offs. He gave a cursory look at the rest of my booty and sent me on my way.

Double doors opened automatically as we left the customs area, and there stood my mum and dad. I had no idea they would be there, and it was 0200 hours, yes, two in the morning. Mum held it together but dad broke down and cried and grabbed me like he'd never let me go. They both were so very happy to see their son.

We all settled down and walked to the car. The drive home was a couple of hundred miles, and I slept a good stretch of it. The Navy had told them of all the arrangements and times of arrival.

CIVILIAN STREET

It was strange to be home and took quite a lot of getting used to. It was difficult to get a good night's sleep for quite a while. The silence was deafening. The lullabies of the motors and engines and blowing air conditioning and the like were missing.

After I had been home a couple of days, Mum and Dad escorted me down to the local pub. Everybody cheered me when I entered, and there was no shortage of beer they wanted to buy me. I didn't drink too much, though, and don't forget—technically I was still under age.

As before, Mum and Dad were very proud of me, but so were the patrons of the pub. They hit me with a thousand questions that came flying in from all angles. It was quite a rush. As time went on, things subsided and I was accepted as one of the boys. My sorties to the bar became normal, which was a good thing. Being a celebrity was hard to process. I wasn't even eighteen years old yet.

Ten weeks gradually floated by, and I had not been reassigned from submarine service. I remembered that if I got to the submarine naval training base, I would pass my physical this time. I was really nervous and getting upset. I definitely didn't want submarine service. It had been relayed to me by the old sea dogs that once a submariner, always a submariner. This was not because they kept you in that service. Apparently, once you've served on a submarine, you don't want to leave. I still knew, though, that promotion was dead slow there, and I wanted to advance to chief someday.

On the Wednesday before I reported for my physical on Monday, I realized I had to suck it up and start getting ready, mentally and physically, for reporting to duty. On Thursday afternoon I watched as the postman delivered the letters around the cul-de-sac and climbed the steps to our house. In England back then, we didn't often get letters. I went to the door mat, and there was a letter from Her Majesty's Service. Was it? Could it be?

Hallelujah, it was! Yahoo, the drinks were on me.

I was told to report for duty to HMS Blake stationed in Portsmouth dockyard. That was strange because I needed to go to HMS Nelson, a shore base just outside the dockyard, first.

I was over the moon and far away. Was my destiny being guided? Why did I get to see a medical commander on board the Bulwark just for a preliminary physical checkup? The chief could have done that. The powers that be must have seen that it was a commander who had given my ears a failing mark, so they changed my drafting? "Take it, run with it, don't look back," I decided. Well, maybe a glance or two.

Monday morning, Dad drove me to the station again. Mum, who was a lot happier for me now that she knew I was making a go of it, waved with a smile. Growing up during WWII and see-ing men go away and not come back had to have been hard for her. I vowed that I *would* be back.

ONCE MORE INTO THE FRAY

My kit bag and green Navy suitcase were no lighter when I set off again, and I was no lighter either. I was now 5'5" and 130 pounds, and I had found some muscles I didn't know were there previously.

We—the train and I—chugged into Portsmouth railway station, and I stepped into the void of the next leg of my life's adventure. The path to the rest of my life was completely hidden as I stood on the rail platform; it was a feeling not for the meek and mild. What was that in the Bible? The meek shall inherit the earth? Well, they could jolly well have it. I was moving on as one of the strong.

I had learned not to confuse power with strength. On the Bulwark, I had seen both the arrogant, angry abuse of power as well as the caring use of power that helped you learn. At the moment I had only the power inside myself, and I needed to use it wisely. I had learned that the more knowledgeable and hardworking seniors were the better seniors. When things went wrong, the lesser guys always blamed their subordinates. The better guys took the responsibility and taught their subordinates the right way. I need to shelve that in the memory banks for my future.

But I digress; I struggled about a mile along the road to the gates of HMS Nelson. This was an old barracks, I mean old, old barracks. After going through the paperwork of checking in and finding my quarters, I dumped my gear and sat on the bed. I wondered what I was in for and why I was not on the HMS

Blake, the ship I had been assigned. Maybe it was at sea and I would have to wait until it came back to port.

As I mentioned, the building was ancient. The only heating in on the second floor of the brick building was an open coal fire at one end. It was January and pretty cold, but the fire was out. I found some materials and got it going, then went to get some bedding and made my bed. There were about thirty double bunks in the long room with the ceiling being about twelve feet high. The one coal fire had a lot of work to do, and who would keep it going during the night? At least the bathrooms were through the door at the end of the room.

I was well into my unpacking and bed making when a few men walked into the mess. After introductions, they told me that the Blake was nearing the end of an extensive four year refit. Aha. So that's why I was in Nelson. The crew lived in the barracks and worked on the ship. I soon found out there were only about 45 of us as skeleton crew. We would crew up when the ship was nearing its time to sail.

The funny thing is that they crew treated me like a regular, normal shipmate. Yes, I was a sailor now for sure.

A new boss. The next morning I took care of some details in Nelson, then struck out for the dockyard. The Blake, although much smaller than the Bulwark, was an old WWII cruiser, still a big ship. The age did not matter because everything was new, including all the armament. She was a sight to see in all her glory. The dockyard temporary lighting, straight wooden ladders, and cranes and wires were all over the place. Blue flashes of welding peppered the arena of the ship, and dockyard workers were everywhere. Wow.

I went up the gangway and walked around, not knowing where anything was. I didn't see any of the lads or senior rates, so I thought I'd go back to the barracks and make some calls. I was walking along the jetty alongside the ship when a voice bellowed, "Where are you going"? I froze on the spot. I recognize that voice. I didn't want to turn and confirm it, but I had to.

Oh, god, no. I was right. It was Toby Cranden, the mean petty officer from the flight deck workshop on the Bulwark. My heart sank, but maybe I would not have to work under him. With such a small skeleton crew, could my luck hold out?

PO Cranden came jauntily down the gangway and towered over me, trying to intimidate. It didn't work so much because I was a sailor now. As we both headed to a trailer office along the jetty, small talk was minimal. I couldn't believe my bad luck.

We entered the office, and after all the introductions and pleasantries, were assigned our jobs. Yippee! I wasn't under Cranden. I was going to work on the MRS3 gunnery system under a chief named Bernie Kossar.

The few electricians on board welcomed me as one of them and explained the general routine of the men and ship. Stand easy, the fifteen minute break midmorning and afternoon, spread itself to thirty minutes and the lunch hour was equally iffy. There was always a game or two of contract bridge going on that had to be completed before work resumed.

The lax schedule was interrupted by serious work, and I was eager to make a good impression with my new boss, Bernie. Another rating on this section, Richard Golding, also had a pretty good handle on the work involved and a good knowledge of the ship. He was quite a character. He and another cohort made cheese buns every morning and sold them at stand easy. They were a good price and saved us from having to run to a dockyard sandwich stand. I'm guessing they made a healthy profit.

The huge computer system had thousands and thousands of special connections with rubber covers over all the ends. All these insulating covers needed to be changed, and the chief kind of felt sorry when he gave us this tedious task, but it had to be completed as assigned. There were special tools to remove the sleeves each connection had without damaging them. However, our fingers ached at the end of everyday—but not enough to stop us lifting a pint of ale.

Talking of lifting a pint of ale, three of the seasoned sailors were in a ten pin bowling team, but one of them had been drafted to another area in the country. They asked me if I would like to join them. I jumped at the chance, and every Tuesday we would go to the bowling alley and play in a league. We had a lot of fun and a great social evening every week. After a couple of beers during the games, followed by a couple of beers after the games, we always ended up at an Indian food restaurant. Normally about twelve of us would go, and it was always a good night. The owner loved us coming in and even bought us all a gift at Christmas. We reciprocated the following week.

Duty watch in the dead of night. At night on the ship, rounds had to be done every four hours by the duty watch. The ship was long and tall, and every inch had to be inspected at 1600 hours, 2000 hours, 2400 hours, 0400 hours, and 0800 hours, by one person. On the nights I was duty, which was every four days, it was scary. The only real lighting down the main fore and aft passageway was string lighting. A protected light bulb was glowing about every twelve to fifteen feet. That is, the ones that were still working. As we were tied to the jetty but still on the river, we moved up and down and a little side to side. This swung the lights and moved shadows around. It also created creaking sounds along with the slap of the water against the side of the ship. Once you add in the stories of ghosts in the admirals cabin and paint shop where people had died, there's your recipe for aaarrrrgggghhhhh.

You could not cheat on rounds either. You had to carry a tape clock, which was a locked box with time marked tape inside that turned as time went by. At points designated around the ship were keys on a chain, each with numbers on them. When you got to the key, it was placed in a keyway and punched, thusly marking the tape and noting the time you were in that space. There was no lighting except by flashlight.

The keys were in these spaces:

- The very most forward position in the paint shop, right in the cleft of the bow.
- The bridge, four decks up on wooden slatted ladders. The diesel generator space, down five ladders from the bridge and through a non-lit passage, down a non-lit shaft on a straight ladder two decks into a pitch black compartment. The deck plates were up, and you had to walk across a crisscross of raised bars, then go between the bulkhead and the generator into the farthest corner. There was no way out but back. This was the scariest, making you feel trapped and corralled.
- The captain's cabin, not too bad but spooky.
- The dreaded admiral's cabin, so noted because a deadly accident had recently occurred there and ghosts had been seen. I needed to walk right across the far corner and around a multitude of material for refurbishing the whole compartment.

I could probably race around all of these positions in about two minutes, but it seemed to take me an hour. I was a nervous wreck all the way around, and when there was a thunder storm with lightening, the scene was set for a murder mystery horror story. I didn't want to be the dead body whose life ended with that freaky grotesque look on its face. The quarter master on the gangway probably just saw a blur as I rushed to and fro around the ship. Maybe the ghost stories came from people like me doing their job. Who knows?

I'VE GOT GAME

Let me change the subject to something of a lighter note. One Saturday when we were both on duty, Richard Golding and I wanted to go to a real football match between Portsmouth and an arch rival I cannot recall this far down the pike. It was a top game and we devised a plan to be there.

At lunch time we came back to the ship with some civilian clothes. A little later, we both left the gangway and went to an empty warehouse in the dockyard. In order to get to the dockyard main gate and not go past the ship, we needed to detour about a mile and a half all the way around the jetties. Once free of the dockyard, we boarded a bus for the sports ground. We just loved the game, which was going well for the home team. Half time arrived, and we were standing there, chatting about the game.

The next thing you know, there was a tap on my shoulder. We turned around, and, oh boy, there was the chief electrician from the Blake. "Aren't you two duty watch today?" he asked.

Now I want you to know there were about seventy-five thousand people watching the game that day. What are the odds he would see us? But he had. "Oh, hi, chief. Yeh, well, er, yes," we answered. "But we have stand-ins to cover the fire watch party we're in. We put in request forms and presumed you signed them."

"Well, no, I didn't see them and I didn't sign them. Why don't you two come to the office on Monday and we'll work this out?"

He didn't buy our story, so plan "B" had to come into play. After the game we retraced our steps back on board and went to work. We filled out the request forms we had spoken of and then placed them on the chief's desk. The forms had the right dates and the names of the shipmates who would cover for us.

On Monday in the chief's office, we didn't actually bluff our way through. He didn't buy our story. In this type of ship scenario things are much more relaxed and free. He knew he had us by the short and curlies and yanked hard. He enjoyed making us squirm and cringe, then sent us on our way sweating bullets but glad to have escaped punishment. I'm sure we heard him laughing at us all the way back to the ship.

I still can't believe it. Seventy five thousand people in a stadium and the chief stood right behind us. Later in my life I learned all about karma and I'm guessing this is how it works sometimes.

STEPPING ON UP

I had been on board over six months, and I was coasting nicely. There was one difference between the other junior rates and me. I don't want to suggest that they were lazy because they were not, but I did show more interest in my job than many of them, and I was dedicated. The ship was approaching the end of the refit period and RN personnel were gradually taking over from the dockyard. The crew was slowly swelling in numbers.

The chief cornered me one morning and said that I should start studying for my killicks PPE. For the uninitiated, that's the *preliminary professional examination.* I told him it was too soon as I had only been an electrical mechanic first class a short time. He said, "So what? You can get ahead of the game, and I'll help you all you need. He was a young chief himself and showed great interest in his workers. Later in my career, I took on this mantle rather to pass it forward. I said, "Okay, I'll go for it."

The next day he gave me all the prep books I needed, and we got to work. The purpose of the PPE exam was to see if I was worthy of getting a chance to take an electrical/electronic course for further promotion. The courses were very expensive, and they didn't want to waste the money on people who weren't likely to pass.

Of course we still had to do the required work on board to test and tune and get this gunnery system ready to fire, although that was still a long way off. We used lunch hours and time after work to study. I also worked in the mess at night and was getting a good handle on things.

The test was written and two and a half hours long, with no multiple choice questions. Instead, you had to sketch and describe or explain a theory, like, for example, "Explain the benefits of back EMF (electro motive force)." The questions were complicated and you had too know your stuff. If you passed the written exam, then you had an oral exam and would be grilled by electrical engineering officers for as long as they deemed necessary. If you were doing well, they continued with more questions, so a short interview was a bad sign.

After a few weeks of pounding me to dust, the chief said, "Okay, let's put in the request for the written." The test was set up, and in I went. It took me the whole two and a half hours, and I had the chief a little worried. I was just very precise and went over my answers meticulously. I wanted to pass so badly and didn't want to let him down. He had put in so many hours of his own time to help me.

Two agonizing days later, I was bowled over by the chief as he crashed into the transmitting station, tripping over the little door step and clutching my shoulders to stop himself from falling over. He finally gasped out, "You passed! You passed!" He was beaming from ear to ear and slapping me all over. His belief in me and his prodding and teaching had paid off. He had nothing to gain from this except the joy of giving and serving.

There was still one hurdle to go, the oral. For the oral, the powers that be needed to set up three officers for my test. This needed to be one officer from my ship and two independents. This took some time to set up, apparently, as I was told the exam would be in six weeks. Now what? I had no idea what they would ask. Oh boy!

The next day the chief came in and said he was pretty sure he knew the first question. He had been asked by our electrical officer for all the inputs and outputs of the radar director, computer, and gun turret for the MRS3 system, along with a block diagram. Were they going to ask about that? He thought so, but that was a tall order, in fact nigh on impossible for somebody of my experience. This meant they thought I was too young and were going to trip me up early.

They didn't reckon on Bernie, my chief. Bernie drew out the block diagram over the next day or so and put in all the inputs and outputs. He sat me down and went over and over the diagram, explaining the drawings. He then got me a job change off of his department onto watch keeping on the switchboard. This meant I could study while on switchboard duty. He then periodically came by to have me draw and explain to him, as well as encourage me. This man was sent from heaven, I just know it. Though never an atheist, I had never taken notice of any kind of religion. Looking back, I know a higher power had a hand in all of this.

So the day came, and I got all gussied up and looking posh. I strode positively into the compartment set aside for the grilling. There before me was my electrical divisional officer and two electrical commanders. I inwardly gulped and sat at the table facing the dynamic trio of dread lords.

They first asked me to sketch and describe the MRS3 system and put in all the inputs and outputs I could think of. All three sat back in their chairs looking pleased with themselves and, I'm sure, looking forward to an early lunch. I was delighted.

I picked up the provided pencil and started to draw my block diagram with lines going to and fro between various points. As I went about my business I boldly gave explanations and insights, more than they likely knew themselves. Almost an hour later, I came up for air to see their bewildered but smiling faces. They congratulated me on a very complete answer..

They then asked me about troubleshooting techniques and many other aspects of the job, but I was on a roll and brimming with confidence. I did stumble on some intense questioning on servos and magslips, and that did get me a tad frazzled, but I felt good about the rest of the session. Three hours later I left the room for them to discuss my future.

The chief was waiting outside. "How do you think it went?" he asked. "What did they ask? Did you do okay? Do you think you passed? How do you feel?" I told him about the first question and how I had aced it. He said, "Then don't worry. You've passed. I just know it."

Not even ten minutes went by before they called me back in. Was a short recess a good thing or a bad thing?

They went over a few flaky answers I had given, explained the better responses, and asked if I understood. I said I did, and then they questioned me to test that. They all then smiled and told me I had passed with a "Very good." They said I had surprised them with the detail and fluidity of my answer to the first question. Hands were shaken all around, which matched the shaking of the rest of my body.

I stepped outside and didn't have to say a word to Bernie. My face said it all and his face was aglow. I have never before had somebody else be so pleased for me.

I wasn't eligible to be a leading hand/killick for almost two years, but there I was poised to be automatically promoted when I was old enough. I had to be at least twenty and a half to be promoted because they wanted promoted people to have ample hands-on experience, not just schoolroom smarts. People who are good at passing tests are not always good at their job.

NOTHING TO SNIFF AT

Life went on. The bowling crew kept on bowling and having fun and Indian food. I went home most weekends when I wasn't on duty. I did have a car, as I had passed the driver's test when I was 17.

The ship was starting to look like a fighting machine instead of an old jalopy. System testing was getting more serious, and Bernie was keeping me by his side teaching me all kinds of troubleshooting techniques for scenarios I might come across.

One day Richard, my other cohort on the gunnery team, and I had a narrow escape from a weird situation. We were down a shaft with a straight ladder in a transmitting station for the gun. This was one of the blocks in my MRS3 diagram. We were given a product called Phospro to clean all the contacts at the back of a huge computer that filled a large compartment on the ship. We were spraying and wiping all morning and decided to go to lunch. When we got to the vertical ladder to climb out, we realized we were under the control of the spray. I started to climb and couldn't do it, so Richard pulled me aside and tried himself. He couldn't either. We could hardly speak and certainly couldn't shout and were going downhill fast. What to do? Dizziness was overcoming us, and Richard started to collapse. We were in trouble, real trouble.

I stepped over Richard and grabbed the highest rung I could reach. I managed to haul my body up and swung my other arm up; I got my elbow onto another rung and hung on. I wrapped my arm around the back of the ladder and slowly lifted my feet to the next level. Creeping slowly ever upward, I slung my elbows over the combing of the hatch and pulled my head into sight of the passageway. Luckily, a fellow sailor saw me and came over. Unfortunately, he thought I was messing around and almost left the area. That was until I weakly raised my arm and tried to speak. He immediately got to his knees and, grabbing fistfuls of shirt, pulled me over onto the deck. I pointed down the shaft and he got the message. He saw Richard and took off to get help. Two mates started to help me to the main deck, but Richard had to get out of the shaft first. Bunches of mates arrived and all was eventually well. Our headaches actually lasted into the next day, but that was as bad as it got. We had a story to tell and have laughed about it ever since.

One side note: After that, we did continue to clean and use the Phospro but had a large exhaust fan sucking away the fumes and another fan pumping in fresh air.

All of the small drawers that slid into the computer had a ton of pins on the back and slotted into the contacts that we had cleaned with the Phospro. They had circuit boards in them that included many vacuum tubes, resisters, capacitors and many other electronic parts. This was state of the art during this period of time. Well, they had to be cleaned and how was that going to be achieved? A huge learning experience was about to take place.

In the dockyard there was a building that housed a special electronic cleaning device. There were three very large metal sinks side by side sitting on top of a long oven. The sinks were to be filled to two thirds of capacity. The left-hand sink was to be filled with a special solution and the other two with warm water. On flipping a switch, the solution was agitated and the electronic drawers set in it were bombarded with electrons at high speed. After thirty minutes of this, they were then rinsed in the second sink and double rinsed in the third sink. The drawers were then placed in the oven to dry at a very low temperature so that the insulation on the wiring was safe. We had maybe one hundred and fifty of these to do, and it took all day. It was a tedious job but very worthwhile.

TRAIN TRACK TRIP

One day I was riding the ship's bike through the massive dock-yard to get some small supplies from the other end of the yard. The yard had its own railway system that wound all over the yard and was actually connected to the national grid. I was peddling away in the rain and crossing a *caisson*, which is a doorway, across the end of a dry dock. My bicycle wheel slid into the sunken railway track, jammed, and I went hurtling over the crossbars. The double somersault with tuck and pike followed by a swan dive would have earned me a gold medal in the Olympics. My crash landing may have disqualified me, though, as I lay concussed on the ground.

The relationship between dockyard union workers and naval personnel was not the greatest. I had always had a great relationship with them, though, because I respected what they did for us. Immediately two hefty dockies were on the ground at my side and redirecting traffic around me. Yes, cars also crossed these caissons. They picked up my bike and slowly got me vertical before escorting me to a close-by dockyard tea room, where they bought me a coffee and snack and sat with me until they were sure I was okay. I couldn't have been more grateful. When they found me, the dockies had been going for a break—two guardian angels just waiting in the wings to look after me.

The next day, having figured they took a break at the same time and place on a regular basis, I returned to the tea room. Sure enough, they were there. I offered to get them whatever they wanted, but they smiled and said that it wasn't necessary. I got myself a snack and a coffee and sat with them. I now had two good dockyard mateys, and that was a wonderful thing. Later when returning to Portsmouth not only on the Blake but other ships, I always sought them out. On occasion, they got me supplies right away when it might normally have taken weeks, and people on board would wonder how I got the stuff. I eventually had the tag of being the ship's specialty expeditor, the go-to guy for the electrical department. It's funny how life works when you can cooperate and earn unlikely friendships.

A sad day. Slightly astern of the Blake was an Israeli submarine being refitted. It had recently been handed back to the Israeli Navy after successfully completing extensive sea trials. It was time to make the journey back to their home land, and off they sailed with great fanfare. I believe it was just four days later when all communication was lost with the sub. Everybody was hoping it was just a glitch, and it seemed like the whole dockyard was silent for the next several days.

The sub was never heard from again and, to my knowledge, was never found, at least not that I ever heard. Even though we didn't really know anybody aboard, our hearts were heavy, It was as if we had lost members of our own family. I had learned that all sailors of the world, regardless of country or whether on a military or merchant ship, are brothers in kind.

It was widely suggested that the sub's crew had removed some installed parts to have as spares. They were again installed by the dockyard. What if they removed something that was not spotted and thusly not replaced?

We eventually shed most of the dockyard workers, whose work we were very grateful for. Most of their tasks had been completed, except for help in testing and tuning the major components, including the two gunnery systems, missile systems, engines and boiler rooms, and all radars, to name just the major responsibilities. Weeks later we took a short jaunt out into the English Channel for a day and back alongside. A day or so later a longer more extensive sortie proved just as successful. Things were going well, and one day soon we would be sailing with the fleet again. The old WWII cruiser had new life.

Stormy crossing. One morning Toby, a leading hand, came into the mess all excited. He knew the captain of the biggest yacht the navy owned, with the tallest mast in the port of Southampton. It's name was Malibu and was taken, during WWII, from a German commander. Toby was offered a weekend trip with two friends to Dieppe in France. Roger Barnes and I were the chosen ones.

Saturday morning we arrived at the Malibu, met the three permanent crew, and set off on the huge, 10 berth yacht. It was a gorgeous day and the seas were calm for the channel. During the trip we were taught all kinds of sailing lessons using those ratcheted turning handles and tacking with such a large boat. My Singapore dingy sailing helped a little but this was so much more.

We spent the evening and next morning visiting Dieppe. One of the crew had a slight tay-tar-tate with a French sailor, which could have got ugly but things settled down okay.

Around 1600 hours on Sunday we up anchored and set out for Alderney, one of the larger Channel Isles. The weather was changing fast, but the skipper knew a tavern owner and wanted to visit.

The sea was quite choppy, and at 2200 hours we lowered the motor boat, tied up at the wharf, and went to a pub. I only had two drinks, but the rest of the group was soon a little worse for wear. I was a tad concerned, but we got back aboard in one piece. Everybody piled below except the skipper, who started giving me instructions on how to navigate back to Southampton in the now gale force winds with no moonlight and torrential rain. He knew he'd had too much to drink.

I haven't yet said the sea was now ugly and angry with large waves. The boat's wheel was very large like those on a pirate ship and I was in full weather gear with just my eyes and nose peeking out. He told me to just keep the boat heading on a particular course and when I saw two lighted towers to give him a call. then he went below.

It was now midnight as we set off with no sails up and just the motor to send us across the way. This was a very dangerous crossing for a novice like me in the busiest shipping lanes in the world. To make it worse, the wind was horrendous and the waves cold and unrelenting as they crashed continuously into my freezing soul.

Fighting the wheel to stay on course was incredibly challenging as we were buffeted from hell to all kingdom come. It's a good thing I was as fit as I was. We were tossed from side to side and up and down through crashing waves as I fought to stay on the given heading. As 0600 or so slid by, I saw two flashing lights on two towers through the mist. Had I actually made it? How I kept the boat on course is another unexplained miracle.

I woke the skipper ,and he got us alongside the customs jetty past the breakwater as I lay slumped below, dead to the world.

HORSES FOR COURSES

Something unexpected happened. I received drafting orders to join another ship in about two months. I later found out that the drafting office had only put me on the Blake as a quick temporary fix after I was removed from submarine service. Now I was to join HMS Bacchante, a Leander class frigate. I was to fly out to Montreal in Canada, where it was going to cover the opening of the world fair being held there. Wow. What a great assignment! Bacchante was then going on a North American and Caribbean tour. Double wow.

Then another bizarre twist came into my life. Two weeks later I received a draft to HMS Collingwood, the electrical training establishment. With it, a note said I had a choice of going to Collingwood for the leading hand course or continuing with the draft to HMS Bacchante. Tom, my chief, brought this news to me and had a determined look on his face. He knew what an exciting adventure I thought the Bacchante would be at the young age of nineteen (Yep, I was nineteen now), and also knew what a great opportunity it was to potentially leapfrog years ahead as far as a future promotion was concerned.

I didn't fully understand the ramifications of this, not even after he explained the situation. He said that this was the chance of a lifetime, that never in his whole naval experience had anybody been given a choice of draft. He told me to grab the chance and go to Collingwood; I would have plenty of time to go around the world later. He badgered me with logic until I finally said I would join the electrical course.

Tom slapped me on the back and smiled from ear to ear, but I was scared. I was going on a course tipped for older people with a rank on their arm. I was already feeling intimidated because their experience and knowledge would be much greater than mine.

I had to wait to see when the final draft date would be implemented, and daily life continued. I could tell that the other killicks were thrilled to bits for me, though some of the lads who were older and hadn't taken the exam were maybe less so. They knew it took a lot of studying, though, which many of them weren't prepared to do. Maybe it inspired them to see a young whippersnapper like me make the effort and pass. Maybe it suggested to them that they should bite the bullet. After all, the money difference was huge.

We finally sailed in a full damage control setting. The ship was not ready to commission yet by quite a stretch, but things like the engine and boiler and stern glands needed to be proved in real time. So off we trotted into the English Channel for a lengthier trip.

A rescue at sea. On day two, somebody spotted an SOS red flare down channel, and we were dispatched to check it out. We were the closest ship and got there first. This was very fortunate for the Indian man in a fairly large row boat. He was about to sink from the weight of the now burgeoning sacks of wet rice that were expanding and bursting. I say fortunate because we had a large crane on deck and could save not only him but also his boat.

We very slowly came alongside because trying to cozy up to something so small with several thousand tons of might is extremely tricky. The captain's skills were up to the task. After getting said individual on board, we proceeded to empty the boat, get strops around it and hoist it aboard.

You may be asking yourself what the heck an Indian was doing in the middle of the busiest shipping lane in the world. It turns out that he was on his way to India. Yes, India. When he asked friends the way to India, they told him to row down the Solent, the river through Portsmouth, and turn right at the English Channel. When he reached the Atlantic, he was to turn left. And oh, they said, "Take plenty of rice. It's a long way."

Now I can only assume his buddies were joking and not taking his question seriously. Unfortunately, he believed them. Is what I'm telling you a load of codswallop? Look, me mateys; truth really is stranger than fiction. We all had a good laugh with him and entertained him in the electrical mess deck. He felt so foolish but held his head high and took it in good spirit. He was a good guy.

JUGGLING JAUNTS

A few weeks later my draft chit came in for me to join HMS Excellent. What? That wasn't the deal. What game were they playing?

As usual, my wise ol' Chief Kossar came to my rescue. He explained that as I was going to leave the ship, they needed to get somebody up to speed with my job before the ship became fully functional and got commissioned for the fleet. The trip to Whale Island, as it was known, was going to be short and temporary.

The only fear now was that this was the seaman training school and very strict. Dress code was tight, and all the military stuff not usually associated with the electrical or mechanical engineering branches came into play.

Playing football. During the three month stopover, I got involved in the five-a-side football league. We played during the lunch break almost every day, and it was a lot of highly competitive fun. My team was deemed to be the underdog in the club final, mainly because of our size. We were good players, though, and fleet of foot.

The game was well under way in the second 15-minute half, and I was racing for a 50/50 ball. So was a monster posing as a human being. He thought I would back off at the last second. I didn't. We clashed head on at full speed. Physics being the way it is, I slammed into the ground going backwards at a speed not to the liking of my body. I lay unconscious on the ground and had to be brought around with smelling salts.

After a few moments, I was up and running again. Soon I actually scored the winning goal—and that's not something I'm making up for this book!

After the game, Monster Man came over right away and asked me how I felt. We laughed and sank the first of many beers. I still have the coin that all the winning team members received. I'm very proud of that little ol' coin; it's in the china cabinet in the dining room.

School of hard knocks. I was soon back at Collingwood again. This time I got to live in fairly new living quarters. There were four people to a large, comfortable room, and the area was spotless. I soon had three other roommates, two of whom turned out to be drunkards.

It was but a few days before we were collecting as a class on the parade ground and, after the daily diatribe from the dais, the playing of "God Save the Queen" by the Collingwood volunteer band, and prayers, off we marched to the classroom.

The course took us from a free and enjoyable life to a desk and chair. Slam! All morning, every morning, for four weeks it was four hours of math, followed by four hours of solid electronic theory in the afternoon. There were eleven different classes and tests to pass. If you failed two tests during the course, you were removed from the class. Everybody except me was a leading hand and would be demoted back to EM1. If I failed, I would just leave the course.

One person passed the electronic test and failed the math test. He was back-classed to the next class coming through a couple of months later and failed the math test again. I suppose his number was up.

The leading hands' duty roster made them duty about once a month—patrol duty, clean camp duty, main gate runner, and general dogs' body. But because I was an EM1, I was duty every four days. "This isn't fair," I thought, so I tried out for the volunteer band, which did no duties at all. It's called a blue card job because the card you hand in when going ashore is actually blue. All I had to do was go to band practice once a week. The other advantage was that I played with the band every morning on the parade ground, which meant I didn't march to the classroom. I just independently ambled down there. In case you're wondering how I managed to join the band so easily, I learned how to play the bugle in the Boy Scouts.

Before one Memorial Day, they asked for a volunteer to play "Last Post" at two different churches. I figured I'd do it as I'd get paid for each event by the hosts. The first one went quite well. I was picked up by a church member and driven to and fro. I did manage to go really high on one note that rattled the ears of all in attendance, but the whole piece was not too bad. The driver offered me two pounds for my troubles.

This is where I got singed. To be polite, I said, "It's okay. Keep the money."

He then said, "Okay, thanks."

Wow. I had just lost two quid. When the next church guy drove me home and offered the money, I smartly said "Thank you very much," and took it.

I found the course tough, and interjected into it was two weeks of leadership training. Although this was actually not part of the curriculum that you needed to pass, it would sure look good on your record if you did well. Plus, it was something I really enjoyed.

Some of the training was on the parade ground; some was practical, with classroom time and then weekend orienteering in the forest. The practical was a series of difficult commando type tasks that each team had to undertake, such as knots and pole lashings to build a structure. Each task was led by a different leader and, largely due to my scout training, I did well.

This made me more palatable to the whole class as a non killick. They could see I was every bit as good as they were and, in some cases, better. This leadership training really helped me through the rest of my life, and not just the Navy.

Bad timing. One messy incident occurred one night in our quad of beds. One of the drunken sots came back a lot worse for wear. Two of us had short-sheeted his bed, folding his bed sheet half-way up so that when he tried to put his legs in, he hit the bottom of the folded sheet.

This turned out to be bad timing on our part. He flew into a rage. On top of his drunkenness, he had just lost a fight, and we could now see that one eye was swollen with a massive bruise. He looked a bit like a painting from Picasso's Blue Period. He grabbed me around the throat and threw me down on his bed and jumped on top of me.

Did I mention that he was twice my size and a muscle boson? He was screaming and yelling about, beating me to a pulp, and had his other fist clenched about to pulverize me. I bellowed back and said I would punch him as hard as I could into his bad eye. I did have one free hand and he knew it.

"You wouldn't dare," he said.

"Is it worth the risk of losing your eyesight in that eye?"

This slowed him down, and I could see his body language change. I knew I had his attention and felt him relax a little as he realized what he was doing to a classmate. He got off of me, and the situation was resolved.

The next morning was a total turnaround for him. He couldn't stop apologizing, and I totally forgave him. "Would you really have punched my bad eye?" he asked.

"Yes," I said, "but only because I was in danger."

As is often the case after situations like this, we became better friends.

A CLOSE CALL

During the course I was taking, there was a two week summer leave. When I took off for home, I handed in my station card at the main gate, as usual, and drove home in my car. I left around noon on Saturday, which gave me until 0800 hours Monday morning.

When I returned to camp around 0100 hours Monday morning, my card could not be found. I had a legitimate leave and was back early, so it should not have been removed by the Navy police staff. The main gate petty officer finally got involved and found it in the "late off shore box."

I explained that I was actually early, not late. He asked if I had put in a request form, to which I answered that I didn't need to. It was automatic for our class to go on weekends if we were not duty. He then told me that a memo went out before main leave that all personnel were to request weekend leave during this two week leave period. So, it seemed, I was 16 hours absent without leave. This means heavy fines and stoppage of pay, plus stoppage of leave, not to mention a black blob on my record.

I was furious. When and where was this memo posted, and how come I didn't know about it? I was told to report to the main gate at 0700 hours to go in front of the officer of the day who would send me, probably, onto commander's report. This just wasn't right, as that was only about five hours from now and I'd need to get up at around 0600 hours to get to the gate in time.

I wasn't happy, but I got up the next morning and trotted off up the main drag, which was very long. I saw hordes of people, at least a hundred. I looked behind me, and more coming, like zombies.

At 0700 hours, the officer of the day arrived, saw all of us, and asked the quartermaster who all these people were and what they wanted. He replied, "They were all absent without leave."

The officer's first words were, "Oh, my God." He was a smart guy and quickly realized that nobody had got the memo. He said, "You are all dismissed." A huge cheer went up, and we all went to breakfast. What a relief, a sensible officer and a storm in a tea cup quelled.

Drafting orders. The last test on the course was taken and passed, and we were now assigned a job in various parts of the camp until our drafting orders came through. I was given a really nice job in an office with a good chief and a couple of petty officers. They wanted to know how the heck I had finished the killicks course and was still an EM1. Not only that, but it would be another six months or so before I was old enough to receive it. Remember, you have to be at least twenty years and six months to be a leading hand killick.

A message came into the office one morning in a brown envelope. It was my drafting orders, and I was assigned to a dream come true. The ship was a Leander class frigate comprised of about two hundred and fifty men. Everybody wanted a Leander class frigate. The name of the ship was HMS Dido and was the first of its class to be commissioned. I later found out that it had not, to this date, had a main dockyard assisted maintenance overhaul and wasn't going to get one soon. They were testing it to see how long it could go without major equipment and rewiring maintenance.

My next adventure was being loaded onto the projector of life for me. I never did get to play a movie of my choosing, but this was probably just as well.

NEW DIGS

Two weeks went by and I gladly watched HMS Collingwood disappear in my rearview mirror. The Dido had its home base in a different naval dockyard than both the Bulwark in Plymouth and the Blake in Portsmouth. Dido was in Chatham dockyard on the southeast coast. There was a naval training school attached to the side of the dockyard called HMS Pembroke. All the Navy cooks and chefs were trained there. I don't think I've mentioned to this point how wonderful, generally, the food was throughout the Navy.

A weekend at home was in the cards as it was on the way to my new assignment. I said goodbye to mum and dad again as Dido was leaving for the Far East the following week. This trip was going to be about nine months to a year long. Talk about jumping onboard and learning on the fly.

I heaved and clawed my way up the gangway. My kitbag, suitcase and tool kit slowed my progress to the brow. I saluted the flag and jumped aboard. I was so excited.

The chief electrician escorted me to the electrical mess deck, where I dumped my gear, and I followed him to the office. I had never been on such a small ship. The passageways were much narrower and the deck heads, *ceilings* to land lubbers, were much lower. When I was introduced to other chiefs in the small office, the first thing they noticed was the two stars on my electrical badge with no hook on my other arm.

I should explain. An EM1 had one star on his electrical badge on the right arm. A leading hand, before completing the

Collingwood course, had the same with an anchor on the left arm. This is why they were called *hooky,* another name for a killick or leading hand. The second star on the right arm meant you had completed the leading hand course. I had completed the course but was still not a leading hand.

Back in the mess deck later while I was unpacking, a very deep, broad midland accented voice boomed out, "What the bloody hell! Jack Frost, how the heck are you?" It was Brian from the mess in Collingwood during initial electrical training—the guy with the shotgun wedding, if you remember.

I was glad to see him, and we sat down over a beer as more greenies came in. It was the lunch hour, and people were coming in for their tot of rum. I was still too young to receive it, but everybody gave me sippers. Brian caught me up on some news about him. He now had four kids, he said, and I wondered, "Does he know how they are made?"

The sad part is that when he came back from a trip to the Far East and went home, the house was empty. Although corresponding normally with him, his wife had met somebody else and moved in with him. He was now divorced and trying to build a new life.

He was holding back the tears as he unfolded this story to me. As my time in the Navy progressed, this became a commonplace thing—the tales and tears that is. People seemed to be drawn to me to share their woes, especially personal ones. I listened and consoled, I never did give advice.

As tot time was unfolding, a tall ginger-headed and full-bearded old man came in. He was grumpy and snarly but greeted me with a smile and downed his third of a pint of grog in one swish. He then left the mess and disappeared in a flash. Brian and some others let me know that he was Arty Shaw, commonly known as Father. This was because he was older than dirt at the ripe old age of thirty-eight. He was at least fourteen years older than anybody else except one guy named Peter. He had apparently been up and down with promotion and demotion several times, from killick to EM1 and back.

I reported back to the office after lunch and the chief took me to my place of work. I wasn't expected to work today, just to unpack and settle in. I was going to work in the transmission station for the 4.5" gun. This was similar to the job I had on the Blake. Chief Roberts seemed a good person and was young and full of vim. I needed to explain my badge yet again. Things were looking good and I felt a great deal of pride and confidence.

ON THE ROAD AGAIN

We sailed a few days later with the next stop being Gibraltar via the English Channel and the Atlantic. This required going through the Bay of Biscay, one of the unfriendliest stretches of water ever. It is rough about eighty percent of the time. I had gone through it on the Bulwark, but that was a big ship and it wasn't too rough at the time. I was about to learn about rough seas and small ships.

We were tossed from here to kingdom come and then some. Later I was treated to much, much worse, but this was new to me. Sometimes you had to really hang on to your hollyhocks as your feet left the deck. Luckily, my mess deck was down aft. The further you go forward, the more the rise and fall because the rise of the bow does not match the rise of the stern. I didn't get sea sick (I actually never did throughout the Navy), but it sure took some getting used to. When I did feel the worse for wear, it was often due to the run ashore the night before sailing.

Gibraltar poked its head over the horizon, and we made a beeline for it. We were only in for a couple of days, but it was beautiful. I did some swimming at the Olympic size pool on naval property just outside the dockyard. We sank down a few beers at our favorite bar, the London Bar, an incredibly unique place with walls and ceilings completely covered with bank notes of all denominations. Gibraltar was always the last stop before coming home from faraway places, and the sailors didn't have enough left to make exchanging it worthwhile. So onto the wall it went.

Before returning on board one night about midnight, three of us were passing a small passageway between two buildings. In our slightly drunken stupor, we decided we wanted to explore. This passage wound around like a labyrinth, going left and right and left again. A long way into exploring it, we stopped and thought about returning to the main street. John decided to light up a cigarette and struck a match. The flame immediately blew out, but there wasn't any wind or breeze. We thought this funny, so he lit another match with two of us cupping our hands around it. The flame went sideways and went out. There was definitely no breeze, and because of the ghost stories that prevailed around Gibraltar, we bolted back the way we came. We were laughing so hard we could hardly stand up as we bailed out in a big snotty heap into the open main drag and relative safety. Oh, our brave military might! We hoped nobody was watching.

Cock of the Week award. Before leaving Gibraltar, I wanted to go across the other side of the basin to visit HMS Sheffield, a destroyer on its way back to Blighty after a lengthy commission to the Far East. I thought they might give me some extra supplies and asked the quartermaster to page the communication petty officer, who arrived very quickly. There before me was an old friend, James Hatton. After warm and hearty greetings, I told him what I needed and he requisitioned the supplies for me without hesitation. It was lunchtime by then, so he asked me to stay for a couple of beers. I had forgotten that we were sailing at 1300 hours, which was creeping up on us without my consent. The next thing I heard was a page for me to report to my ship.

I had started a tradition on board Dido of awarding a weekly trophy to the person who made the silliest mistake. The trophy was a large plastic cockerel, which was the logo for the Courage Brewery that supplied our beer. Ergo, the award was called the "Cock of the Week Award." It was very popular with the crew.

Back to the story. I rushed down the gangway of Sheffield and raced across the caisson to the other side of the basin. I looked up and saw everybody in their white uniforms lining the deck for a ceremonial exit. It was a long way to run and as I passed the bow of the ship, I noticed everybody dressed in a blue uniform. This didn't register too much as I heard somebody yell hold the crane. The crane was removing the gangway. I jumped onto the gangway and stormed up and onto the flight deck.

This is where it got weird; I didn't recognize anybody at all. Looking aft, I saw the Dido with all the personnel dressed in white. I had boarded the wrong ship. It happened that HMS Achilles was leaving port at the same time as us, heading back to England. Hence the blue suits.

I said, "Oops, wrong ship," and ran back down the gangway. It was a few short yards to the bow of Dido so I could already hear the cheering, laughing, and clapping of everybody lining the sides. The applause continued all the way down the Starboard side until I reached the top of the gangway and disappeared below deck.

I thought I was going to be in trouble, but the whole scenario made it more of a joke. The commander did call me to his cabin later, but it was to tell me I was going to be the recipient of the fabled "Cock of the Week Award." There wasn't a sailor aboard across all ranks, including the officers, who didn't slap me on the back and thank me for a good laugh.

WHO SAID PORT SAID?

We topped up our supplies and refueled before setting off across the Mediterranean Sea heading for Port Said. Going through the Suez Canal on a frigate wasn't much different than with the Bulwark. The traders, while anchored waiting for the convoy to form, were easier to deal with because they were just a few feet from the top deck to the water. The Gully Gully men, as the magicians were called, came on board for the trip through the Canal. They had special permission to sleep on the deck. Their wizardry was quite amazing, and they give a great show to the lads. They were called Gully Gully men because as they complete their latest trick, they said "Gully, gully, gully." I still don't know what it means. Maybe it's the same as abracadabra

The Red Sea swallowed us up and cooked us before whisking us into the Arabian Sea. I swear it's called the Red Sea because it is red hot there. On we pushed and were headed for the Maldives Islands, which are a cluster of islands right on the equator, southwest off the tip of India and Sri Lanka. These islands are actually a series of atolls, so all the islands are protected by a reef, which is the rim of an old volcano.

The strangest thing on approach to an atoll is that the first thing you see is palm tree tops poking out of the sea. As you get closer the trunks appear, and then you see crashing waves as they hit the yet unseen reefs protecting the land. The reason for this is, for the one we visited, was that the highest point of the atoll was nine feet above sea level.

This visit was a "showing the flag" exercise to let the locals know we still had their back. They were under British protection and appreciated the occasional acknowledgement of that. The atoll had only one female, and she was quite an elderly English woman who looked and spoke as if from the old British Empire days. She could swear like an old mariner and drink any one of us under the table.

We had grand days on the most pristine beaches of all creation—not a toffee paper or slick of oil, just pure white and yellow flour-like sand. The waters were warm and the beer cool. I could have jumped ship right then and there. We played football and a spot of cricket, old chap. Swimming was unbelievable as the water was warm, calm, and smooth as a baby's bum. Life in a blue suit was just fine.

PROMOTION INTO TURMOIL

The massive Straits of Malacca were heading right for us. The seas were open and calm, the wind at zero, and the skies cloudless, so it was a surprise when we picked up a May Day distress signal. Two freighters had collided and one was in danger of sinking. We were the closest ship, which meant that if we got there first, we would have salvage rights. Even in a long Navy career, it's extremely unlikely that you actually get salvage money, but here I was getting my second chance at it in a few short years.

When we arrived, we were shocked at the scene before us. Two very long freighters were stuck together with the bow of one jammed exactly in the middle of the side of the other. Once again I remind you, smooth water, no wind and totally clear skies in the middle of the day. How in the world did they collide? The assumption was that they were both on auto pilot with nobody on the bridge and no lookouts. Even then, the auto pilot still should have sent a warning, but of course if the crew were snoozing what then?

We rescued the crew of the listing ship and stabilized it by stopping the water flooding in and pumping said water out. I say this rather glibly, but it was a bigger task than it sounds. We then stood by until tugboats and rescue workers steamed out from Singas the next day. This time I was not expecting a large cache of money from the salvage money pot, but I seem to remember getting just a few quid. That was enough for a couple of rounds of beer.

Having played the hero, off we set for the dockyard of Singapore and Sembawang village. We were going to be in port for about three weeks so had plenty of time do and see an awful lot of things. This time there was more of a check list in my head because I was now old enough to be promoted to leading electrical mechanic.

On the day I reached twenty and a half, I was on captain's report. I thought I was well respected. I had a reputation for working long hours, and I had absorbed so much by asking questions. Much of the work I got involved in I didn't have to do, but did anyway. When the chief was working, I would stay and watch and assist, sometimes working until two and three in the morning and restarting work at 0800 hours. The captain sang my praises and gladly promoted me on the spot. This promotion at such a young age came with many life learning lessons lining up to teach me.

The grumpy old leading hand of the mess deck, Arty Shaw, was grumpier than ever toward me and very jealous. He was in charge of not only the regular electricians but also the other leading hands, so he could hold one over on me if push came to shove. My job was to avoid putting myself in a position to give him that chance.

Darrin Joyce was a first class electrician who was always very obtuse and negative. He kept everybody at arm's length and was generally mean. Naturally, my character clashed with his, and he tried to goad me into situations where I needed to make difficult decisions and tried to make me look small. Being a new killick in the same mess as the people you were once on a level with is definitely tricky. This was a minefield of personnel and situational traps. I learned that the trick was to keep my head high, believe in myself, and not be afraid to take charge.

A bigger problem. Dealing with Darrin and Arty was tricky enough, but then came the hammer blow. A new electrical officer took over from the original about a month later. He was a sub lieutenant and had come up through the ranks, so really knew his stuff. I don't to this day know who said what to whom, or if it was just his own idea, but he made me leading hand of the mess deck. Wow.

At the ripe old age of twenty and a half, I was now in charge of six seasoned leading hands, with one being the original old man of the sea. I believe Davy Jones was his grandson. Arty Shaw immediately took all of his bedding to the workshop and basically lived down there. He needed to come to 3L, our mess deck marking, to get things from his locker and to get his daily tot of rum, but that was all.

I had a mess meeting right away and asked for their support. I asked them to give me a chance and said that it was going to be a learning curve for us all. Darrin, of course, got all pedantic and snarly, in addition to his usual sarcasm and typically mean comments. To my surprise, several of the more mature sailors jumped on him and lashed him down pretty damn well. Except for Arty, the killicks each spoke to me a little later and told me they were in full support of me. It turns out they hadn't liked the way Arty had been running things for a long time.

I quickly discovered that the hardest part of my daily duties was to get everybody out of bed in the mornings. Call to hands was piped at 0700 hours, and everybody had to be in the main electrical workshop my 0800 hours, where they were checked off on a clipboard by the main chief electrician. I would get up and turn all the lights on and head to the bathroom. By the time I got back, half of the lights would be turned off again. They knew once I turned them back on again, they stayed on. It was one of those unwritten unspoken rules that everybody adhered to. This had gone on before I was in charge, but didn't realize how difficult it was to get the troops moving. I was held responsible for getting everybody there on time.

The other main morning task was to organize mess cooks. Two people every day would skip the morning muster and clean the mess for one hour. I would make the list out and give one special task to do other than the regular daily cleaning. These two were also responsible for setting up the mess for tea and coffee at *stand easy* in the morning and afternoon. Two other people who were at least twenty-one would get the rum ration. At 11:45 hours, a message would come over the *Tannoy*: "Up spirits." That was the cue to get the rum *fanny* and head forward to get the bubbly.

Was I learning a lot or what?

THE CAPTAIN'S VISIT

It's amazing how people look for leadership. If any kind of question came up for any reason, I felt my crew looked in my direction. None was more obvious than when it was announced that there would be a captain's rounds coming in two weeks. This meant that the captain would visit each mess deck and inspect it to a very high level. Everything had to be spic and span. Even all the stainless steel lockers were polished to the max. It was my job to organize every job and think of every detail to be dealt with. Arty, of course, didn't help a lick. His job was to sit back and hope I failed inspection.

We were all up late on the Friday night doing what I thought were the last minute items. We were, however, nowhere near finished. Thank goodness the captain started forward and worked his way aft, making us the second to last mess deck and giving us a couple of hours longer than the rest.

It wasn't enough. When the captain was in the mess before ours, we still had tons of junk and stuff to get rid of. I was sweating like a pig getting into my number one uniform to report the mess ready for inspection. Opposite our mess door was a hatch with a vertical ladder going down one deck, thank goodness. The lads dumped all the remaining gear and mops and all and sundry down the hatch and closed it seconds before the captain's entourage came into view. They must surely have heard the noise.

I sprung to attention as the captain approached, beads of sweat running down the sides of my face and neck. "3L mess deck ready for rounds, sir," I crisply sounded out. He said good morning, saluted and I stepped inside. He asked how I was handling my new position and various other points of interest to him, which I thought was cool. By his body language I sensed that although the mess was good and clean and tidy, it wasn't to the standard of captain's rounds. Since this was my first, I hoped he would let it slide and give me a pass. He smiled and kindly thanked me before moving on to the final mess aft of us.

On passing the hatch that had saved us, he asked, "Shouldn't that normally be open?"

I said, "Yes, sir. I'll see to it as soon as you've finished rounds." I'm sure he was letting me know that he knew what I had done. Oh well.

We were at sea, and I was pacing up and down the flight deck/helicopter deck as the other mess members gradually came to me to see how things went. "Did we pass?" they would ask.

"I don't know yet," I would say.

Finally the junior electrical officer walked up to me. He put his arm on my shoulder and told me that we had got a re-scrub. We had failed. I was mortified, but he told me not to worry as it was my first time and things would improve next time. He was so supportive and positive for me. I really knew he had my back and was so very grateful.

The redo was the next day, along with two other mess decks, and was done by the first lieutenant, also known as the ship's commander. He was second only to the captain. This time we were very much ready, and the commander was pleased enough to pass us. This was a blessing, no thanks to the infamous Arty. I'm sure he got a lot of satisfaction out of seeing me wriggle.

LIFE IN THE FAR EAST

We were back in Singapore and I was starting to become more involved with other aspects of life on board a ship. I was recognized as somebody who kept fit and would attend the almost daily volunteer keep-fit class on the flight deck. This was run by the sergeant of the small contingent of the Royal Marines on board. I would also often get up before call to hands and go running before breakfast. I also played deck hockey at sea and volleyball and participated in the five-a-side soccer games.

I tell you this because it led to me being asked to attend a rugby training session on the Singapore dockyard playing fields. There were acres and acres of them, including a good- sized outdoor stadium right across from the HMS Terror clubhouse bar. It held at least three thousand people, and inter-ship games were well attended.

I said, "Thanks for asking, but I've never played and already do quite a lot." He pleaded with me as they were one short to form a full team. "Okay, okay," I said as I folded like a piece of limp seaweed. That afternoon off we trotted to my next adventure.

It became very obvious that I had never played before. However, they really liked the speed at which I ran to catch up with the opposition and tackled them. I could also outrun them when I got the ball. I was on the team. Oh boy.

I was shocked when they let me know the first game was in two days' time. We played at night under the lights with half-stewed shipmates cheering us on. The beer flowed as we flowed and unfortunately lost. That didn't matter much to us, and our shipmates didn't care either. They enjoyed the game, and were proud to be Dido.

The third half, as we called it, at the bar lasted all the way to last orders, and we all stumbled back on board ready for the hangover in the morning. It was very accommodating and came on with full force. The chief, who had watched the game, enjoyed making more noise than usual and watching me suffer.

I was now a rugby player. Because of my speed and willingness to give up my body to tackle any sized person, I later became the home town hero on many an occasion. I collected many a fine bruise while dishing out my own brand of punishment to the opposition. This was fun, brutal fun, but fun.

Off to Hong Kong. Hong Kong was our next stop, and I was looking forward to that. I just loved the Chinese, as well as Singaporeans and Malays. Maybe I had been Asian in a past life. The hubbub of the island, the bartering, the smiling faces, the sites, and the good runs ashore all added to the scene.

I took another trip to the top of the peak on the peak railway and then headed for a place called Aberdeen. There were three of us on this trip, which required a long taxi ride to the other side of the island. We passed by a beautiful sandy beach, which was protected with a shark net in a long, arching line. The sky was a crisp azure blue with a couple of puffy pillowed clouds leisurely backstroking across the serenity.

A few short miles down the road, our dream world was shattered as we exited the taxi. Frantically swiveling our necks from side to side, we were hoping for an oxygen mask. Incredibly strong, pungent fumes were forcing their way up our nostrils and were mind altering.

Other than the shops along the dockside, Aberdeen is a floating village of sampans. They were all somewhat tied together, and people stepped across from one to the other. Now think about where all the sewage went. Yep, straight in the water. I wanted to puke as there was nowhere to hide, nowhere to run. This area was a tourist attraction but I figured the tours must have oxygen masks available to all members.

Out in the middle of the bay were the famous floating restaurants that we were told had really fancy, expensive menus. Across the way was a huge hillside covered in graves that were themselves covered in plants and flowers. It was a wonderfully colorful panorama.

After an hour or so, our burning nostrils were begging us for mercy. We hailed a taxi and piled in.

On arrival back at our traditional haunts, we sought out one of our favorite family café style sidewalk eateries. They used just a wok and small fire, but the food was cheap, plentiful and delicious. It was fun to watch the sea of people and chat with the little kids playing around us, giggling and mildly mischievous as they ran around having fun. Then, with our appetites satiated, we popped into the China Fleet Club for a few beers and finally rolled back on board. It had been a good day. Recognizing and appreciating other cultures and getting among the real people is exhilarating and broadens the mind.

Into the South China Sea. The day before sailing we had a rugby game against the Army garrison. The ground was rock solid clay and had about three blades of grass. We did win this one, but I managed to break a couple of ribs and bruise a few more. The pain was almost unbearable when I sneezed or laughed. Being onboard a moving ship was bad enough but it was even more so with Chief Brian Andrews around. Every time he saw me, he would make faces and burst into a false laugh while pointing at me. I couldn't help but laugh and ended up clutching my chest in agony. Brian got much joy out of doing this at my expense. It took a good few weeks before I got back to normal, much to Brian's chagrin.

Sadly, we eventually shucked the reins holding us to the jetty and slid away silently into the South China Sea. By this time, I was one of two electrical leading hands that were designated as capstan driver. On the focsle, the deck at the pointy end where the two anchors are, the anchor chains go around the two capstans. A tee bar is slotted to a keyway in the deck and when turned controls the speed and direction of said equipment. The spinning capstans can be disengaged from the anchor chains to spin on their own when coming alongside, for example. A *hawser*, or large rope, would be looped over a bollard on the jetty, and the other end would be wrapped around the capstan. With the turning of the capstan, the ship would be pulled slowly to come alongside safely. I received orders from the commander from on top of the bridge.

The other main use was when refueling at sea, commonly known as *RAS*. A small line would be fired from a gun between the two ships. This would be used to pull a larger rope across, which was wrapped around the capstan and the wires to pull over the hoses. Again, the timing of the pulling and the speed were relayed to me from the commander on the bridge top.

The Dido had a wonderful reputation around the Royal Auxiliary Fleet, the replenishment ships. We were very efficient and worked the wires and hook-ups with speed and accuracy. The merchant men loved us. On one occasion when we were trying to beat the record for hook-up and break-away I was defying the commander, who was becoming more and more furious with me. At one stage of the operation he wanted me to go to the third speed. The two motor generators were just below my feet on two deck, and I could hear them straining. If I went to the third speed there was a risk of burning them out. The whining of the equipment was too much, so I signaled with my hands, "No." He put three fingers up again and shoved them forward strongly. I again signaled, "No."

At the conclusion of the RAS I was paged to his cabin. The senior electrical officer's cabin was opposite the commander's, and I stopped there first to explain the situation. He came with me to see the commander. I have to say that the commander listened and begrudgingly agreed with my assessment of the situation. My senior officer later gave me a pat on the back for sticking to my guns and saving the motor generators.

I was not intimidated by power and used my technical and common sense. This type of mental strength did not go unnoticed in many a situation during my service on Dido and future ships, though I wasn't aware of it at the time.

We did, at a later date, break the RAS record, by the way.

THAI ONE ON

We happened upon Thailand and Bangkok for our next stop. This time, being a smaller ship, we docked right in the city area. The first night in port, a cocktail party had been arranged for the officers and shore side upper crust British patriots. Local Thai officials and dignitaries were also invited. I was asked to help serve the drinks on the flight deck where the party was being held.

Many of the officers were plying the women with drinks and doubling up on what they asked for. The women were instantly aware of this. Unfortunately for me, they would ask me to down their drink for them, often to drink half of it and hand it back. Dutifully I did this which, as the evening went on, became a problem. Fortunately, I outlasted the party and was helping to clean up when the junior electrical officer who was officer of the day noticed my inability to walk a straight line. He told me to finish and get below for the night.

When I got below, the lads wanted to take me ashore, which I resisted. Still, I went along to a bar just outside the dockyard gate. There, the Thai locals were whooping it up more than one would expect. It turns out they were celebrating the end of the dry season and welcoming in the monsoon season–a national event. At midnight, the start of the monsoons, all the Thai people began dowsing each other with water, supposedly because it was no longer going to be scarce. We joined in this fun and everybody got soaked.

I was way out of it and not especially in control of myself when a few of the women of the night grabbed me. This was also a tradition, supposedly. They stripped and soaped me down while whooping and hollering and singing a native song. Everybody was having a blast.

They did throw me some towels at the end of the song, and I was helped getting dressed. I was also assisted back on board and crashed for the remainder of the night. Later I told some of the officers about the drinks and the ladies. They had wondered how the women were holding their liquor so well.

A serious development. On the third day in port, something more serious happened. I was the duty electrical killick when I was summoned by the senior electrical officer, the officer of the day, and the captain. There were other departments there also as we were told an intake valve to the turbo generator in the boiler room was clogged. This is where water was pulled in to cool the generator. The divers were to be going down to remove the valve and take care of the situation.

When the valve is taken out, sea water floods into the boiler room at the pressure of the ship's weight. We needed to gather all the submersible pumps aboard and get them into the bilges of the boiler room. Hoses would then be needed to go up two decks to the main passageway and from there up one more deck, through an outboard watertight door and over the side.

Once we were ready, the divers took out the final piece underwater and, look out, there came the river. It didn't take long for the pumps to be submerged and kick into action as the water surged up the hoses and over the side.

The critical situation here was that the water cannot get to four inches above the bottom deck plates above the bilges. The likelihood of the boilers blowing up was very high after that level. We were under our own power alongside and not hooked to shore facilities. The water would get into the boilers and explode for sure.

I set up a watch system with my duty electricians and myself to stay in the boiler room. I needed to know if a pump stopped working or some other repair was needed. The water was slowly rising in the bilges as we couldn't quite keep up with the intake of water. We were almost holding our own so it was a race against time. How quickly could the divers clean and replace the valve? A couple of hoses split and spewed filthy black water everywhere. The easy fix still took a valuable amount of lost pumping time, and the water kept coming.

Other incidents kept us busy all day, and the four of us were getting ragged and tired. Then around 1900 hours one pump shut down completely and needed repair. The water was at the bottom plate level and things were getting dicey. The divers were getting close to finishing, but we needed this pump in action. I hooked up the repaired hose to the pump and yelled to the guys on two deck to switch on.

At this moment in time an idiot came into my life. It was time for the daily mess deck rounds by the officer of the day. The mess was to be clean and tidy with a junior rate saluting and reporting "3L mess ready for rounds, sir." Well, we had been pretty busy at this juncture in time, so of course the mess was not readied, and nobody was there.

The officer of the day had sent the duty mid-shipman (trainee officer) to do his rounds for him. Dumbo was now standing at the top of the hatch shouting down for me to come to him. I yelled that I'd be there in a moment but I was busy right then.

At this instant, my junior rate flipped the switch for the submersible and all hell broke loose. I had not clipped the hose onto the pump all the way, and the enormous pressure the pumps exerted blew the hose straight into my head. Not only that, but the water—black, oily, greasy and just plain nasty water—powered into my mouth and up my nostrils. I was half, no, three quarters, choking to death, and my eyes were also in bad shape.

Bozo was now getting obnoxious and still demanding that I obey his direct order and come up the two decks of ladder immediately. I screamed at him an emphatic, "No!" I managed to tell my junior to turn off the pump that was now spraying water over everything within forty feet. I reconnected the hose and got the pump on again.

I then climbed the ladder soaked in oil and grease, still choking and gagging, to meet the idiot of the century. He was still standing there all blustery and important, ready to dress me down. At this point, I did use the much-used special naval dictionary and borrowed several words from it. He still wanted to know why my mess deck wasn't ready for rounds. I should have shaken like a golden retriever getting out of a pool and dowsed him in slimy, oily dredge, but didn't. I sniffed in his face as he asked what the heck I thought I was doing. I then asked if he was drunk or something. I also asked if he knew, as the substitute officer of the day, what was going on with the ship today. This is when he told me to get cleaned up and report to his cabin.

An hour later, the divers had the valve back in place. The valve had been jammed up with plastic bags that everything in Bangkok is sold in. They apparently end up in the river. We just needed to keep the pumps running to drain the bilges. The water had reached an inch above the plates and all was well.

I now degreased myself and got dressed for the showdown with the idiot. My senior electrical officer had heard about the incident and headed me off at the pass. I was invited into his cabin and told to relay what took place at the boiler room. On completion of my story, he congratulated me on a tremendously difficult job well done and asked me to give his thanks to the rest of my men. "Leave the rest to me and go get some shut eye," he said. I thanked him and headed out for the mess.

The next morning, the idiot came down to my workshop. I braced for a stiff argument because I was not going to back down or apologize. No sir, not a step backward, not me. To my surprise, he put out his hand and vigorously shook my arm off. He was very sorry for the night before and admitted that he should have been more aware of the situation.

He continued to tell me that things were not going so well for him as a trainee officer, and he might not make his apprenticeship. One reason was that he was not assertive enough and needed to be stronger. That explained a lot. By this time, I had slowly walked with him to the gyro compass room, which was small and had a door that closed. We had a long heart to heart. Young officer trainees had no experience of life on board and knew less about anything on a ship than anybody. That is just the way it was. "Let people do their job," I said, "and slip in a suggestion if you have an idea to share." I suggested that he ease himself into this special society of knowledgeable sailors and get accepted. Only then would he be listened to. I told him I thought he was a good person and to believe in that. From that point onward, we were the best of friends, or as much as that was possible between the lower deck and officers.

I was beginning to see how good things could come out of bad situations. I also realized that I had just backed off, just like I said I wouldn't. I had given him a chance and heard his side of the story. You never know what is really going on in someone else's life behind the scenes.

Throughout my Navy life, people came to me to unload their sorrows and problems. Even as a young killick, crew members from all departments, even some younger senior rates, seemed to gravitate my way. Maybe it was my face or something, but they would tell me of their wife or girlfriend problems. Loneliness and yearning for their loved ones was very common. Mainly, I just listened and empathized with them. Sometimes, though, what they wanted to talk about was a senior rate giving them a hard time in their department. On this one, I was very careful.

I often asked them what they would have done if they were in charge. This type of thing went on for the duration of my time in service to the Queen.

BEIRA PATROL

We bade our short stay in Bangkok a farewell and headed for our home base in the Far East, Singas. We did spend time doing inter-ship war exercises as was normal during any length of time between ports. We also hooked up for training maneuvers with naval forces of all kinds of allied nations. When a large exercise was imminent, we were shadowed by Russian ships and aircraft. I was always amazed at how close the opposing planes would fly. If they opened their canopies, they seemed close enough to shake hands.

During this time in Singapore I spent a lot of time playing sport. I ran more often, played five-a-side soccer, spent time at Aggie Westerns relaxing and swimming and, of course, played rugby for the ship's team. We won some and lost some but as I said earlier, the "third half" and its camaraderie was the most important. Morale on Dido was the very best. This was very apparent by the support all the sports teams got and also by how successful we were at everything we did. Everything the Dido was involved in was done well—RAS, sport, gunnery shooting, all sea exercises. This was the result of a great captain and the rapport between all ranks. Life in a blue suit was good.

I haven't, as yet, mentioned Beira Patrol. We did a stint on patrol off of the coast of Beira. This is a port on the coast of Mozambique in the Mozambique Channel. On the other side of this channel is Madagascar. Mr. Ian Smith many years before had decided to take over Rhodesia from the British. The British wanted majority rule for independence, but the white population, in the minority, wanted to continue in charge. One action taken was to blockade oil tankers feeding the port of Beira. This was the only oil supply pipeline to the landlocked nation.

The patrol was to last six weeks which, if you add the time taken going to and from patrol, is a long time at sea. The approximately eight weeks at sea meant many RAS's. This, however, did break up the boredom and monotony of the endless going up and down the channel. We mainly played plenty of games, and keep-fit classes were more heavily attended. Deck hockey competitions were well-supported by spectators, and the competitions were brutal. The flight deck, as you can imagine, was extremely rough. We only wore sandals and shorts for these events, so when you went flying onto the deck from a rough tackle, layers of skin came peeling off. The semi-finals and finals of these knockout competitions were like gladiator aftermaths. Blood and chunks of flesh were scattered over the deck, and the seagulls had a feast.

The tug of war competitions were the best supported. The flight deck wasn't long enough to have two ten-men teams pulling against each other. A block and tackle on an eye hook were placed in the deck about five feet in from either side. The rope was passed through each block so both teams were side by side about 20 feet apart pulling in the same direction. The deck has a superb rough surface with a fantastic grip. Consequently, to gain even a couple of inches on the opposition could take forever.

All these competitions were between the different mess decks, which included teams from the two chief and two petty officer messes. The wardroom, or officers' quarters, also had a team. I was a member of my mess's team. These tug of war events could go for well over an hour. While still pulling, the team would be fed food and water by other mess members. This was when the other team would try to gain an inch or two in case concentration lapsed.

The yelling and screaming of support for one's team was tremendous. Even if you lost, you were hailed a champion just for enduring the match. Sometimes, when a tug was over, it seemed that only skin and bone were left on the bodies, with all liquid sweated out of the carcasses. The evening meal after these events was well attended, and much food was engorged.

The most sought-after trophy was the famous "Beira Bucket." There were at least two ships on patrol and sometimes a third on stand down. They were called Faith, Hope and Charity. (Cute, don't you think?) When two ships were exchanging positions, they would meet and vie, through a multitude of games, for this heralded trophy, which was just a two gallon metal bucket. The winner would have the crest of their ship painted on the side.

The deck games included volleyball, tug of war and deck hockey. Stilt walking was another skill to be mastered—not easy on a rolling ship. Board games were played, along with some innovative ones. The best of these, I recall, was filling a forty gallon oil drum with sea water. The teams would be given small buckets to send over the side of the ship on ropes. The trick was to tie the rope so the bucket landed on the water sideways and pull the hitch. The bucket got water into it much quicker this way. Then we would pull up the bucket and spill it into the 40 gallon drum. There was a definite art to this competition, and a lot of practice went into this before the big day.

Not all fun and games. We did get serious on a couple of occasions, when an oil tanker would try to run the gauntlet. On one occasion, after multiple warnings and getting permission from London, we fired across the bows of one tanker. Another time the tanker, which was Russian if I remember correctly, pled with us to go into Beira because they had a very sick sailor aboard. After much negotiation between Beira, the ship and London, we ended up going alongside the tanker and taking him aboard us. We then went to the three mile national limit of Beira and handed him over to the Mozambique authorities. I was part of a team that was designated to board other ships so had the job of helping with the transfer.

We all felt very sorry for the dear old soul because he was rather elderly and couldn't speak any English. Here he was, as a Russian citizen, being transferred to a British warship and on to god knows where. He looked rather terrified. We tried to make him feel at ease as much as possible, but probably to no avail.

Once a tanker tried to have us believe that their fresh water tanks were contaminated with sea water. We went aboard and dipped their tanks. The water was just fine. I was also part of landing parties, which might be used for things like setting up kitchens in a tsunami disaster situation or helping in earthquake or hurricane relief efforts. With our explosive training, we could even blow up unstable walls to make an area safe.

Getting mail once a week was quite an event. The Fleet Air Arm or Royal Air Force would fly really low, as near to the ship as possible, and drop waterproof containers with the booty inside. Immediately after the drop, the sea boat would launch and pick it up. I remember on one occasion one of the capsules broke open, and there were letters all over the sea. The sea boat crew had a net and did as good a job as they could scooping them up. Of course, some of them had a pretty good ink run, but mostly one could get the gist of the message. I seem to remember the Captain giving the Air Force a shellacking over the error.

APART FROM BONAPARTE

The end of Beira patrol was upon us and having been relieved by another Leander class frigate, we were on our way to St. Helena. This is the very small island where Napoleon Bonaparte was exiled by the British. We docked with great fanfare, pomp and circumstance. The islanders were glad to see us and know that they had not been forgotten. The one day stay was not nearly enough time for us all to explore and enjoy the beauty that abounded, so port watch got the morning from 0900 hours to 1500 hours to explore, and starboard watch from 1600 hours to midnight.

I went ashore with port watch in the morning with three of my mess mates. We hiked up what I suspected was a million or so steps to a monument at the top of a very large hill. The sun was bright, and we were soaked to the skin way before the top. The journey down was just as torturous but, hey, we did it. Fresh pineapple juice with a good sandwich was the order of the day as we sat in the shade of a very large tree.

While perusing the wares of the few shops, we got to chatting with the locals and found out about Napoleon's house way up in the hills. It was a museum and well worth visiting, they said. They rustled up some transport for us, and off we set.

It was a long but beautiful drive, and we finally arrived at a white, picket-fenced acreage with a fairly small, single story house in the center. A flag pole had the French flag straining on the lanyards as the wind was brisk on top of this hill. We were told that the British had actually made Napoleon's house officially French territory. The inside of the house was very primitive and the furnishings sparse. It seemed Napoleon was not given the luxuries of an emperor or national leader.

A big problem on shore patrol duty. When we got back to the ship, I was designated to be in charge of the shore patrol for the starboard watch run ashore. There was only myself and two other junior rates to look after about 125 sailors. These men would have fewer hours of daylight to explore the area, so I knew the two bars in the small village would be well attended.

I kept the patrol in the main area of the island where most of the island's residents lived. The early going went well, and all was quiet on the western front. Around 2100 hours, things got noisier and more rambunctious, but I let the scene alone as everybody was in good spirits. When we passed the 2300 hour mark, I started to move among the lads to nudge them to start heading back to the jetty. The last boat was to be at midnight, and the ship was sailing early the next morning. Naturally, the normal thinking lads saw the wisdom in this and moved out. Fifteen minutes later, I was nudging a little harder with a stronger and more persuasive argument, and more saw the common sense of getting back. This left the diehards and the more drunken element of the group to coerce back.

A concerned sailor came to me at this point and said his friend had decided to desert and run off into the night. I immediately went to both bars and yelled out the situation, telling everybody to move out now. I was well-respected on the ship and the sternness in my voice and the knowledge that time was about up anyway got them to head out and call it a night.

I managed to gather a couple of the locals and asked their advice on probable hiding places. They suggested a place or two, but soon we were out of time. I had a ship to shore radio, so I asked that the last boat be delayed. I received an affirmative.

Luckily, I noticed a small commotion up a lane, which was all residential. I called the other two patrol members and made haste in that direction. A slightly worried woman stood outside her house and said one of our lads had just walked in. I asked her permission to go inside and proceeded to do just that.

I sat down and just quietly chatted matter-of-factly with the man. I explained that on such a small island, he couldn't hide forever, and where would he get food and water? If he stayed, how would he live, where would he work? The idea was to pose all these problems for him to think about. Don't forget, he was there because he had been drinking too much alcohol.

I could see the wheels turning. "Look," I said, "if we go back right now I will not report this incident." Then I shut up to allow him to roll his way out of the self-imposed corner. Finally he said, "Okay, let's go." I breathed a sigh of relief and we headed to the jetty. I apologized to the home owners and asked if there was anything they needed from me or the ship. He had done no damage, and they let the matter go.

The last boat was now full, and a big cheer went up as we jumped aboard. Keep in mind, though, that it was full of lads who had drunk the most. Just before approaching the companion ladder on the side of the ship, a fight broke out between three or four of the also-rans. The bay at this point was very choppy for a boat of this size, and we were being tossed around and soaked with spray. There was going to be trouble with coming along side in this condition as the officer of the day and the first lieutenant were at the top of the ladder. I ordered the coxswain to take the boat around the ship and back to the ladder. Once on the other side, I yelled at the lads to quit fighting and sit down. If they did this, nothing would be said. A small cheer went up, and by the time the boat came back to the ladder, all was well again. I was the last to get on the ladder, having helped every staggering drunk to precariously make the jump onto the small platform.

At the top of the ladder, the first lieutenant told us, the shore patrol, to line up at ease. I thought, "Uh-oh. Now what? Here comes a tongue lashing for the way things went." He called us to attention and just started heaping all kinds of praise upon us. He knew of the desertion problem and had seen the fight. He really liked the idea of me telling the coxswain to take her around the ship. He also talked about how we resolved a very serious issue with a potential desertion. The two patrolmen and I certainly earned our wings that night.

OIL AND WATER

That morning we weighed anchor, leaving the beauty of St. Helena, and reluctantly headed for Freetown in Sierra Leone. As we came alongside the jetty and tied up, there was an air of "Uh-oh." This was not exactly a glamour spot for the normal oxygen-breathing, fun-loving humanoid. It was just an oil tanker filling port, and we were there to refuel for the continuing journey to Gibraltar and on to Chatham dockyard in the U.K.

We were to be in port for two days, so a small group of us went ashore just out of curiosity. There wasn't much to see, but we waded through about a half mile or more of inch deep crude oil to get out of the dockyard. This stuff, the life of the civilized world, is super thick, super smelly and super slick. It was all we could do to stay upright.

Outside the dockyard the merchants along the road were on their haunches on the ground, their wares spread on colorful cloths on the ground for all to see. They spoke fairly good English and were very animated. Mostly, they showed excellent, hand-carved wooden animals, handmade colorful clothing, animal skin products of all kinds, and numerous clockwork animated toys. Everybody wanted a slice of our money but would actually take anything in exchange. I gave up my shirt for a wonderfully carved wooden elephant. Probably, if they'd had their way, I would have gone back on board stark naked with a sack full of booty. The bantering and bartering was brutal but fun.

We found a little hut type place that sold a cold beer and some decent food and rested for a while before heading back through the mire. When we reached the gangway we were not allowed back on board until we had removed our footwear. I decided that my shoes were beyond recovery, so I ditched them in a dumpster right next to the gangway. Then on reaching the flight deck, we had to put our trappings in a large plastic bag. The bag was full of other people's goodies and laced with some kind of white powder. Apparently the animal skin items and the clothing were possibly infected with some kind of bug. The authorities had warned the ship about this, unbeknownst to us minions. We could retrieve our souvenirs three days later.

Heading back to Gibraltar. The next day Freetown disappeared over the horizon. We then headed to our good old staple diet of Gibraltar. The fresh cool sea breeze swept through our nostrils and restored our sense of smell. I walked to the focsle and leaned against the guardrail right in the peak of the brow. The shush of the waves slapping against the ship's side as it rose and fell, carving its chosen path through the calm waves, was music to my ears. A fine misty spray cooled my skin as it caressed my face. I had to leave this envelope of paradise as I knew there was work to be done.

Oh, boy, was I in for a shock. Two days out at sea and around that bump on the West coast of Africa, things got dicey. It was very stormy and grey, but that wasn't the real problem. The waves were extremely long and getting extremely high. Eventually the waves were 120 feet from the peak to trough bottom, and the ship was really heeling over dangerously. Other ships of the fleet had joined us for an exercise and sometimes we couldn't see them.

One night I was resting as best I could—nobody could sleep, despite being very tired. My top bunk had the roll bar up to keep me in the confines of the bed. There were two clips that stopped the bed from swinging down to make the top and bottom bunks a seat. The ship rolled so far over that these clips, unbeknownst to me, fell away. When the ship rolled back the other way, my bed kept going and folded me between the bunk and the bulkhead. I screamed, thinking the ship had turned over, and Brent, on the bunk under me, screamed because I had landed on him. The mess lights went on because of the commotion, and everybody was in hysterics while trying to extricate me from my situation. Brent and I were a little bruised and shaken but okay, and things calmed down again.

The next day I had to go on the flight deck to disconnect some waterlogged equipment. It was shorting out the rest of the speakers on that circuit and had to be taken care of. I swung back the eight clips pinning the exterior watertight door closed. I'm not sure what I expected, but I opened the door to find a wall of water right next to the guard rail and towering 120 feet above me. I immediately jumped back inside, slamming the door and jamming the clips back down while swallowing as hard as I could to replace my heart to its rightful position in my chest. It took a few moments to recover, but eventually I slowly reopened the door. This time I at least knew what to expect. It was still scary, for sure, but I made my way aft and took care of the situation. I think my bowel contents did stay in place, but it was a close call.

Several days later, things had calmed down a lot as we moved north and away from the area. The tip of the peak of the Rock of Gibraltar poked out of the Atlantic and continued to rise above the waves. The land spread out before us, and we were soon back on terra firma.

A kerfuffle at the London Bar. Gib was where the home bound ships normally stopped. The main reason was to refuel, but the lads used it as a last minute chance to buy something unique for their families. We single goof balls used it as a last minute excuse to run ashore and get drunk. As I made more and more stops in Gibraltar, I always promised to drink lightly on the last night in, but it never happened.

After we went ashore, we hit the famed London Bar first. After a couple of pints, we moved on to find a more obscure bar, somewhere we hadn't been before. We found a really neat place that by this time of night had just a few customers, none of which were military. We engaged in light friendly conversation and were enjoying the change of pace when, all of a sudden, there was a great fracas just outside the pub door in the tiny cobbled alley. Along with the landlord and the other couple of customers, we went outside. There we witnessed a rather large older man wielding a chunk of two- by-four and about to strike a cowering young Gibraltarian. They were speaking Spanish, so all wasn't clear, but it seemed that the young man may have more than courted the older man's daughter, maybe even made her pregnant. We didn't want an international incident involving Navy personnel, so we left it to the natives to wrestle and talk the man down.

When all the kerfuffle had died down, the landlord bought us all a free drink. After downing it, we bid everybody farewell. "No, no, no," the locals said. "You must stay." It turns out they were mortified that we had been subjected to such a local scene. So we stayed. We were there until four in the morning, well-oiled and worse for wear.

The communication sea checks were to be completed by 0700 hours, and these took one and a half to two hours. We were sailing at 0900 hours, and they need to be confirmed correct two hours before. I stayed awake and gulped down a couple of cups of coffee before my co-workers showed up.

The Bay of Biscay was smiling like the Grinch of Christmas, rubbing its hands and licking its chops. The forecast was not good. Sure enough, once we cleared the shelter of the bottom of Spain and started to pass Portugal, the waves were merciless toward my hungover head and stomach. I did survive but not without some misery and pain.

A channel night party. We were to enter and traverse the English Channel overnight, as is normal. We pitched and rolled more than I wanted, but it was better than the Bay. That evening we decided to have a channel night party in the mess. We had been collecting beer over several weeks, albeit illegally, and invited the senior rates into the mess along with the junior officer. A couple of hours later everybody was well oiled and having a blast when somebody suggested having a "dance of the flaming butt cheeks" competition. A big cheer went up, and four brave volunteers, of which I was one, opted to compete. The idea was for participants to roll up two sheets of newspaper and place it between their butt cheeks. The ends were then lit at the same time, and the last man left with a burning newspaper won the match.

When competing in these competitions, I generally won; it was all in the rolling of the paper. Too tight and the flame went out and you lost. Too slack and the flame burned too quickly and you lost. The clapping and chanting and yelling was raucous, to say the least, and I won again, not red-faced but red-cheeked.

The following morning I was fine and took my position up on the focsle as designated capstan driver. The ship always had a standard close down to a certain level with required personnel in set positions when in close quarters with land. In order to sail to Chatham dockyard we had to sail into the mouth of the Thames and then onto Chatham. I was on the capstan in case we have to drop anchor in an emergency stop.

A break in Chatham. Chatham was going to be our host for a couple of months now. The crew had been doing a lot of sea time and, along with the ship, needed a well-earned break. The dockyard mateys were the greatest help in refurbishing and restoring the ship to its former glory after a long trip. They were truly a blessing and did a lot of planned maintenance that couldn't be done at sea. They also repaired, replaced, painted and generally got us back to a healthy square one. I understood this to the nth degree and appreciated their help and cooperation. Unfortunately this attitude wasn't shared by many of my shipmates. I think they were too attached to the equipment and thought of it as their own. So, guess who got great service and assistance from the dockies?

One of the foremen, Gary Dean, and I had developed a wonderful rapport. He smoked a pipe that was always with him, so I always made sure he got a supply of tobacco in his office every month. This was totally illegal, but, hey, who was going to know? To protect Gary, I always left a bag of tobacco cans on his office chair when he wasn't there. This way he technically didn't know where it came from. He, of course, always looked after me and did me a lot of favors. He would get me extra supplies I knew I would need on board before going on a longer trip. This way I always looked good to the officers and captain.

The close by watering holes was glad to see us back. The Anchor Pub had the infamous Black Daff, a rather portly lady of the area who always wore a large black dress. She would envelope and devour young sailors who were looking for their first sexual exploit and didn't care who, how or where. The Ship pub up the road from the Anchor had Sweaty Betty. She was also rather portly with a propensity for a damp complexion. Neither ladies were light in the bust department and would grab a young sprog by the back of the head and thrust it into her crevasse. This was done to the raucous laughter of all and was sort of a rite of passage and indoctrination to the scene for blushing newbies.

TESTING AND TUNING THE SHIP AND CREW

Time and tide wait for no man and we were ready for the world again. The lock gates were beckoning, and we were to go for that dreaded work-up in Portland. Many crew had departed and been replaced so the ship crew needed to be whipped into a lean mean fighting machine again.

John Roberts, our chief, was exceptional at his testing and tuning and preparations. During a gun firing practice one day, a plane was towing the target drone on about a 300' wire trailing out of the rear of the plane. The idea was to get as many target triggered bursts (TTB's) as possible. The targets exploded the shells if they got within a normal plane kill distance.

We were getting puff of smoke after puff of smoke; it was fantastic. Then we actually hit the small towed drone. The gun radar picked up the wire trailing the aircraft, and the shells started exploding around the wire while getting closer and closer to the plane. Panicked messages from the pilot soon had us cease fire. This had never happened before, but was our system good or what?

Many months later in the Atlantic, we were firing at a remote controlled plane. A team of experts was testing this new form of gunnery practice and were on board for observation. They weren't too pleased when, at the first testing, our system scored a direct hit on the 7,000 pound sterling test plane and sent it in pieces into the *oggin* (sea). We thought it was great as it showed how good our system was. We recovered the large wooden propeller and kept it as a trophy.

Back to Portland, some firing from a German frigate went awry. They were meant to hit a towed target at sea. Somehow their system got one hundred and eighty degrees out, and on firing, their shells hit the mainland. Fortunately they landed in a farmer's field and only one cow was killed. I'm sure the irate farmer was compensated for but he was still pretty mad.

A week later the same frigate was to fire at a target being towed by a tug boat. It's a good thing they weren't firing at a plane. Somehow the radar locked onto the tug boat and three shells later it was sunk. Again they were somewhat lucky, if you call that luck, because nobody was killed. I wouldn't like to be in their shoes for the next few weeks.

A testing disappointment. I was disappointed during our work-up harbor week. That's when we were tested on all the aspects of the ship's capabilities for landing sorties, hurricane relief and such. The new highly heralded movie, *Tora, Tora, Tora*, was premiering in London, and the ship and been awarded ten tickets for the ship's company to attend in uniform. I was one of the lucky recipients and was raring to go. But on the day of the event, we had a major problem with the wind speed and direction equipment up the mast. We were sailing the next day, so I had to stand down from the movie and work up the mast. Even worse was the fact it was raining with a good stiff wind in tow. I had to take one for the ship and suck it up.

After the work-up, we returned to Chatham for a well-earned rest before setting off on another venture. During our time there I brought my car to the ship. The parking was quite a way down the jetty, except for five spaces next to the ship. One had a "Reserved for Captain" sign and one a "Reserved for Commander" sign. Looking around the dockyard, I found a plain "Reserved" sign and placed it in my boot (trunk). I got lucky and parked by the ship soon after and from then on had that spot. I would place the "Reserved" sign on the spot before leaving and put it in the boot when parked. Then I didn't get soaked when it rained while coming from way down the jetty.

This went very well for me until the last couple of days. I was taking the sign out of the car just as the commander came along the upper deck. A voice barked out, "What are you doing there, Frost?"

Climbing back into my skin, I replied, "I was just moving this sign out of the way." He didn't buy it, and we had a little contentious discussion about my ingenious ploy.

One night during our stay, one of the electrical petty officers who lived on the married patch asked me to babysit. I agreed and stayed the night, as it was quite a distance. When we were waiting to catch the bus back, the bus went sweeping past us, completely full. This was a problem, as I needed to be onboard by 0745 hours, and the chief's seaman/regulating police had always hated electricians and particularly wanted my head.

Charlie's wife ended up taking us back, but the clock was now ticking way too fast. There was a time check on board at 0745 which went like this: *Stand by for the time check at 0745, stand by, stand by ... NOW... the time is 0745.*

As we raced along the jetty, I heard *Stand by for the time check.* I also saw the chief at the top of the gangway with my station card in his hand, waving it at me. He would charge me even if I was only two seconds late, the old buzzard. I raced up the gangway and got to the top as the word *NOW* was said. I was on time, exactly. I snatched the card from the chief's outstretched fingers and said, "Thanks, chief" with a great big smile on my face. He grumbled as he shuffled down the port side.

Two months later, on cue, we went through the lock gates into the tidal river and left Chatham in our wake. This time we were on a tour of Europe via the North Sea and the English Channel.

EUROPE AND MORE

The leading hand of the mess deck job was clicking along nicely. I'd had to put my foot down on a couple of people and incidents, but most seemed to approve of my actions, at least privately. It's funny because sometimes I could feel the mess members looking and waiting to see what I would do. Sometimes I would act, while other times I'd let something slide and speak privately to the people involved

We were to hook up with an international flotilla of ships to do many and various types of sea borne exercises. The group came under the umbrella of "STANAVFORLANT" which breaks down to "Standing Naval Force Atlantic." This was different from NATO, with which most people are familiar.

Our first stop after maneuvers in the English Channel and southern end of the North Sea was Antwerp in Belgium. This was a fascinating stop where I chose to go on a day trip to Fort Breendonk. "To where?" you might ask, as I certainly did.

Fort Breendonk was built in the early 1900s for the Belgium Army. However, during the 2nd World War the Nazi regime made it into a concentration camp. It was now kept up as a museum lest we forget the atrocities of that terrible period in history. I don't know if I have ever been so moved either before or since that day. They showed us exactly what happened, including the interrogations and torture rooms and routines. They also had real live tapes of some of these that they played. It was disturbing, to say the least. We visited the cells whose walls were covered in messages of hope. Also on display were the areas where hundreds of prisoners were hung by the neck with wire. There is so much more to share, but you get the picture without me getting more graphic. I urge you to take a look for yourself, maybe on Google or similar outlet. How can human beings even think about such things, let alone carry them out?

We were only in Antwerp a couple of days and we were busy getting ready for a serious shooting exercise. The testing and tuning and, for me, also getting the film cans ready, was an eighteen hour a day ordeal for several days.

Yes, we filmed shots of the shells exploding. The camera was set on top of the radar director and ran at 300 frames per second. Its job was to film the shells' explosion proximity to the target. I had to put the film in the cans using a black bag. In other words, I threaded the film through 10 or 12 rollers and sprockets without being able to see what I was doing. If I didn't get it right, all records were rendered useless. No pressure though.

I remember during one of these shoots sitting in the transmission room on a stool, falling asleep. The transmission room is where the users of the equipment line up the radar on the target and decide when to fire the gun. We maintainers of this equipment were actually better at this than the official users, but don't try telling them that. Anyway, the electrical officer was sitting next to me when I fell asleep from exhaustion, and he caught me on my way to the deck. Everybody laughed, but he ordered me to go to my bunk and sleep. I told him I'd rather stay and sat on the floor out of the way. When you have put so much time and effort into a project, you want to see the results and the action as it happens.

A stop in Hamburg. The next stop was up the river Rhine to Hamburg. Quite a lot happened here, some of which I didn't fully understand. First, I had a great couple of runs ashore with the lads. We went to the Reeperbahn, which was a very long red light district with eight hundred clubs and pubs. There were also two streets with guards at the entrances, and you had to be eighteen years old to enter. The ladies in the balcony style windows were very friendly and plentiful. They also had an incredibly small amount of clothing on; I hoped they had adequate heating in those rooms. I didn't find out for myself, and we moved on to have some fun in the beer halls.

The rugby team members seemed to drift together like shifting seaweed in the Sargasso. We ended up in a bar with a large balcony that had about twenty stair steps going up each side. We had a routine of singing, "Hi Ho, Hi Ho. It's off to work we go, with a shovel and spade and a hand grenade, Hi Ho, Hi Ho..." and so forth. It was the seven dwarf show, so we would all be on our knees. Fifteen men singing this song at full throttle while ascending the stairs on their knees was quite a spectacle. Coming back down on the knees was quite a feat. Still singing, we crawled out the front door and into the road of the Reeperbahn, stopping traffic. This was crazy stuff, but the bar patrons were now outside cheering us on. Once back inside, the barman bought us all a drink as I think we boosted his sales buy a chunk. People were now pouring into the bar to see what all the fun was about.

The next day we were to play rugby against the Hamburg rugby club. We had no idea what we were in for. The bus picked us up at the ship and took us to this enormous sports consortium. The club house was huge and this place, apparently, had a dozen teams or more.

Having changed and eagerly run out onto the field, we were confronted by a team of Godzillas. This was going to be like feeding sardines to the sharks. Sure enough, by half time, the score was sixty to zero. Were we having fun yet? Did they know we were just a small frigate, barely able to put a team together? Did they know that we had just spent thirty of the last thirty-five days at sea? Guess what the score was at full time: one hundred and twenty to zero. It turns out this team had won the German Amateur Cup for the last three years. This was their training night. We thought it a little off to do this to us and were a tad perturbed. They were good men, though, and at least were sorry. They hadn't been the ones to set up the event, and one could blame our own people for not explaining our level of play.

Now for the good news; the club house was set up for everybody to have a bang-up meal with free booze until 2200 hours. They entertained us and fed us like nothing I have ever experienced before or since. It was a good day all round, and the German people were wonderful. At around 0100 hours, I could barely stand and remember being told to wait on the jetty just aft of the ship with a group of the team. The very large scrum forward, who was a mid-shipman, was waiting for the officer of the day to leave the gangway. When he did, the middy swung me up over his shoulder and carried me onboard and down to my mess deck. He poured me onto my bed, and the lads did the rest to look after me.

The next morning had no right arriving so quickly. I wasn't in the best of states but did manage to arrive in my place of work on schedule. The chief made fun of me and created all kinds of noise. I just wanted to curl up and die.

Cold and cruel seas. Into the English Channel we went with the rest of the flotilla of Stanavforlant. After a major exercise involving ships, aircraft, and submarines, we ducked into Rotterdam and got more shore respite. The seas had been cruel and the refueling routine brutal. As often would happen in the colder climates, we would don heavy duty foul weather gear. This didn't stop the freezing waves from crashing over the bow and drenching us every few seconds. Sometimes the waves pushed us around mercilessly. We also almost literally froze our butts off. We would laugh about the fact that both cheeks would start to quiver uncontrollably and wouldn't stop. I never did ask if the bridge occupants could see our rears wobbling.

The other thing was, after being drenched and slapped around for an hour or more, our faces were caked with salt. When showering, which was mainly to unfreeze our bodies, it could take five or six soapings of our faces to get the salt out. I think it penetrated all the way to our brains. I kind of enjoyed this capstan job, though. Maybe I'm just a natural masochist.

The Russians always followed us; the bear in the air was ever present. This time we had a couple of their radar ships in tow along with a warship. We jammed their radar as best as we could, while they tried to jam and interfere with our equipment. It was a constant giant game of cat and mouse.

Adventures in Amsterdam. In Rotterdam, the ship organized a weekend trip to Amsterdam, which included train fare and hotel. Not many took up this offer, a couple of greenies and I did, greenies being electricians. It was a nice break from the ship, and Amsterdam had plenty to offer in entertainment.

While walking back to the hotel at a late hour on the second night, we were accosted. We had been warned that a gang, of sorts, might follow the Stanavforlant group around and could cause trouble. This might have been them, I don't know. What I do know is they threatened us and tried to rob us, and I did take a punch in the face. We yelled and cursed at them and took off like a bullet from a gun. We made it to the hotel lobby and fell in a big heap right there. The desk clerk called the police, and we made a report but didn't expect anything else. The police were very kind and told us how sorry they were. It wasn't their fault and we got the feeling they really cared for their city.

The train ride back was a catastrophe. We had checked on the train times earlier in the day and determined we would catch the last train at 1201 hours on Sunday. Great, all set then. Well, at 1203 we asked the station people where the train was. They asked, "What train?" It was then we learned the 1201 was 1201 Sunday morning. Monday's first train was 0600 hours. Now what? There were about twenty of us, and we were all going to be late. I got the four of us greenies together, and we agreed to get a taxi. It would be very expensive but divided by four would be okay. We did make it aboard on time and explained what happened for the rest of the crew. We were a little miffed that the rest were then excused when we had paid a boatload to be on time. Oh well, that's life in a blue suit.

Off to the Arctic Circle. Rotterdam came and went and we headed for the Arctic Circle. I had been to the Arctic before, but every time it is different, depending on the time of year. I did get a "Blue Nose" certificate again for crossing the Arctic Circle; it was kind of neat to receive these little mementos to carry forth.

It was a long haul up the main drag of the North Sea, and the weather was inclement. The skies were clear, but the seas were angry; maybe Neptune's brother of the north was restless. We needed to refuel ship, and it was always best to sail into the waves for greater steerage control, especially when alongside a fuel tanker. This meant the waves would come charging over the bow relentlessly for a good hour while we drank our fuel.

The focsle crew was almost invisible, hiding under multi-layers of clothing and foul weather gear. Our noses and eyes were peeking through a small hole in the hoods, the eyelids weighed down with ice. The larger chunks of water were hitting us as they uncaringly pounded their way across the deck. The finer spray turned into little shards of ice before they attacked us like the Chinese death of a thousand cuts. The buttocks, naturally, were doing their dance of joy, acting as if they were belly dancers in Turkey or quivering like a recently banged cymbal in a rock band. Did I mention that we were cold? We were cold. I'm still wondering if I'm a masochist because this, for me, was a thrilling experience—a little dangerous with a lot of adrenaline. What a rush!

Another experience in the Arctic Circle was so diametrically opposite to the rugged hustle and tussle of refueling that you would think I was on a different ship in another part of the world. Before turning in for the night, I always took a trip to the bridge to make sure all was well. Besides the dedication to my job, I hoped it would save me being woken during the night to fix something up there. I got a shake most nights for some reason or other.

On this night's foray, it was around midnight when I ascended the four short steps from the half deck below to the bridge. There before me in the night sky was the aurora borealis in all its grandiose glory. It is the most beautiful sight I have ever seen. We were in complete darkness at sea with no city lights. The only way I can describe it is this: somebody poured a billion pounds of flour in a big circle from space and it was sifting down, slowly filtering to earth. Then a multitude of green, orange, red, green and purple floodlights penetrated the curtain of flour. Add to that, somebody carefully stirring the air, making it undulate and move in exceedingly slow circles. I was in awe. Is there a God, or was I just the luckiest man alive?

JOB CHANGE

With our exercises completed for now, we headed for the sanctitude of Copenhagen. By this time I had been moved to a new job on board. They move junior rates—anybody below petty officer—around ever so often so they learn the different aspects of ship-borne electrics. The workshops on board are heavy electric, domestic, gunnery systems, sonar and communications. I was transferred to communications. My chief wasn't too happy as I was well-trained up to the point where I ran a lot of gear on my own.

My new petty officer, Jim Austin, was pleased as punch. He knew what he was getting and was ready to celebrate. Communications included, telephones (there was a phone exchange), all microphones and amplifiers, the gyro compass and all its repeaters, the magnetic compass with repeaters, wind speed and direction indicators, all low voltage machinery along with the low voltage switchboard, all sound powered phones (like the field phones in the old war movies) and all the comm's headsets and interconnecting units, of which there were hundreds. The ship's log was also on our list. The log is a piece of equipment that sticks out the bottom of the ship and registers its speed using piezoelectric technology.

Jim Austin, myself, and two second class electricians were the only team members, and there was a tremendous amount of work to do, especially on an older ship. Dido was one of the first of its class, and the Navy wanted to know how far it could be pushed without a major refit. Consequently, there was even more maintenance and repair to be done. Jim was always getting called to the bridge, ops room, or boiler and engine room in the evenings. I would go to where he was called to assist and learn more quickly. The lads in the mess called me a groveler as I didn't have to go, but I wanted to learn and quickly. Once up to speed with the gear we could divide and conquer more repairs daily. Jim loved this idea and we instantly became a great team. Jim had a photographic memory and was very talented. This was another good move that allowed for my rapid promotional progress through the Navy. There had to be a god or guardian angel controlling this.

Jim was also the editor of the ship's newspaper, which meant he did everything. The paper came out once a week while at sea. I helped him with that as well after I came on. It was a lot of fun and was all done in the evenings in our "spare time." A box was placed in the main drag on number two deck outside the Wardroom. This was the drop box for anybody who had a story we could put in the paper about seeing somebody doing something dumb. They could remain anonymous; we didn't care. There was also the "Egbert" cartoon and stories of general interest. We made two or three copies for each mess deck and one each for the senior officers. When we distributed them, we were mobbed by the mess members clamoring to read them first. One reason was to see if they had been implicated in any dumb deed.

Copenhagen was a very clean city; I got to see the "Mermaid" in the harbor and many other sites. One night another seaman and I were invited to a large family party, which was fabulous. Two women at the party invited us back to their place, where they enjoyed our company for the rest of the night.

The problem then was that there was a ship's parade on the jetty in the morning in full, official number one uniform with inspection, at 0900 hours. We made it back by 0845 hours, looking like we had been pulled through a hedge backwards, but we straightened ourselves out somewhat. We hadn't slept, so my eyes were fighting to stay open as the captain stood in front of me. For the first time in my naval career, I was not proud of myself. I had a feeling the captain wasn't too happy either. It was pretty obvious I was not ready for inspection. Afterwards we were the talk of the ship, but this time for all the wrong reasons.

A major problem. Having tasted the delights of this wonderful city it was time to move on. At this point we were relieved of duty from Stanavforlant as another RN ship took over. This turned out to be very fortuitous for the Navy. The night before sailing we had a major problem. Naturally, I was the duty electrical leading hand.

We had already developed one bad diesel generator on one of the four switchboards which could be interconnected. This night we suddenly, without warning, had a bad section on the switchboard of the good generator. That meant that if the turbo generators lost power because of a major steam failure, we couldn't bring on the diesel generators to power the ship. In other words, we would be dead in the water without power or steam and not allowed to sail in that precarious position. Can you imagine us being in the middle of the North Sea and becoming a dead floating nightmare? The embarrassment to our captain, crew and Royal Navy would be horrendous. We would also be ridiculed in every pub in Chatham, and the tug boats coming out to pull us in would have a huge task ahead of them.

The junior electrical officer John Stone, a senior and smart chief electrical mechanic, and I had a meeting of the minds. The good switchboard needed to be cross connected to the good generator. There were hundreds of connections that needed to be disconnected and then reconfigured—a monumental task that also included manufacturing connections to be bolted together to carry 500 kilowatts. With this amount of power on a connection, the surfaces had to be absolutely perfect. Any minor gap would create sparking and very quick disintegration of the connector.

The three of us rolled up our sleeves for a long night. Did I say night? We worked through the night, the next day and night, and the next day, in all seventy-four hours without sleep. We did stop to eat and drink but that was all. There was too much information to hand over to another team to continue.

The job done, it was time to test our work. Nervously, we turned each circuit on, one at a time, and kept an eye on the huge fabricated connectors. All was well in the neighborhood.

Some time later, when I was in petty officer training school, a chief came by the PO's club and dining hall to congratulate me on a job well done. I said, "What job?" with a quizzical look on my face. He then handed me a commanding officer's citation for the diesel generator job. It had taken time, as it had to go through Admiralty House and all that jazz. I was flabbergasted and over-joyed, especially as it came with a check for two hundred and fifty pounds sterling, a lot of money back then. The job was also a story in the fleet electrical news bulletin, so our team was now famous. I would like to have enjoyed it while still on the Dido, but that's just my ego talking.

Moving on. With the generators fixed on the Dido, the crew were ecstatic, especially the married men, as we could now go home. The wives of the married men had previously been told of our earlier arrival, so it was imperative to let them know we'd be late. Many of them live in Chatham and were always on the jetty when we arrived. It was a tough life for families in the Navy. With the whole world to cover and keep as safe as possible, we were away so much. We single men loved it, though; at least I did. Free food and lodge while tripping around the globe? Sure, it was longs hours and hard work much of the time, but look at the reward. I was as happy as a clam at high tide.

Coming up the river into Chatham we hit another snag. Thick pea soup fog engulfed the whole area. We were well aware of this problem before heading into the river, but the captain wanted to give it a shot, knowing of all the families waiting to meet us. He tried to get in the lock, and the ship's speed was just enough to maintain steerage. As capstan driver I was ready, if ordered, to drop both anchors immediately. The rest of the focsle crew had their eyes peeled along with mine. This was a risky move by the captain, but he trusted his crew.

In the end the fog became so dense that we had to back up to the nearest buoy in the river and wait until morning. We had a great captain who respected his men, and we all knew he had done his best. He had stuck his neck out at high risk for us, and we knew and appreciated it. This is why we were considered the best in the fleet.

The families were informed of our delay and had to come back the next day. On arrival, no one would have known we were late. All the wives and children were thrilled to bits. Yesterday was in the history books and forgotten. I was greeted by Gary, my dockyard friend, and we had a beer and snack in the mess. We then got to work on hooking up the ship with all the necessary wires.

The dockyard mateys were tremendous. They got both of the diesel generators and switchboards back to square one. The rest of the ship was spruced up and looking great. The equipment throughout was in fine shape, and we were rested for the next leg of our adventures.

Gary Dean, my dockyard electrical contact, came by to thank me for a restock of some tobacco, and we had a couple of beers together. He asked if there was anything he could help with, and I did have a question. We wanted to have a full length mirror in the mess and I wondered if he knew how or where I could get one. He thought for a moment and said that HMS Salisbury was close to coming out of a major refit. There was a mirror in the captain's cabin, but that's all he was saying.

The next day I took another mess member with me, both of us dressed in just boiler suits, no cap. I didn't want the name of Dido being connected to our skullduggery. Into the captain's cabin we snuck and unscrewed the mirror from the bulkhead. Between the two of us, we carefully negotiated the narrow passageways and made it to the gangway. This is where things got a little hairy. We couldn't believe our bad luck as the new captain's car pulled up on the dockside. Of course he got the right of way up the gangway and was whistled aboard.

"Is that my mirror," he asked cheerfully.

"Yes sir," I said, trying to stay cool.

"Well, don't break it, and bring it back nicely refurbished, lads," he said with a broad smile and a thank you.

"We'll look after it for you sir," I replied, and off we trotted with sweat running down our spines. I didn't lie. We did look after it. That was a close one though.

ROYAL DUTY

Our next venture started with a trip to Scotland, where we were to escort the Queen, who was celebrating her birthday, on the royal yacht. We were shuffled off to a small town just south of Aberdeen during her visit. On returning to sea, the Dido did a sail-by while firing a twenty one gun salute. The captain asked if anybody could play the bugle. This was to make the whole thing more official as bugle calls signal the start and finish of firing. I stepped forward, not having played for a couple of years. The ships side and superstructure was lined with sailors in their official #1 uniform. As we passed by, we were to remove our hats and roll them in a circle while yelling, "Hip, hip, hoorah," three times. It is to be noted that we were to use the correct pronunciation for the Queen, shouting, "Hoorah," not "Hooray." I really don't think she would have known the difference, what with the distance from the yacht and the prevailing wind. I can lay claim to the fact that I played for the Queen of England.

A tragedy. After being released from royal duty, our next job ended on a very sad note. We were exercising off of the Mull of Kintyre in Scotland. The helicopter pilot had to put in a minimum number of night flying hours, so the senior engineering officer and the pilot set off to see the lights over close by Northern Ireland.

The chopper was guided blind by the ship. There was a switch on the radar table that turned off the land masses temporarily so the shortest way back could be plotted. However, this switch didn't get turned back on, and the pilot was flown straight into the Mull of Kintyre mountainside.

We didn't know this at the time; we just knew it had disappeared from the radar table. I was awakened along with many others. My task was to get all the arc searchlights up and running as we were to be searching the sea. Most of the crew ended up around the ship's upper deck looking for any signs. When daylight broke, the Shackleton aircraft that were deployed saw the engineering officer on top of a hill, waving. On arrival at the scene, the rescuers found that the pilot and the officer rolled with the chopper to the bottom after hitting the hill. When the engineering officer came to, he found the pilot dead. His throat mike had choked him. He was a young upcoming star in the wardroom and was genuinely liked. Any crew member in contact with him had nothing but praise for his style of leadership.

The keys to the city. At one stage in my deployment of Dido, the ship was to be honored by the city of Bolton. During World War II the citizens of Bolton donated enough funds to the government to build a warship. That ship, when built, was named Dido. Our Dido was the next generation Dido, but Bolton wanted to recognize us and give everybody on board the keys to the city.

In order for us to get to Bolton we docked in Liverpool, the nearest port to Bolton. Yep, Beatle country. On arrival, I did my usual deed of hooking up shore phone lines. This involved meeting the civilian phone company employees on the jetty. We jawed a while and swapped stories before we got to work on the hook-up. On completion, I bought two cartons of cigarettes as a thank you. The head man offered me a new phone of any color. It just so happened I had been asked, at our last Chatham visit, to try for a colored phone for the captain's cabin, so I accepted their offer. They put five different colored phones in a box for me and we parted ways.

The keys-to-the-city celebration was a huge deal. It involved us marching in a parade carrying rifles with fixed bayonets. Normally, military personnel cannot do this on British soil. This was the only exception. It showed that the city trusted us, which in turn showed good faith. The streets were lined with thousands of people and we all felt very proud.

After the parade, a civic luncheon was held where food and booze flowed excessively. Speeches were heralded and coats of arms and plaques exchanged. There must have been eight hundred people at this function. Part of the deal for having the keys to the city was getting a lot of freebies. Each sailor was given a proper document stating he had a key to the city, and it lasted for a life time. Some of the free items were bus rides, bowling, cinemas, and anything owned by the city. I have never been back there but, one day, who knows?

I put a green phone in the captain's cabin and thought that good. Later in Chatham, the captain's wife came on board. She didn't like the green phone and asked for a blue one because it would match the furniture better. Did she know this was a war ship? Did she know the only Navy color issue phone was black?

But the next day the captain had a blue phone. Word got back to me that the captain wanted to know how the heck I got him what he wanted and so fast. I told him, "That's for me to know. Don't ask questions." Hey, I needed a little mystique in my life. He chuckled, knowing I had a reputation for getting anything people wanted.

Off to the Americas. After Bolton it was back for a brush up and reset in Chatham. Then off to places I hadn't visited before–the Americas and the Caribbean arena.

We first stopped at Portsmouth in the English Channel. The wind was blowing like crazy, and bringing the ship alongside was going to be tricky for the Captain. As capstan driver, I was going to have to be on my toes. The wind was blowing us away from the jetty, but we did get close enough to get a rope to the dockyard workers. This allowed us to get the extremely thick and strong wire called a spring across to them. After placing the end loop over a bollard and our end around the capstan a few turns, we started to pull ourselves in. The wire was not only pulling two and a half thousand tons through the water sideways but also that added weight from the wind. The tension on the wire made it sing like the Vienna Boys Choir, and it was twanging and vibrating way too much for my liking.

The captain ordered everybody off the focsle except me and the seaman petty officer. With that much tension, if it snapped, the two of us were going to be cut in half. As we were nervously looking at each other, the expected happened. The wire separated with an ear-splitting crack, and we hit the deck, pronto. To our amazement the wire didn't whiplash at all but just dropped with a flop to the deck. Looking along the deck at each other, we were mystified but grateful.

What happened? To this day, we don't know why we didn't die. Was there a guardian angel or a god protecting us?

TROUBLE IN PARADISE

Before sailing, we had picked up a couple of electricians to replace the two that left in Chatham. One was a regular electrician with a few years under his belt. Savvy and strong in character, he was married with two young children. The second was a young electrical artificer joining his first ship. An artificer does four years of electrical and electronic training, just like a university degree type thing. Their road to promotion is quite fast; the problem is; in the early stages they actually know nothing. Bookwork doesn't cut it on board a ship.

Tom Parks fit in very quickly and easily. He was a really good man, worked hard, knew his stuff, and was a joy. Although he was a very nice person and tried his best to please, Harry Potts was weak-willed in nature and by his very body language and demeanor invited ridicule and derision. He was not accepted in the mess by several people, most of all by Darrin (pain in the neck) Joyce.

On the first day of sailing out of Portsmouth, Harry's first day on board, the sea was fairly calm. Within thirty minutes of sailing, Harry was found in his bottom bunk sleeping. That was bad enough during working hours, but there was a pool of puke lying on the floor by him. I was called to the mess to deal with this, with the group of agitators giving him a hard time.

The joys of leadership were upon me. I got him out of bed and explained that no matter how he felt, his mother was not on board. He needed to get a bucket of water, cloth, and mop and get his mess cleaned up right away. This may seem harsh, but I needed to appease the rogues and teach him about life in a blue suit. I stayed with him to make sure all was completed and to keep the wolves at bay. Once done with the cleanup, I took him to the upper deck to appreciate the joys of fresh sea air. He felt much better. I advised him that next time he felt bad to go to the sick bay. That way he was out of sight of the brotherhood, and the doc might let him lie down there to recover. A trip to the upper deck was good for the soul too.

With that crisis tucked away, there was always something going on with Harry and Darin. Darin rode Harry for as often and as long as he could. I did as much as was possible to protect him, but I was an incredibly busy man at sea. Some of the other lads did their share of shielding him also. I now shudder to think of the karmic pile Darrin was stocking up on. Later in his career, some of this karma came back to roost and it involved me.

At sea, we had the traditional exercises with ships in the area. Once on our own, heading west, we played cat and mouse with a passing submarine. We lost the game, as is usual with a submarine, but did quite well, really.

On we chugged to the Azores. This was basically a refueling stop, but I was very interested in the islands, which are where Sir Richard Grenville lay while waiting to fight an armada from Spain. He ended up being surrounded by much larger Spanish galleons that got too close to him. Their guns fired over Sir Richard, and the small British warship decimated the fleet. Their lower guns fired and hit the galleons below and at the water line.

These short stops at small islands were also intended to show the flag and reassure the populous under our military protection that we had not forgotten them. We were always well received in these situations, and a good run ashore was had by all.

A visit to Bermuda. Our next stop was Bermuda. The island was definitely British; even the police wore the British bobby uniform with the large bulbous hat. It was a beautiful and serene place, but sadly the site of another tragic event in my history.

At call to hands one morning Tom Parks was not in the mess deck. I went to the gangway; he wasn't late off shore until 0745 hours However, as the minutes ticked by he was now AWOL, and I was concerned. He wasn't the type to be late, so where was he?

About 1100 hours I was working on the upper deck when an ambulance pulled up alongside the ship docked in front of us. It was a British merchant ship. While ashore, Tom had befriended some of the crew along with others from the Dido. As the other members of Dido came back on board, Tom stayed a little longer and got very drunk. The merchant seamen were thinking of Tom and didn't want him to get into trouble by coming on board us in that state. To be clear, he actually would not have been, but because we were Royal Navy with much more discipline, that's what they thought. They kindly took him aboard their vessel and put him in a spare bunk.

The next morning when they awoke him to get back on Dido in good time, Tom was dead. He had vomited while asleep on his back and choked to death. Ironically, had he come aboard us, we would have bedded him and taken turns watching him through the night.

This was a very unfortunate accident, and nobody blamed the merchant mariners. We knew they had his best interests at heart. We had a kit auction for his wife and children. This was a tradition passed through the ages. The crew bid on items of kit, and when the bid was won, the item was thrown back in for re-auction. This went on until the crew had given as much as they could.

I had the job of organizing this and handed the proceeds to the paymaster officer to forward to the family. Tom had only been on board for a couple of months and, as I said before had been a well-liked and dedicated worker. I weep as I write this event and it's nearly fifty years ago.

A hurricane. As tragic as this incident was, life on board had to go on. A hurricane was looming, our path to the Caribbean under siege. The next couple of days we spent a lot of time battening down the hatches. Every moving object was either tied down or put in drawers; the drawers were then connected and tied so they couldn't shunt open. I had a word with my men and asked them to work with me physically and mentally. This meant working two days of sixteen to eighteen hours each. They didn't even blink and said, "Let's get to it." I really believe that they knew how hard I worked with the long hours at sea and stood by me when I needed them.

The ship was starting to barge through the waves as opposed to slicing through them. The bow was rising and dipping with more prominence. The clouds were swirling, and the white caps were heaving blankets of spray over the ship. Darkness was falling during the day. The wind was huffing, puffing and whistling. I have been through a hurricane before but that was on a carrier. How would I handle one on a ship ten times or more smaller?

By the next morning, the seas are massive and powerful. The ship shuddered as it smacked into the next mountain of water. The bow was thrown into the air before crunching back down below the next wave. Walls of water crashed over the 4.5" gun and onto the bridge windows before whipping across the superstructure and lacing the flight deck.

Most sailors stayed in their beds and mess decks. Work was only required by essential personnel and watch keepers. I was called to the bridge and ops room a few times. Jim, my petty officer, had always been called before, but by this stage of me being on the department, I took over the first call out. This allowed him more rest, me more experience, and everybody won. If I needed a hand on technical issues, he was right there with me in a heart-beat. We were a great team, and it showed.

Being called to the bridge allowed me to stay and watch the show. One had to hang on but the spectacle was quite amazing. How did twenty-five hundred tons of metal stay afloat in the water? One moment all you could see was water, and the next all was sky. Getting to and from locations was tricky. Not only did the ship pitch and dip violently, but it also rolled in the same fashion. I was literally staggering from bulkhead to bulkhead and trying to forge forward at the same time. What land lubbers probably don't think about is that movement is literally twenty-four hours a day and unrelenting. It makes for a very tiring experience as your muscles are constantly working to stay upright.

Meal times were interesting. The cooks made us soup and sandwiches which we lived off for the duration of said storm. Us savvy individuals thanked our cooks for all they could do under the circumstances. The less informed, of course, grumbled and whined. These people more than likely stayed in their bunks for the duration of the storm except to eat. If they didn't like the rough seas, they shouldn't have joined the Navy. That's life in a blue suit.

Having plowed through the worst of the hurricane, life started to normalize somewhat. It was still very rough as the seas take a long time to settle down again. Things were more manageable, but the amount of work to fix all the upper deck and superstructure microphones and speakers was enormous. The seaman branch were chipping and scrapping paint for the next week or more.

The sun finally arrived on the scene, and we ate regular meals again. Harry Potts finally crawled out from his den, where he had gone into hibernation. He couldn't even get to the dining room for a sandwich. A few men brought him some sustenance, but he mostly would look at it and dry heave a few times.

MUSTIQUE AND MAGIC

Before visiting the Caribbean we stopped at a small privately owned island called Mustique. It was owned by Colin Tennant, a British aristocrat, and had a very exclusive and expensive hotel. Merely rich people couldn't afford to come here, only the extremely wealthy. For example, Princes Margaret had been known to visit.

We anchored offshore, and we were going to scrape and paint the whole ship's side. We looked terrible from the storm and wanted to look good on entering our first port of call for our whirlwind flag waving tour of the Caribbean. We were invited to go ashore, but the hotel was off limits. Maybe the out-of- bounds was because even the ashtrays were very expensive. To ensure nobody went there, a shore patrol of two was stationed in the foyer. I was the first days' patrol along with Harry Goldsmith.

Things were quiet when Colin came by to say hello and thank us for keeping the crew at bay. During our chat, somehow, we got to mention we hadn't had mail for a week or two. He asked where it was, and I told him it was stuck in St. Vincent, a larger island north of Mustique. He said he could soon fix that and made arrangements for his plane to pick it up and land on his private airstrip the next day. Sure enough, the next day we had mail. Wow.

Colin then mentioned his shore radio was not working. Harry and I fixed it, and he was very grateful. I will always remember how light and casual he was and how he treated us as equals. The following day, a launch came by with Colin aboard. Naturally, the skipper welcomed him at the top of the companion ladder, especially as he had two bottles of whiskey.

Along with me, most of the crew were painting the ship's sides. There was some gesticulating, and the skipper pointed at me and waved at me to come forth. On arrival, Colin handed me the whiskey as a thank you for fixing the radio. Lower deck crew cannot have liquor, but the captain approved it, and all was well.

Colin also arranged a barbeque on the beach closest to the ship one evening, run by the locals native to the island. They cooked a pig on a huge spit, and all the regular trimmings were provided. Was this the life or what?

The day before we left I got to go ashore with a few friends and went to a fantastic beach nearby the hotel. It was totally deserted, and so we skinny dipped and sunbathed, protecting only the delicate parts from getting burned. The white power sand along with the crystal clear water and quiet whimsical waves made for an unbelievable outing. Did I die and end up in heaven?

Our paradise vacation came to an end as we up anchored and set sail, looking all pretty and sparkly again.

Back to reality. Out on the open sea again, we were to have a live firing of the anti-submarine depth charges. The three barrel firing was normally done with practice rounds, which are lighter than the live rounds. To get the same distance, a lighter pack of firing cordite is used.

I was in the forward petty officers' mess when we heard the whoof of the depth charges being sent on their way. They were fired over the mast from the stern of the ship as when attacking a submarine a ship is charging straight ahead for the target. The next second a panicked sounding voice came over the main broadcast system as the ship healed over to the max. "Standby for hard heal to port, hands to action stations, hands to action stations." Then, *woompata, woompata, woompata.* The three depth charges exploded really close to the ship, and the ship side bulkhead bowed in and out three times.

The heavier live charges had been sent on their way by the lighter cordite units. The shells, apparently, barely cleared the mast and landed in the water not far from the bow as the ship charged forward. I don't recall the status of the number of heads that rolled for that mishap, but I thought I heard a couple of frames of ten pin bowling being played.

The final act for the ship's company was to return all the stuff on the decks to their former place and inspect all the compartments below the water line. We needed to make sure the outer welding and riveting was still intact and no leaks were present. Once again the ship building and dockyard civilians came through as advertised. No leaks and no problems were detected.

We reached the hole in the wall on the edge of the Caribbean. This is a rock formation in the sea right on the brink of where the shallower Caribbean Sea starts. There is a very large archway right through the rock hence the name. This continental shelf is a life saver for the islands. When exiting the Caribbean the ship literally starts to rock and roll the second you pass this phenomenon. The color of the water changes from turquoise to deep blue and you can see the line of demarcation.

DOING THE RIGHT THING

With that scare in the books, Barbados came steaming towards us with open friendly arms. We were ready to step onto terra firma and rest our bodies. A small group of us went ashore and hit the local bars. I knew that tomorrow I wanted to hit the workshop running so didn't over indulge. A game of darts and other pub games tend to slow down the bubbly consumption and make it a more enjoyable run ashore.

Having got on top of the worst of the maintenance and repairs, I was able to take the following afternoon off. This time off is called a make and mend. It goes back to the older days when the sailors were given time to sew and repair their clothing. They were away for very long stretches and spent months at a time at sea.

Three of us went into town and looked around the shops, then headed toward the beaches. A taxi took us to the third best beach in the world at the time. Like the Maldives, the sand was like talcum powder, the sun was smiling, and the azure blue water was warm. The waves barely made a noise as they lapped at the shore line and hissed to a stop before scrambling back to deep water. There was a small hut type bar nearby, which we made the most of. No, we didn't drink alcohol, but some of the soft drink concoctions the cheerful islander stirred for us. We relaxed on the sand, kicked back, spent time in the water and baked our skin. Once we were cooked to medium rare, we sauntered back to the ship and that night I slept like I'd never slept before.

That weekend I took off Saturday afternoon for another beach with some mess mates. At this particular beach, which was much wider with more sand, there were all kinds of commercial boating rides. After chilling for a while, we wandered the beach watching a tremendous amount of bouncing flesh as people played ball games and laughed and cavorted about. How do those small pieces of cloth keep all the white parts under cover?

We came upon a Barbados native working on his boat and looking a little down and out. For some inexplicable reason we stopped to chat with him. I now know why, how and what was going on. Those nudges from God happen even when you think you are not religious or spiritual. He or It doesn't differentiate or judge, just uses who is willing and able.

This boating man's face was in bad shape. One half was badly scarred with fresh wounds and one hand and arm was bandaged. On asking, he told us he was trying to fix a problem on his boat when it burst into flames straight onto him. He ran a parasailing business on the beach and was now out of commission. Well, we couldn't let that go by. We asked if we could help and he squeezed out a smile of gratitude.

Using his tools, we got to work stripping down the offending parts and rebuilding them after sanding and cleaning them. Two hours or so later, we crossed our fingers, got the boat down to the water, and flashed up the engine. She burst into life as if nothing was going to stop her. His name slips my mind after all these years, but the injured man was a little less injured now. He offered to give us all a free ride with the parasail. I jumped at the chance, but the others declined.

He had a floating platform a hundred or so yards off shore, which is where we started. I stood on the platform all harnessed with a carabiner clip in my hand. The boat was taken around to get the sail inflated and in the air, and when he steadied the boat next to the platform, I hooked up and away we went. I don't know how high I was, but it felt very high. No noise of any kind could be heard, it was so peaceful and serene. The views were spectacular as he took me first one way along the beach and then the other. It was a glorious view to the nth degree.

Now to get me down, he brought the boat alongside the platform where an assistant placed the long rope under a pulley. The boat then gently pulled forward as I slowly descended to the platform. On arrival back to the beach, I tried to cajole the others into a ride but to no avail. It was so exciting and exhilarating I wanted them to enjoy it with me.

We had a bottle of beer with our new found friend and said our goodbyes. He was so grateful and happy, but it was not only a gift to him but a gift to us. I was starting to understand I was not alone at any time in this physical world or body.

A rugby game with a surprise. We did have a rugby game arranged for us to play. In a couple of weeks the Barbados National Team was going to play in the Caribbean Cup knock-out tournament, and they needed some real game experience. I figured this was a set-up for a thrashing just like in Hamburg.

We were bussed to the rugby club arena, which was much more elaborate than I expected. In the clubhouse, the whole team was flabbergasted to see before us the mighty Gareth Edwards, the greatest rugby player of all time. He was the Pele of soccer or the Djokovic of tennis. He was vacationing with his wife and heard about the game.

One of the lads offered him a place on the team, sort of tongue in cheek, and he said, "Okay." We were gobsmacked. Did he just say yes? This was the same as having the royal family to dinner. Everybody cheered as we went off to get changed.

The game went quite well, and we held our own for a respectable defeat. Gareth was absolutely incredible. The wizardry of his moves was dazzling, as was his brilliant kicking technique. He spun the ball in a spiral just like a quarterback only with his foot.

He joined us for the third half of drinking and was as humble as they come. He was gracious, classy and a gentleman. The club put on a wonderful spread for us and did themselves proud. We all wished them well in the tourney, said goodbye to Gareth Edwards and headed for the ship.

There was a small yucky incident the night before we sailed. Brandon Blunt came off shore totally wasted and climbed into his three tier top bunk. It was the wee hours of the morning with everybody asleep and the lights out. Unfortunately, he didn't pull the roll bar out to the side. This stops a person being rolled out of the bunk during rough weather or by just turning over.

A few moments later there was a loud crash as Brandon hit the deck. As leading hand of the mess deck, I leaped out of bed and was first on the scene in my bare feet. I mention the bare feet because the lights were not on yet. I stepped forward, and thick, slimy and smelly goo oozed between my toes. The lights came on and sure enough I was standing in his puke, and everybody just about barfed up themselves. My throat filled from my stomach but I managed to hold it all down. Despite our rule of clean your own mess, Brandon was totally incapable. The leader has to take the lead, so I got it all sorted out for him. I can still smell the stench as I recall the story.

WALLET DRAINING BEER

We all enjoyed Barbados and its people but it was time to sail again. This time we are off to the French Island of Martinique. Why would we go to a French Island in the Caribbean? It turns out there was going to be a summit meeting of the five major Western countries, with leaders Giscard d' Estaing, Helmut Schmidt, James Callaghan, and Jimmy Carter and, if I remember correctly, Giulio Andreotti the Italian Prime Minister.

On arrival in Martinique, we started to prepare for the big event. One notable addition was the so-called Russian merchant ship that docked right in front of us the next day. It was known as a listening ship with all its fancy listening devices hidden in plain sight. Our answer to that was to put all our radar sets on at full power to jam them up real good. The inhabitants of the island more than likely lost any semblance of radio and television reception.

On the big day, MI6, the CIA, and other security units of the big five combed the ship and kept us at bay as much as was feasible. We did still, after all, have to get around the ship. We were told that three particular hotels were out-of-bounds because all the dignitaries were staying there.

That lunchtime Colin Brown, my best pal and run ashore oppo, and two others went ashore. We carried our bathing togs in case we ended up on a beach. On sauntering through the township, we happened upon the three out-of-bounds hotels. We decided to take a look in the pool area, but nobody but a waiter was in view.

We ordered four beers which came in liter bottles and cost about four francs each, then spent quite a bit of time in the water and relaxing.

When dusk approached, we asked the waiter where all the action was, and he told us of the nightclub upstairs around from the pool. Off we went. There was a door at the top of the stairs with one of those cloak and dagger sliding spy slots. We knocked and a security man let us in. Inside there was a small carpeted room with a desk and another door, locked.

The security man did not speak English nor did we French, so sign-type language ensued. He indicated that we needed a key to a hotel room to gain entry. At this I put my hand in my pocket as if getting my key. I expressed surprise that I couldn't find it and gestured to Colin to check his pockets. On doing this, we looked at the poor man standing there and pleaded for us to be allowed in. He did relent and said we could ascend the plush and extravagant stairway that was beyond the second door.

At the top of the stairs we laid our eyes upon an incredible scene. There was a quiet band serenading in the corner next to a beautiful wooden dance floor. The rest of the floor had four inch high pile on the carpet, or so it seemed. People in gowns and thousands of dollars' worth of attire sat at ornately decorated tables. The atmosphere was out of this world, at least out of our world.

The bar was just across the way, so we headed in that direction. I ordered two beers, and the bar tender popped the caps. I figured the drink would be more than by the pool so put a twenty franc note on the bar. The non-English speaking bartender rubbed his fingers together and indicated more would be needed. At this I put up another twenty with the same result. I did this two more times before he was satisfied, which meant these beers cost me eighty Francs. Naturally, the other two didn't order anything.

Feeling somewhat underdressed and definitely underfunded, we sat at the closest table and drank crow, I mean beer. One of my friends asked to share our drink and I said no way at forty francs a pop. We stayed as long as it took to devour the liquid gold and scarpered out of there as fast as an express train.

Down the road a little we entered a small bar and ordered some more four-franc beers. Oh, how much better they tasted! A couple of English-speaking women joined us, and we enjoyed their company. After a while they wanted to do business with us, but we were short of their required fee. We did have enough between us for Colin to enjoy one of them and her wares. The bar closed at this point and I waited outside, rather tired and drowsy. It was after two in the morning, so I sat on the ground and dozed off against the wheel of a truck.

I awoke and checked my watch to find it was past three o'clock. I dozed some more and Colin still hadn't come around. I needed to stand and give my rear end a break from the stony ground and stretch my legs. Going to the other side of the truck, there was Colin fast asleep against the other wheel. I woke him and asked how long he'd been there, and he said over an hour. We laughed our heads off and made our way back to the ship.

The next morning the buzz had got around about our expensive beers. We had gone against the order of the hotels being out-of-bounds. Had the officers got wind of it?

I was in the main passageway on two deck when the first lieutenant, i.e. the second in command, said, "Good morning, Frost. Glad to hear you enjoyed your beer last night." He chuckled as he headed into the wardroom. Yes, everyone probably knew of our adventure.

Martinique was a really poor island as was, it seemed, any French-owned island at the time. We were not sorry when it was time to sail just three days later.

Off to Virgin Gorda. Off to the British Island of Virgin Gorda we went. Before meeting our next port of call, we were asked to find a desert island for the Royal Family. They were on a tour of the Caribbean and wanted a place to rest up privately on the Queen's birthday.

The navigator and the captain came up with an island named French Key, and we made our way there. These desert islands were surrounded by coral reefs and small inlets here and there. The Dido inched forward very delicately looking for a close-in safe anchorage for the royal yacht. It was dicey, but we finally succeeded and anchored ourselves to go ashore.

Each watch had three hours to go in by sea boat and swim, play cricket, sunbathe, or whatever. A few of us went further down the pristine, talcum powder beach and just chilled. We ended up skinny dipping and challenging the sun to our lily white parts until shortly before it was time to go. Before leaving we etched a huge sign in the sand saying HAPPY BIRTHDAY. We didn't know if it would last until Her Majesty arrived but gave it a shot.

Getting back to the ship was a little more uncomfortable than the outward trip. My two red cushions that were previously white were warmer than before.

A couple of weeks later, the captain received a message, from the royal yacht, thanking the Dido for their message. The sandy message had lasted!

Now onto our original stop of Virgin Gorda. On the way, we needed some solid food stores to replenish our refrigerators so were heading for a rendezvous with a RAS ship. We were also going to check off an annual requirement for practice transferring a man from one ship to another. After getting all the ropes and pulleys and blocks and tackles rigged up, an actual sailor had to be pulled across the treacherous gap between the ships.

Of course, dummy here volunteered to get into the bosuns chair, as it was called, to be swung across and back. Going over from the Dido was smooth and simple without incident. I got onto the deck and waved ecstatically to my crew mates, and they waved back. I didn't know at this juncture what they had planned for my return trip.

Halfway back, the dozen or so men pulling on the rope started to pull the rope up and down, which caused me to start bouncing. Eventually I was going up and down like a yo-yo ranging thirty feet either way, up and down. The water was clutching at my butt on the downward sway as I was yelling at the men that payback is a bitch. It seemed half the ship's company was watching, clapping and laughing and cheering. Anyway, I once again gave everybody something to talk and laugh about.

DEFEATED BY A SCORPION

As was often the case with islands, the first we saw of Virgin Gorda was a small rock on the horizon, poking out of the sea. The rock became a mountain and then we saw the land around it. Virgin Gorda, one of the British Virgin Islands, was not a military port, and our showing-the-flag visit showed the people that we cared about them and had not forgotten them.

They were having their annual island race two days after we arrived, so I decided to enter with a small team of runners from the ship. I kept fit on the flight deck each day, and what with all the ladders that one climbs and descends by the hour, I felt I was in pretty good shape.

On the day of the race, early in the morning, we were picked up by an islander and driven to Devil's Point at one end of the island. The race was called the Peak Race, and it became apparent why when we were shown the route. Devil's Point was at sea level and the race to the other end of the island, about eight miles, took us over each mountainous peak and back to sea level.

Before the race a squall was going to hit our part of the island, and we were to seek shelter. Five of us ducked into a very small canvas shelter on the sandy beach. Suddenly somebody shrieked, like a little girl, "SCORPION!" We all stood up and burst out of there like there was a grenade about to explode. The shattered remains of the shelter lay around the sand in pieces. We looked around for the scorpion, in case we were standing on it, and there it was. This tiny, frail scorpion, at most three inches long, had just destroyed the might of the British Empire. We strong, brave bastions of the Navy had fallen to a critter smaller than my hand. How embarrassing was that?

After the squall passed, a loud horn obliterated the silence, and we headed for the starting line, along with a hundred and forty or so runners. The starting gun burst into action, jolting us forward. One hundred yards down the road, it seemed we were running perpendicular to the beach. It was so steep that most of the runners were walking this part of the race. I decided to keep running, even though taking shorter strides than normal and running from side to side a little to help with the grade. This enabled me to keep near the front runners somewhat. At the top of this strength-sapping stage, there was a long and just as steep descent. I found running directly down hurt the toes so once again zigzagged my way forward. It seemed that all the front runners were doing the same. I'm sure we descended faster doing this.

Although starting early in the day it soon became very hot, and the water drained out of me like a cataract spilling over a cliff. Fortunately, the race organizers were experienced and had plenty of watering holes along the way. I would grab two containers, drink one, and pour the other on my head and across my chest. We ran the contour of the island which took us up and down many mountainous hillocks and valleys. I had fun, even though my aching, hurting carcass begged for me to stop.

I knew I was in a good position, not to win, but to do well. Looking from the top of the last pinnacle I saw the finish line in the distance. A string of runners were laid out before me, and I thought I could catch two of them before the end. My addled brain said, "Don't do it. Coast in and be pleased with what you have. Nobody is close enough behind you to catch you if you fall and break a leg." The burning torch that had recently been thrust down my throat got hotter and rougher, but I found myself thinking, "I'm not stopping now. Let's do this."

I tried to lengthen my stride; that didn't work. I tried quickening my steps; that didn't work either. I tried taking in more air, but that just fanned the flames in my neck. I was closing in on one runner, fast, but so was the finish line. We crossed the line together, shoulder to shoulder. As I crossed the line and collapsed in a snotty heap, the shouting and yelling of my shipmates was ringing in my head. I had come in tied at eighteenth.

The incredible spread of food and drink were a welcoming sight after a cooling dip in the pool re-energized my prune-like skin.

ON GUARD

Next we headed to Belize. There was a sinister side to this particular visit as we were used as a guard ship. The Guatemalans were invading Belize to take it for the expansion of their own border. Guatemala was to the east and had the Pacific for a coastline. Belize was to the west and had the Caribbean. The difference was that Belize had oil off the coast, and Guatemala did not.

On arrival in the bay of Belize City, we needed to anchor two miles off from the docks. The reason for this was awful. The water was so polluted with sewage it was actually brown. We couldn't have this water being sucked up into our turbo generator cooling systems. This was also a concern when we went ashore by sea boat. Imagine, or not, the water splashing over the gunnels as we rode to shore.

Just outside of Belize City, we Brits had a marine contingent and six Harrier Jump Jets. Dido was to provide the naval gunfire support to the marines if called upon to repel an invasion. We did relieve another frigate, and after a few weeks we would ourselves be relieved.

Rugby and hockey. A rugby and hockey game was arranged between us and the marines. Why did we keep playing these muscle bosons that spend most of their time keeping fit? We were bussed to the killing grounds and after stretching and flexing took to the field for the slaughter. We lined up to start the game, but as the referee was about to blow the whistle, a young marine ran onto the field and handed the referee a note. We had to get back to the ship ASAP because the Guatemalans were invading at the far southern end of the country.

We up anchored and sailed for the south before everybody was back on board. I'm glad the seas were very smooth because we put the pedal to the metal at thirty or so knots, which makes for an extremely rough ride if the waters are even mildly rough. It was a long journey and when we got there waited for the marines to give us coordinates for our guns to spit their fiery fury. This didn't actually happen as the Harrier Jump Jets took care of the situation and sent the intruders packing.

We stayed for another thirty six hours before the intelligence units confirmed the Guatemalans had fled all the way home. The crew members left behind had been loaded onto a convoy of trucks and driven to a rendezvous point close to where we stood by for action. This entailed being driven through the jungle on those bumpy dirt roads, just like in the movies. The more than one-day trip was torturous for those sea-faring, non-landlubbers.

The rough camping was bad enough, but when they found out that the trip was to be reversed, that was even worse. Yep, by the time they had reached their destination, we were on our way back to the city. Back through the jungle they bounced and jostled, teaching them that it's best to get back to ship quickly when it calls.

PIRATE INVASION

Once we were relieved by the next ship up, we set sail for the magnificent island of Grand Cayman. We were warned before-hand that the islanders were celebrating an island holiday—Pirate's Day. Their plan was to attack and take over the ship and capture the captain. We were duly warned.

As we approached the jetty, we saw a large armada of sailing and fishing boats filled with people dressed in all kinds of pirate get-ups. They also had guns firing off realistic but safe bangs and smoke. The captain had ordered us, before approaching the jetty, to drop the rope netting over the starboard side. The screaming, yelling pirates started to scramble up the nets as soon as we were tethered to the dock. Then they tried to climb up the nets and over the side. At first we knocked them back into the water with fire hoses, but they wised up to this. They started coming over in gangs at the same time, and we were eventually over run and defeated, the battle lost. There was a big bash on the jetty later and great fun was had by all.

Grand Cayman was truly a beautiful Caribbean Island. Looking over the side of the ship into the still, fairly deep water, one could see the bottom of the ocean. It was as clear as if there were no water at all. You know those fish tanks in restaurants and people's homes with tropical fish? Well, you could see all those type of fish just swimming around in the biggest fish tank of all.

The island was famous for its turtle farm, which some of us visited. The farm actually served up meat from turtles, legally, and sold the shells. When I purchased a shell, I was given a certificate to prove I had bought it legally at this farm. A few of us also ate at the restaurant and had turtle. It was kind of chewy and not that great.

The only drawback to this paradise island was the squadrons of mosquitoes and horse flies that took off at dusk. They swooped down like Stukas in the London Blitz. We did find out that after a couple of beers they didn't like us. They didn't seem to like alcohol, a good excuse to drink.

Injury on deck. Before I take leave of Grand Cayman I would be remiss not to mention one more incident. We floodlit the ship, a huge undertaking that demanded a lot of work. We did this on many a flag waving visit to highlight the ship and show it off. It looked really cool and majestic at night. Ten-foot poles were extended from all along the side of the ship, including from the superstructure, mast and funnel. Five-hundred watt bulbs were housed at the end.

I was on one deck when an electrician on two deck dropped a large shackle. Yep, you guessed it; I was right below and softened the impact on the deck—for the shackle, that is. I found out that a head wound doth bleed profusely. Blood ran down my head, over my shoulders, and down my back and chest. I made haste to the sick bay, where the duty doc got me sorted out. The pain was zero for the first few minutes, but then my senses kicked in and ouch, it hurt.

By the way, a floodlit ship looked absolutely terrific. It was all worthwhile, blood and all.

AMERICA THE BEAUTIFUL

After more exercises with the US Navy, Brunswick, Georgia, was our next pit stop. On the way there, the weather and seas were pretty rough, and the temperatures were dropping. One night, when I was duty leading hand electrician, I was called to the boat deck. It was 2000 hours, cold and dark. Waves coming over the bow were being swept over the boat deck and sea boat.

At the start of each four hour watch, the sea boat motor had to be started as a test. At 2000 hours, the motor didn't work. The sea boat hung slightly outboard of the ship on the davits— standard procedure at sea for speed of lowering in an emergency. Getting into the boat with my understudy meant climbing onto the cold wet davits, throwing my tool bag across the gap, and then stretching my legs across and grabbing something. The waves below seemed to be beckoning me with curled fingers. We were soaked to the skin within point three seconds and already freezing cold.

After an eternity, it seemed, of lying flat on the boat bottom and oily bilge, I found the problem. The Bendix, which thrusts forward while spinning and engages the engine shaft via two sprockets meeting, was stripped. In harbor and in safety, this would be a small job, but not here. I reported my findings to the bridge, and a few minutes later the senior chief electrician came out to us. I explained everything to him and he said to let him know when we were done.

A new Bendix was found and delivered to the boat deck in really good time. We got back across the chasm of death and in incredibly difficult conditions got the boat working again. It was now past 1100 hours, but I quietly knocked on the senior chief's mess door. When he opened the door, he saw two soaking wet, oily, black hands and faces, drowned rats that were shivering uncontrollably.

He told us to get below and cleaned up then come back and see him. When we did, he came out with three glasses of rum, each with more than one shot in it. He then spent time listening to our challenging escapade and thanked us profusely.

That was the joy, for me, of being in this kind of life style. One day I was lying on a sun- drenched beach soaking up life with powder yellow sand, beautiful shells, clear blue skies, and a cool iced drink. Less than twenty four hours later I was freezing cold, soaked in bilge water, and looking at a black sea and thunderous skies. I really did enjoy both scenarios, one the luxury of life and the other the joy of accomplishment.

Several days later the sanctuary of the port of Brunswick sucked us into its safety. After recovering the equipment, not only on the upper deck but internally also, we set sail for Wilmington, North Carolina.

A bone-chilling journey. It was now very cold, and we spent as little time on the top deck as possible, though drinking in the cool, fresh sea air was a treat. I also enjoyed the sounds and might of the waves and bracing against the wind. It all made me realize that this was truly a great life to lead. It was a lot of hard work, but you get out of life what you put into it.

We were to traverse the river going up to Wilmington early in the morning, very early in the morning. As the capstan driver, I was to be on the focsle with the anchor party at 0400 hours. The journey was around four hours, and it was bone-chilling cold. After less than an hour, we were frozen to the marrow. My butt cheeks were quivering uncontrollably, and they played like drumsticks on the inside of my leggings. My fingers were like french fries just removed from the freezer. Hours later there was the jetty and the resting place, where I could get below and thaw out in the shower.

The welcoming committee had really done a number for us. There was bunting everywhere, and it seemed all the township was out to greet us. A band oompahed us to a stop, and people cheered and clapped and sang; it was a sight to see for sure. However, we were again "raided" by the locals and the captain taken hostage. To get the captain back, we had to promise to attend a fish fry that evening.

That evening, we were whisked away in uniform to the fish fry. Well, I had never seen anything like it in my life. There were these continuously connected shelters like at a flea market going so far you couldn't see the end. This was on both sides of the wide walkway. All the shelters were full of every kind of edible fish in the sea—scallops, crab, oysters on the half shell, as well as coleslaw, shrimp, salads of all nature, fries, baked potatoes, refried beans and, at regular intervals, beer barrels with taps. All of this was free, can you believe that? Free. We were absolutely amazed at the generosity of these folk.

Something unusual, at least for a Brit, happened on the way back to the ship. At around 0100 hours, a bunch of the locals and a few of us were sauntering to a place where there were some taxis. As we passed a warehouse with a loading dock, a few guys came tumbling out and arguing, just like in the old cowboy movies, and a gunshot went off.

The townsfolk surrounded us like a shield; it was so quick it was like iron filings flying to a magnet. A cop car skidded up, and the perpetrator was gone. Where the cop car came from so fast beats me, but we were grateful.

WIPED OUT

Blighty was our next port of call via the obligatory stop in Gib, and we prepared for our long journey home. Many of the towns-folk in Wilmington came to the dockside to give us a warm send-off, and it was appreciated. I have nothing but praise and admiration for Wilmington and its residents.

The cool journey down river was not as bad as coming up river, as it was later in the day. However, it was still long and bitter. My cheeks still did their familiar war dance in my leggings, and out to the Atlantic we sailed.

During some rough weather we encountered, the windshield wipers on the bridge windows decided to call it quits. This was bad news for me and Jim, as it meant a long job on the bridge top. Before going up to purgatory, we got all of our ducks in a row. We had the spare motors, tools on small rope to tie down, harnesses for us to clip ourselves down, spare rope to tie down the removed covers, and our foul weather gear donned. It was raining, the waves were crashing over the bow and dowsing us, and the temperature was unkind, to say the least.

The wipers had two covers protecting them. Each cover had about thirty bolts going around the perimeter, which were well rusted in place. Lying on our stomachs, we proceeded to try and release them from their grip. This was easier said than done, as you can probably imagine. The bolts that sheared off had to be drilled and reverse jimmied out. We were drenched to the skin, soaking wet, freezing. The salt caked on our faces was so thick we looked like a licking block for cows. Hanging over the bridge front and seeing the warm comfy people on the bridge, I could imagine them thinking, "I'm glad that's you out there and not me."

In a dry, sheltered harbor, the job would have taken, maybe, about two hours. But in these conditions, we had to work all of eight hours—another test of endurance and strength that was part of my enjoyment in a blue suit.

Onward we ploughed as the Atlantic put up a fight. Gibraltar opened its arms to us as usual and gave us a safe haven for a couple of days. The Bay of Biscay threw us a quick sucker punch before we traversed the English Channel and made it safely home to Chatham.

Back in Chatham. We stayed in Chatham for several weeks while getting the ship ready for another trip to the Far East. We were going to traverse the Suez Canal again, but this time my butt jiggle would be for another reason. We would be the first ship to go through the Suez Canal after the Egyptian/Israeli six day war.

The war put all kinds of nasty stuff in the narrow waterway. There were unexploded munitions, burnt out trucks and tanks, supply vehicles, and god knows what else. The British sappers, mine and explosive people, had spent at least six months clearing the canal. We trusted our military sidekicks to the max, but we still closed the ship down to a maximum watertight, warlike state. Thankfully, we made it through safely.

While in Chatham I did get a few games of rugby to play. But one afternoon, I was approached and asked if I would be willing to play field hockey. Dido had a game against another ship and was short one player. Many crew members were on leave before our Far East trip, so we were a man down.

I said no at first because I had never even picked up a hockey stick. I didn't know the rules and didn't have a clue what to do.

"That's okay," they said. "You're quick, so you can chase down their fast players. We'll wing it." I relented and a few of us got ready and went to the fields early. I practiced trying to whack that small white ball. I could hit it within four swipes most of the time.

During the game I did become useful in the way they hoped. When one of their men broke away, I could catch him and provide interference while they caught up. Another tactic was for my teammate to whack the ball all the way down the wing, and I would be the first to get to it. Then I could mostly hit it across into the penalty area in front of goal. This at least gave us a chance at scoring.

I had fun and a good run out. Yep, I became a permanent member of the hockey club. Now I was playing hockey and rugby and was also part of the running team, the cross-country team, and the tug-of-war team. In my spare time I caught a wink or two of sleep.

More bad news. Sadly, another piece of bad news blew through the ship. Jonathan, an engineering apprentice, had gone home to visit his girlfriend for the weekend. He was a very hard-working and well-liked member of Dido. On Monday, though, he was late coming back from the weekend and was absent without leave. This wasn't who he was; what was he playing at?

After midday wandered by and he was now over four hours late, the engineering chief phoned his home. Was there a reason, family-wise, why he hadn't returned to the ship? They told the chief he hadn't come home at all that weekend. Now what?

Eventually the police were called in, and they traced his one hundred and thirty mile motorcycle ride home. An enterprising policeman saw a gap in a hedgerow and investigated, only to find Jonathan. He had driven off the road, gone through the hedge where nobody could see him, and died. It was thought that he fell asleep while driving home. This was a shock to all of us, and he was sadly missed. Why did it always seem to be the good men that we lost?

More help from Gary. Life had to go on. About a week before leaving the safety of the dockyard, I went to see Gary with a wish list. One of the items I wanted was one hundred feet of twenty core waterproof telephone cable. He looked through the Chatham dockyard stores and found none and then searched the other dockyards. Nobody had any. He did get me the rest of the items on my list before we left, though, and I was thrilled to bits.

The ship was ready and we were in the lock, which was filling to raise us to the level of the river, when I received a call out of the blue. "Jack, Jack, hold the ship! I've got the phone cable!" Gary said. Oh boy, I couldn't hold the ship. I stood at the back of the flight deck looking for him and saw his little white truck flying along the dockside at a rate of speed that defies logic. The lock caisson on the river side was now open, and we were edging forward. Gary screeched to a tire burning halt on the jetty and yelled, "Throw a rope! Throw a rope!"

A seaman nearby had a rope with a Turk's head on it and threw it to Gary. Gary then tied the phone wire to the rope as the stern of the ship was now past the caisson and into the river. The seaman and I pulled like crazy and dragged the cable over the jetty and through the water, and it landed like a big fish on the deck. I waved and yelled to Gary, and I could see the proud pleased look on his face as his mission was accomplished.

MIDDLE EAST MAGIC

So it was now down river to the Thames, hang a right, right again at the English Channel and go west young man, go west. Taking a sharp left past Lands End (that's the toe at the west end of England), off we went back to Gib. The scowling Bay of Biscay took its usual swipe at us as we trundled through its waves. Then, having given Gibraltar a glancing blow, we headed for Port Said and the Suez Canal via a seven day stay in Alexandria.

There were a couple of highlights in Egypt. The first was an organized bus trip through the countryside to the Giza Pyramids, which included a visit to the Cairo Museum. I signed up for this excursion and was very excited when the day of the trip arrived, but I hadn't realized that Alexandria was so far from the greatest pyramid of all time. The bus was not air-conditioned, and sand and dust filled the air from the open windows. We quickly learned to breathe only through our noses.

The sparse countryside was so different from anything I had seen before except, maybe, for Aden. The farmers were doing their thing in what can only be described as biblical ways. Oxen were the main machinery. I saw some walking round and round an aquifer pulling up water for the fields. Many others were pulling plows and carrying loads upon their backs. Some camels were evident but not as plentiful as the oxen and mules. The whole journey took us back to Jesus' times and ancient history.

Way out in the middle of nowhere, the bus pulled up into a tiny village. I was thinking "Bedouin village" but weren't they nomadic? We all clambered off the coach and were escorted to an area of mostly tents with trestle tables to sit at. The Arabs were extremely friendly and spoke quite good English. They offered us the local Egyptian food, which was nothing like any of us had seen before, and there were no utensils. They were amused by our confusion and showed us how to eat the strange fare. The local beer was brought into play, which helped. In between mouthfuls, I chugged swigs of beer, determined to finish the meal.

The Arab villagers cheered me on, and a few of us cleared the main dish eating hurdle and were offered desert. As far as I know, I was the only guinea pig who dared to engage in this venture. I prepared another bottle of beer and awaited my fate. When dessert arrived, I looked at it, smelled it, and almost tossed it—not the dessert but my stomach contents. It smelled and looked like dog poop rolled in a chapati and covered with sour, lumpy cream. I have to say it was disgusting but, cheered on by my ship mates and eagerly-watching Arab villagers, I bit into it, swallowed, and gushed down a river of beer. Everybody clapped and laughed at my miserable attempt to appease our new-found friends. They slapped me on the back and shook my hand. To this day I wonder if it maybe really was camel dung pie.

On to Cairo. The unusual food stop over, it was time to bid farewell to the oasis pit stop and trundle on to Cairo. This was another bustling city with both modern and ancient mixing as one. On pulling up outside the museum, we were told we had two hours before we departed for the main event, the pyramids.

The biggest and main exhibition was Tutankhamen. It's hard to describe the wealth and opulence abundantly clear in these artifacts. There were three massive boxes that fit inside of each other with no room to fit even a cigarette paper between the separate sides. The monumental and massive statues and headpieces of the early Egyptian era were so incredible to witness. I could have stayed a week just visiting the museum, but the two hours were soon up, and I reluctantly stepped aboard the bus.

It was a relatively short ride to the pyramids. At first all you can do is stand there in awe at the immenseness of the wonders standing before you. My trance over, I proceeded to an area close to the Great Pyramid and some vendors. Several Arabs were vying for our business, some with the offer of a camel ride. "I gotta do this don't I?" I thought.

We haggled over the price and the time of the ride and finally came to an agreement. The bartered price was ten Egyptian pounds. I straddled the hump and the camels' handler mushed the beast to its feet. Having given the vendor a twenty pound note, I asked for my ten pound change. He said no, it was going to be twenty pounds. We got into a shouting match about his dishonesty, and I wanted my ten pounds. This is when his buddies got called around, and they looked threatening enough for me to capitulate and take my twenty pound ride. This is the first time in my worldly travels that a bartered agreement was reneged upon. I paid for a guided tour of the main pyramid and joined up with around twenty others in my group. We were first asked if anybody was claustrophobic. If so, they would go at the head of the group. After climbing up the very low, long, steep and narrow tunnel, we arrived at the main chamber.

I was immediately cloaked in a swath of absolute silence. You know that ringing in your ears when there is silence? That wasn't even present; I experienced a still and stunning out- of –the-body feeling of bliss. The English language doesn't have the capacity to transform this magnificence into words. Even as others were walking around this colossal room, I felt alone. I could feel the weight of the millions of tons around me, truly one of the Seven Wonders of the World, probably *the* wonder of the world according to Jack Frost. It wouldn't be correct to say this moment had to pass as we were escorted out because I can capture that feeling anytime I want to revisit it. Is that what some people might call soul travel?

There was a large opening in the side of the pyramid where thieves once broke in, and that is where we exited. This entailed a tricky, short climb down the stepped outside of the exterior wall. I was still in la-la land when we clambered back aboard the bus.

It was early evening as we were driven back into the city for a meal before heading out and leaving for Alexandria. This time we were taken to a really fancy, top notch restaurant. The silverware was actually silver, and the tablecloths were actually cloth. During this meal of delicious food, we got a neat surprise. Omar Sharif was in the restaurant and knowing we were Royal Navy came over and shook our hands while chatting at quite some length with us. That was an exciting extra to this very enlightening tour.

SUEZ AND MORE

As the first convoy after the six day war, our traverse of the Suez was a historic day, to say the least. We were shut down in Damage Control State One, Condition Zulu. This is the state of readiness for a battle, as I mentioned before. All went well as we entered into the Great Bitter Lake and the Little Bitter Lake. On we went to the Red Sea through the second part of the canal.

Simon Town was on the agenda this time around. South Africa was a new port of call for this world traveler. My uncle moved there from England thirty years earlier and nobody in our immediate or extended family had seen him for twenty-five years. He lived in Cape Town, which was a one hour or so train ride down the track.

While still out to sea on the way to Simon Town, we received a May Day. A ship called the Griqualand was on fire and needed help. We were the first on the scene and, as we discovered later, the only ones responding. The ship's forward hold contained bitumen and was on fire. On the focsle above this was stacked lumber that was now burning.

On arrival, the ship's crew was in a life boat attached to the stern. They were overjoyed to see us and awaited our sea boat to come along side and pick them up. Our captain decided to fight the fire from our upper deck and maneuvered to let this happen. Unfortunately, this almost caused us to collide with the stricken ship. The swell was so bad that when we got close enough for our hoses to be effective, our two vessels slid into the same trough. There were literally only inches between us. The skipper backed off and we tried a different approach. We sent a fire party across with all the required equipment and started to fight the fire from on board. A second fire team soon followed.

After several hours we were making good progress and seemed to be winning the battle. Then, suddenly, the front end of the ship under the lumber exploded. This sent a forest of burning wood all over the ship and raining down on us firefighters. The chance of the ship sinking was now a real possibility. We were immediately ordered to abandon ship, posthaste.

We backed away from the immediate vicinity of Griqualand and waited for instructions. Griqualand was now getting close to the shipping lanes approaching the port of Durban. The South African authorities certainly didn't want a sunken ship in the lanes. Communications were set up between the South African government, White Hall in London, Admiralty House, and HMS Dido.

The upshot was that we were to sink the Griqualand by naval gunfire. This was an exciting event for the ship's company but probably not for anybody else involved. Our gun crews were ordered to their stations and we prepared for action.

The captain decided to take full advantage of this opportunity, and we were to use this as real time practice. We were not going to sink it ASAP, but slowly. First, we did all the safety procedures like making sure no ships were beyond where we were firing, for instance.

The Bofor guns were the first to burst into action. These are small 40 millimeter World War II type guns that you see in the movies. I seem to remember us firing twenty-seven rounds into the superstructure. Then came the big boys, the 4.5" guns. After the fifteenth shell exploded into Griqualand, that was the end.

The ship went down just like in a cartoon. The stern went down first, followed by an upsurge as the ship shot upward and became perpendicular. It then very slowly and silently slid beneath the waves. Call me nostalgic if you wish, but it was an incredibly sad sight to watch. The sea was empty and the waves just carried on like nothing had happened. It was just like somebody taking their hand out of a bowl of water.

THINGS AREN'T ALWAYS BLACK AND WHITE

After getting under way again, we rounded Cape Horn and nuzzled up to Simon Town. Apartheid was still in effect in those days, and we were given all kinds of rules to abide by. Breaking some of these rules could get you thrown in jail immediately and, years later, a court case would be assigned. This would lead to a sentence of years of hard labor. Hard labor in South Africa was brutal. It would mean beatings and slaving while breaking rocks or other hard tasks in the blazing heat of the desert. As I didn't relish this, I have to say I was intimidated.

The first time I went ashore, I went to see if I could track down my uncle. I had got his address from home before leaving England. I went to the train station for a ride to Cape Town and got my first scare. Some of the seats on the platform had "Blanca Only" signs, and some had "Non Blanca Only" signs. I stood and waited for the train and took no chances. The train arrived, and the carriages had the same designations. I just followed the white folk onto a carriage and sat down. That seemed safest.

It was a fairly long trip and the scenery was gorgeous. Cape Town rolled up, and now to find Uncle Doug. "Three Anchor Bay" was the area, and I found a bus with that written on the front. The driver said he would give me a nod when we got there.

Doug's house was at the very top as the road turned back down. I knocked on the door and waited. There was no answer, so I wasn't sure what to do. The neighbor heard me knocking and came over to see who I was. I explained everything to him before he told me they were just out for the day. He said, "Please come stay with us until they return."

It was November 5, Guy Fawkes day in my home town, where it was celebrated all night long with parades, torches, bonfires and tableaux firework displays. The neighbor was from England and always celebrated the fifth, so he had fireworks to set off. We were out front enjoying the fireworks when my uncle arrived. He didn't know who the heck I was, but he and his wife, Audrey, invited me in.

He was just overjoyed to meet me and got out the good stuff—you know, the good whiskey. After some food and more chatter he said, "Why don't you stay the night?" Okay, this was great. We talked our hearts out until 0100 hours, and he happened to mention the ghost they sometimes saw in the house. That chilled me somewhat but there you go.

An hour or so into my sleep, I was awakened by a strange voice. It sounded human but kind of spooky. I laid awake much of the night, afraid of the ghostly voice. When I stepped into the kitchen in the morning for coffee, there sitting on a perch outside his cage was the family pet. A grey parrot welcomed me with a "Good morning, Charlie." Yes, it was the parrot I'd heard talking during the night. My uncle had set me up!

At the train station when Doug dropped me off, things got tricky. The train filled up, as it was rush hour, which included about ten million school kids. The white carriages were full, with me and two other white folk still on the platform, so a railway porter came along, emptied a carriage of black people, changed the sign, and told us to board.

This was very embarrassing for me, but knew I would be in trouble if I spoke up, and it wouldn't have changed anything. I did apologize to the black people who were close to me, but they just looked at me. I guess they were used to it.

I made it back to the ship on time and was the center of attention as my mates had a zillion questions. I couldn't wait for the weekend, as that was when I got to Doug's again. I had a week end pass to stay from Friday evening to Monday morning at 0900 hours Normally this would be 0800 hours, but the train schedule would have made me late. The powers that be gave me that later extra hour. As in general life, you are given certain privileges if you row your boat correctly.

Friday evening Doug had invited some friends round for dinner, which was a splendid affair. We played contract bridge and had a few bevvies for most of the night. The next day he planned to take me to some friends who owned a farm on the other side of Table Mountain. It was called Table Mountain because the top was completely flat. When the clouds formed above the mountain, they draped themselves over the edges, giving the appearance of a table cloth.

These friends seemed to live a more sparse life than Doug, who was a diamond mine manager. They had a huge acreage, though, and were very entertaining. I believe their main goal was to get me drunk, and it took a while. We swapped tales and stories while playing golf on the putting green outside the main part of the farm house.

As sunset fell, I witnessed a beautiful scene. The sun fell directly behind Table Mountain, and halfway down, thousands of shafts of silver light fell into an arc around the sun and glistened in a glorious shower of light. It was a magical moment of awe inspiring splendor. It didn't last long, but the memory will last forever.

The next day, Sunday, Audrey and Doug drove me around some of the sights and explained a whole lot about apartheid. We went to Lions Head, a huge rock formation that—surprise, surprise—looks like a huge lion's head. We drove high above Muizenberg Beach on a country road. This gave us a wonderful panoramic view of the whole beach area, which was gorgeous. We also took a cable car ride up to the top of Table Mountain — a scary ride, for sure, but worth the heart pounding as the view was absolutely phenomenal.

Sunday night we went to a very fancy restaurant for a slap up dinner. In Cape Town a restaurant could not sell alcohol back then. However, you could bring in your own bottle and have it served at your table. So we brown bagged it, yes.

Monday Doug dropped me off at the station, and we parted ways very good friends.

Back on board, I needed to knuckle down and get ready for sea the next day. I did take a break to go ashore to buy my mother a gift. My parents were coming up on their twenty-fifth wedding anniversary, and I wanted to buy her something special. Gold and diamonds were a lot cheaper in South Africa, and I wanted to surprise her with a gift she would never be able to afford.

The jewelry store I walked into only had black people behind the counter. Could I speak to them and do business? I didn't know but started to look for something for Mother. I saw this great broach with a tiger's eye diamond set in a gold surround. Although expensive, I wanted to buy it. It was perfect.

A very nice, attractive black assistant came over and asked if she could help. I wasn't sure if she could legally assist me. This sounds so stupid, but the warnings about tight rules made me paranoid. I actually asked her if that was okay. She smiled a mammoth smile and put me at ease. I made the purchase and went on my way.

GETTING ALL THE BREAKS

After a stop on Beira Patrol we set off for Singapore and, on the way, stopped at Gan in the Maldives Islands, where we refueled. We had now been at sea for seven weeks plus and would be at sea for another week. That's a long stretch for the legs to be off terra firma.

But we arrived safely in Singas. For reasons unbeknownst to me, our sports leader has arranged a game of rugby the following day. Was he crazy or what? We needed to get our act together and settle in for a few days. Then came the news that we also had a field hockey game that same afternoon. Were they trying to kill me or just find out my limitations?

Unfortunately, a small group of us went ashore that first night in port. We decided to go all in, and after a couple of pints in Terror we headed for Singapore City and the Brit Club, a watering hole for the military on the waterfront in the city. Boogie Street, which was closed off from traffic at midnight, really opened at mid-night and closed when the sun rose. It was noted that you were not a real sailor until you had seen the sun rise over Boogie Street.

It was a real den of iniquity. All kinds of bars were open up and down the street with tables and chairs across the roadway. You needed to keep one hand on your wallet and the other covering your crotch. Some of the women were actually men with hormone additions to enhance their boobs. The telltale differences were the Adam's apple and a slightly squeaky voice. They took medicines to tighten their vocal chords.

The dangers on Boogie Street included being coaxed away, beaten and robbed. The loose women were generally not inspected for the ailments they could pass on, and Russian spies were in the fray, trying to learn of ship and other military movements. We just needed to be aware of our surroundings.

Our group didn't need or want any of the extracurricular activities; we just wanted to relax and enjoy the show. One time a really old toothless man came to our table with a small string type instrument. The three strings on it were awful as were the scratchy notes that wailed from them. We actually paid the man, not to play, but to go away. That may have been his ploy all along.

At around 0600 hours the sun rose over Boogie Street and we taxied our way sixteen miles back to the ship. After an hour or so of sleep, we headed to our respective workshops a lot worse for wear. It was Saturday, so we only had to work for an hour. One hour later I was back on my bunk snoozing. I was playing hockey at 1400 hours.

An out-of-body experience. Despite our lack of sleep, the hockey game went quite well, up until one of the opposition whacked my leg so hard it broke his stick. Not wearing shin pads, I crashed to the ground like a dying elephant, giving a blood-curdling shriek. The pain along with the sound of the stick breaking had everybody thinking my leg was broken, but it was in one piece. I couldn't finish the game and it looked like I would not be playing rugby that night.

But when I went to the killing fields to meet up with the team and let them know what had happened, the horrified captain said there was nobody to replace me. He begged me to at least start the game and see how it went. I agreed and got myself ready. I trotted around with a few of the guys to test my leg and loosen it up. All seemed to be well enough to play.

We were going to play a team selected from the ANZUK Forces. This stands for Australian, New Zealand, and United Kingdom Forces. These men trained every single day, while we had just been over eight weeks at sea with no rugby training. Add to this the fact that some of us had just seen the sun rise over Boogie Street and holy cow, I knew it was going to be a massacre.

The game got under way with about four thousand spectators baying and yelling for each team. Cutting to the chase, there were three minutes left in the game with no chance of us winning. This is when catastrophe struck. We were attacking strongly at their end of the field with our fullback going with the play. I swung back to cover his position in case they countered quickly. Sure enough, a 250 pound Mauri, muscle bosun sprang from the fray and came pounding down the field like a raging bull, straight toward me.

Our motto was "Man or ball shall pass, but not both," so I dove out at full stretch as he tried to avoid my tackle. I was stretched out level with the ground as his knee struck under my chin at full speed, along with his two hundred and fifty pounds.

I did hear the crowd's "Oooooohhhh." Then, for the first time in my life, I was hovering above my body looking down at the team swarming around my lifeless carcass. I could see and hear everything that was being said. This included, "Is he dead?"

The next part is what I was told, as I was unconscious at the time. After about fifteen minutes they carried me, to thunderous applause, from the field. I was then put in a taxi and was on my way to the Terror Base Hospital. On the way there, my color changed to very pale and grey, and the two people either side of me were getting worried. One of them shook me a little and said, "Come on, Jack, let's get you to the hospital." At this, my head rolled, my body rocked forward a bit and a large glob of blood fell to the floor. Had he not nudged me, I would have probably been dead on arrival, as they say. The first thing I remember was being given morphine in the receiving area and leaning forward to launch a large wave of sloppy vomit that shot across the tiled floor like a flood from a bursting dam. It must have covered forty square feet or more. The attending nurse rushed to my tormented face, and assured me that was okay. Bless his little cotton socks. That was the first of multiple moments of kindness I was to receive over the next six plus weeks.

I had no idea what was going on but was watching the faces of people as they saw me for the first time. It wasn't encouraging. I wondered what I must look like. I was put in an ICU area, hooked up to all kinds of equipment, and told that they would be taking my blood pressure and pulse every fifteen minutes throughout the night. For this they apologized in advance and were so kind. I still couldn't talk but nodded slightly to acknowledge their message.

I was still wondering what my face looked like as I could barely see through my eyelids. I also knew my cheeks were puffed out to the max, and I could not move my mouth. A couple of times during my mainly sleepless night, I cried to myself. Was I going to be disfigured for life?

The next morning, I was helped to the bathroom. I wasn't keen on visiting the bog as there were, more than likely, mirrors there. I didn't want to face the reality of my condition. That reality came to bear as I looked in the mirror. My face was like a puffer fish on steroids staring back at me. I gasped and grabbed the sink before me. When I got back to bed, I wept.

Later, after multiple tests and X-rays, I was informed they were to going to send me to Changi. To me, Changi was a former Japanese prisoner of war camp. Why was I going there? I still couldn't speak; the x-rays showed I had a double broken jaw. It turned out that Changi was the home of the Singapore military hospital.

CHANGI HOSPITAL

The ambulance arrived, and off I went. I had been warned about this, but it was worse than I thought. Once we turned off the main road to the city, the road was like a giant mogul ski run. The pot holes bounced us around like a ping pong ball in a spinning lottery basket. My loose jaw was wobbling around as I tried to hold onto the vehicle to reduce my movement. The driver was going as slow as he could because he knew the condition of his cargo. He was so thoughtful and apologized all the way to our destination.

I was transferred to a wheel chair that transported me to a ward on the third floor. The nurses very gingerly and respectfully got me into a bed and settled me down. Although this was the next day after my accident, I was still not with it. I still felt dazed, confused and not in control of my situation. I tried to sleep in between the now thirty- minute checkups and was feeling sorry for myself.

The following morning I was seen by a dental surgeon, a major in the Australian Army. He determined my initial course of treatment and told me I was to have surgery to wire my jaw back together once the swelling was under control.

I still couldn't talk but could murmur and mumble. I also couldn't eat, and I had tubes going up my nose and down my throat to help me breath. For some reason, I found myself wondering how the rugby game had finished. Where that rational thought came from, I'm not sure.

A few days later, under the anesthetic I went and popped out the other side wondering how I would look now. It turned out I now had four rows of wire going in and out of my top row of teeth. There were three rows of wire doing the same in my bottom row. Wires were then going up and down connecting the two rows together from my left hinge to the right hinge. Steak dinners were going to be off the menu for a while.

After five days of being totally mollycoddled, it was time for me to stand up and start walking. I had spent most of my time sleeping up to this point and needed to fend for myself. I visited other patients to get acquainted and started to settle into my new life.

After drinking breakfast each morning, I visited the dental surgeon, a great person who did not push his rank of major on me. He didn't introduce himself as *Doctor*, either. I appreciated that. I didn't introduce myself to people as *Electrician Frost*, after all. My teeth and wires were water jetted clean and my chin inspected for alignment and progress.

Now that my face had deflated and I at least looked somewhat normal, I made myself useful around the place. My daily self-imposed chores included going down to the main hospital kitchen and bringing all the meals to our ward. We had our own dining table and chairs with a wonderful view down river and over the mangroves. I would lay out the knives, forks and spoons along with the plates and napkins. Some people had specialized meals while some had the regular menu. I divvied this up for my guests and sucked down my own pureed main course. I had a half tooth to the front right break in the jaw and got most of my sustenance through that gap.

After a meal I would then clean up, place all the plates and cutlery in our kitchen, and return the trolley of food dishes to the main kitchen. Then I'd wash said dishes and put them away.

On one trip for food, I visited the Mauri rugby player that loved-tapped my jaw. I had been told by a visiting shipmate that he had broken his knee cap. I tracked him down and we had a, dare I say it, good old chin wag. I reminded him that he didn't score and we had a good snicker.

At the end of the first week, a Navy chaplain came to see me. I wasn't Catholic so wasn't sure why I needed my last rites read. It turned out it wasn't because he thought I was dying. He wanted to know my state of mind and consciousness. He probably thought about God a lot more than I did, although after leaving my body and watching and hearing everything, I took one step toward curiosity.

Before he left he told me that I was going to be leaving the ship and flying home once I was able. This shook me to the core, as I wanted to stay on board. The ship was going to New Zealand, where I had not been before. And then the Dido was going to the opening of the Sydney Harbor Opera House, where we were to be guard ship for the Queen. What a bummer.

He did offer me one ray of hope. In a few days' time the admiral of the fleet was doing a walkthrough of the hospital. Maybe I would get a chance to speak to him. Now that, I knew, would take an act of God. It was a huge hospital, and he would only visit a few selected areas. The likelihood of him stopping to speak with me was a million to one.

The walkthrough was underway and we were all cleaned up nice and tidy for the maybe visit to our ward. The door to the ward swung open and behind a large entourage of uniformed personnel came the admiral. Wow! He looked at me and made a beeline for my bed. Whhhaaatttttt?

He asked what happened, and we exchanged pleasantries for longer than one would expect. As he turned to leave, he asked if there was anything he could do for me. Whhhaaaatttttt? Was he kidding me? I told him of my dilemma and wishes for my near future. He said that a replacement was more than likely already arranged, but he would make some phone calls and try to arrange for me stay on board.

Whhhaaattttt? This whole scene was totally improbable. How could this be happening? Was there a god after all?

The next day I was informed I would be returning to the Dido as long I could be released from the hospital before it left for New Zealand.

The next morning I spoke with the major, and he thought long and hard about this. He told of his reservations, as even if he took the wires out of my mouth it would be tricky. I would have lock jaw and would not be able to eat normally for several months. Also, since my teeth would be wired together for a while, what if I was seasick? He said he would talk about this with the ship's officers.

The following morning he gave me the good news. The ship was prepared to cook me special meals from the wardroom galley. The ship would also make sure my welfare was uppermost in their minds. If my wires could come out in time for sailing, everything was a go.

This showed me how much respect everybody onboard had for me and it was very humbling. It was more than I ever could have hoped for. This decision had huge ramifications for propelling me into my future with the Navy, but more on that later. I was ecstatic.

Hospital routine. On the ward I had started to look after patients as they came and went. I would clean the floors and help the nurse make the beds of those who couldn't make their own. I was in charge of handing out the one beer a day we were allotted, as long as medications allowed it. I had a list of recipients who did have to sign for the bottle. If they didn't want it, I got them to sign anyway and collected the bottles in a locker I had procured. Thus I became the beer baron of the ward and now and again we would party at night. I know, I know, I was a bad boy, but we did have fun.

I was informed that the ship was leaving for two weeks of exercises with the surrounding allied countries and the Philippines. I was told to hang a towel out of the window at 1400 hours as the ship was going down river and would pass the hospital at that time.

I was so excited; I saw the ship coming and poked the towel between the jalousie slats. I didn't have to wave as the wind took care of that. As the ship drew level, I was shocked to see the 4.5 inch gun turret rotate to point the barrels at me. Then, even better, they dipped the barrels three times in my honor. This brings tears to my eyes as I type, even fifty years later. What an honor and how thoughtful of the captain.

A couple of week earlier I had been moved down the hall into the furthest four bed room. One afternoon a young boy was brought in and was going to need an operation. Though I didn't know it at the time, they put him with me so I could help him out, mentally. He was about ten years old and was likely intimidated, being with a bunch of hairy assed older military men. I took him under my wing and when he wasn't sleeping played with him quite a bit.

His operation had an unfortunate but not permanent side effect. He would wet the bed, especially at night. The nurses put a small alarm on the bed to alert them at night. Being military, I slept very lightly and could hear when it went off. Before the night nurse arrived, I would get the young man up and strip the bed. The nurse and I would then remake the bed and things went quickly.

I had my own refrigerator, which was always stocked with milk, yogurt, eggs and all kinds of fruits. I had my own blender to mush up all these wonderful foods. I could have as much as I liked and when I liked, it was up to me. Sometimes they would offer to make me a drink, and I accepted. The trouble was I never knew what they put in it. When I asked, they would just giggle and run off. This was a game they liked to play with me. Were they maybe trying to kill me?

One thing I had to do for myself was rinse my mouth with salt water every hour on the hour. Then I rinsed my mouth with bicarbonate of soda on the half hour. Believe it or not, I did this religiously.

A monumental moment in my stay occurred when I was allowed to visit the ship. This was after about week five and the ship had returned to the Singapore dockyard. The major went to the dockyard area once a week, where there was a dental office. He said I could go with him and spend the day on board. I did have to make sure I took my wire cutters. I carried them all the time in case I spewed up. I could choke to death if that happened.

He dropped me off at the gangway and told me to make sure I got back to his dental office by 1600 hours. This was about three miles from the Dido and the ships land rover would take me back. It was great to see all my mess and ship mates. They had a thousand questions and were glad to see me.

At the right time I was driven back to the dental office. I discovered he was working on his last patient and wouldn't be long. I sat in the waiting room where he was told I would be. Thirty or forty five minutes later an orderly walked by and asked what I wanted. I told him I was waiting for the major and he would be here soon. "Oh!" he said. "The major has left for Changi. He left a while ago." I was stranded.

I asked if there were any bus connections between the two places. He knew of a bus that went so far and then might have a connection to Changi from there. This was my only option, so off I went to find the first bus stop. I did get to the hospital about an hour or so later and walked into the ward. The duty nurse grabbed and hugged me saying, "Thank God you're okay. We've all been worried sick. You must phone the major immediately. He is worried also." I called him at home with the number they gave me. The phone didn't even ring once before it was answered. He was just beside himself and was apologizing time after time. Yeh, he had forgotten me and realized it several miles down the road. He figured, because he knew the kind of person I was, that by the time he drove back I would have found a resourceful way to get myself back. He was right.

The next morning I walked into the area where we always met and he wasn't there. That was strange because he was always waiting for me every morning at the same time. Well, he was hiding behind the door. He got down on bended knee and asked for forgiveness. He was so funny, and we had a good laugh about it. He truly was a gentleman.

I really became the man of the ward over the six plus weeks and even taught the new night nurse the routine. The matron would come each morning to inspect the ward, and I reminded the nurse of things not done yet. Then I helped to get them done. Another thing I did was take on the task of stripping all the wood cabinets and varnishing them. That was a huge job, but it took up the spare time on my hands.

Finally, it was time to have my wires removed. That morning was horrific. The major had said earlier that they didn't put me under to remove them, which was disconcerting in itself. After giving me twenty-four, yes, twenty-four injections, he went to the task at hand. He took the wire cutters that I had been carrying and went to work. Guess what? They were blunt and wouldn't cut the wire. The major was furious. I wouldn't have wanted to be in the orderlies shoes for that one.

He cut out the up and down wires first as my mouth rendered forth pints of blood. I was sure I was going to be drained of the red stuff before he finished. He then cut the horizontal wires, of which there were seven, down the middle. The scary thing was when he asked me to grip the arm of the chair tightly. He then grabbed a wire in the middle with pliers and pulled. I could feel the wire running in and out of my teeth. The blood rained down my chin like something evil was chasing it. We took a break after each two rows, that's two wires each side.

Once the nightmare was over, I was mentally drained and so was my blood.

BACK ON THE BRINY

Forty eight hours after tearful but cheerful goodbyes to the hospital staff, I was back onboard. Sadly, my first piece of news was quite awful. One of my closest friends was being transferred to Changi by CASEVAC chopper as I was on my way back. CASEVAC is casualty evacuation, and it generally means something serious. My friend had been in a rush and stepped on a watertight door combing while jumping forward. He crushed his head on the top of the combing. It hurt and he had a headache but didn't think anything more about it. Later, while eating lunch he stood up, screamed a hellacious scream and fell to the deck. He had cracked his skull and was dead on arrival at Changi. With a wife and two kids, this was extra, ultra-sad. As many friends as I lost during my stay in the "mob," I had to start believing in my own guardian angels.

Unfortunately, time and tide wait for no man and a few days later we said our farewell to Singas and headed for Sydney, Australia. I had a lot of catching up to do with everybody. I could talk through my clenched teeth quite well but tried to keep it to a minimum.

I hooked up with the officers' chef and told him the kinds of things I would need to eat. He was super accommodating and looked after me like I was royalty. I ate mostly pureed food, but he always made me some great scrambled eggs each morning.

My department petty officer was glad to have me back and take some of the weight off his shoulders. My fitness left much to be desired at first, but it wasn't long though before I was back in the saddle. The trip down to Australia was preceded by New Zealand and was generally uneventful as we passed through rough, smooth and indifferent seas. The dolphins and flying fish danced around the bow. The dolphins played in the waves curling away from the bow along with diving under the bow and resurfacing on the other side. The flying fish were fun to watch as they popped up and skimmed across the water like a flat stone skipping along after being tossed. Some of them seemed to fly forever. The beauty and grandeur of the ocean never ceased to amaze me. Was this the life, or what?

The captain decided he wanted to sail through Cook Strait. This was a stretch of water between the main South Island and a small island just off shore. Cook Strait is very narrow as shipping waterways go and fairly shallow, depending on the tide. The wonder of this passage was that on both sides mountains shot skyward right from the shore line. I was expecting Jason and the Argonauts to come zooming into view at any moment. Or maybe the Sirens were to be heard to tempt us to our fate. Neither happened, and we made it safely through.

Our first port of call in New Zealand was to be Nelson. Nelson was a relatively small town at the north end of South Island. There wasn't a lot to do there except drink and be merry, but one thing was happening during our stay. The English Lions were playing the All Blacks in New Zealand. For the uninitiated, this was the biggest rivalry in rugby during that time period. The Lions had not beaten the All Blacks in New Zealand for quite a while, but this was meant to be the year to break that duck.

The game was very close, but the Lions won the day. What a feat for the Brits! Four of us walked into a local bar, in uniform, and immediately started crowing about the great Lions win. That was a mistake. The entire group of disappointed Kiwis started throwing beer cans and bottles at us, and things looked like they were going to get nasty real quick. We didn't throw any back, took it in our stride, and started laughing. The cascade of missiles stopped, and they roared with laughter and welcomed us into their fold.

We barely bought a drink all night and had a great time chatting and spinning old sea dog stories. They gave as well as they got with their own hair-raising stories at sea. The bar closed at 2200 hours, which we thought a little strange, especially in a rough and tumble society such as this. But then the "back room" unofficial bar opened.

We actually went through a side door, where there was another bar. The only rule was that, to keep it legal, you couldn't pay for a drink. You may think the landlord would be out a lot of money, but the way around this was that people left a large tip for the drink that was served. At 0400 hours, we spilled out of the bar and slithered back on board.

After four days of Nelson, we gratefully slinked out to sea and made our way to the capital of New Zealand, Wellington, which is at the south end of North Island, and then to Auckland farther north on the North Island. I had more sober runs ashore at both places, sightseeing and enjoying cultural sites.

Off to Sydney. The next leg of our journey was the trip to Sydney, Australia, for the opening of the Sydney Harbor Opera House. We were also guard ship for the Queen and the Royal Yacht.

On the way to Australia, there was a loud knocking noise under the ship along the keel line. The skipper eventually decided to stop the ship and send the ship's divers down for a *decko*. This may seem a simple task and it normally would be. But have I mentioned yet that this sea area is the most shark infested area in the world? Every kind of shark is available to have a diver for lunch. This includes the great white and hammerhead sharks, two of the most aggressive. This was a dangerous mission by any account. Much planning went into the dive, and the divers, with their lookouts, proceeded underwater. They discovered that a length of the actual keel had ripped away from the ship's bottom and was flapping from side to side. The flap needed to be cut before it tore even more, so the divers now needed to be under water for a lengthier period. The task was completed without any untoward incident and we continued on our way.

OPERATIC CULTURE

A week or so later we sailed into Sydney Harbor with great fanfare and pomp and circumstance. We lined the upper deck in our
number one uniforms and had bunting flags flying. The Sydney
Harbor Bridge flew over the top of us as we passed the famed
new opera house. The dockside was nearby, and we eased alongside to a swath of people greeting us. The city was all abuzz with
excitement over the official opening of the Sydney Opera House
in twelve days' time.

Three of my mess mates and I had applied for a week of
leave, and we were going to hire a car to tour the country a little.
The initial idea was to drive to Alice Springs, but that was quickly
squashed. We were speaking to some locals about this trip, and
they started to ask all kinds of questions: How many vehicles are
going? Do you have shovels and spades, water tanks, multiple
gas tanks? What kind of radios do you have? How many spare
wheels have you got? You know the road can disappear under
sand drifts, right? We decided to just tour around the shoreline
and outer perimeter of the country.

When we drove to a bank to change money, there was a sign
on the sidewalk that said *Two Hour Parking*. Fifteen minutes
later we exited the bank to see a policeman writing us a parking
ticket. We explained we'd only been parked for fifteen minutes.
At this, he told us that after 1600 hours this road became a freeway, and there was no parking on the freeway.

We proudly told him we were on HMS Dido and had come
in yesterday as guard ship to the Queen. Also, we were in for the

opening of the Opera House, as had been plastered all over the front page of the Sydney newspaper. His reply was something I cannot put in print, but he had obviously read the special naval dictionary. We couldn't believe he treated a visitor to the city in such a fashion.

We headed to the east coast and Port Macquarie, a large city in New South Wales north of Sydney. After traveling through some outback style country, we stopped at a wild animal refuge. Although we didn't see any animals on the road, the scenery was fantastic. In Port Macquarie, we saw a large billboard for the new rock opera *Jesus Christ Superstar.* I had bought the LP for this and loved the music so thought we would go to the play. We asked and searched all over the city, but nobody could tell us where it was showing. Finally, we spoke to somebody in a diner who said it was actually showing in Sydney. We were amazed that it was being advertised so far away. The waitress said, "It's only 250 miles away. We go there for a night out; it's not that far." We laughed at this and went on our way.

On our way over the Blue Ridge Mountains to Tamworth, we stopped at a community on top of a mountain about thirty miles out of town. The road was very stony and very narrow with a horrendous drop off all the way to the top. On eventually making the top, we found lush green grass, colorful flowers and shrubs, a small group of colorful houses, and what seemed to be a clubhouse and lawn bowling green in pristine condition. We entered the club house and within minutes were warmly greeted and afforded great hospitality. We were also challenged to a game of bowls, which we lost handsomely.

The next morning the locals suggested we not drive over the mountain because there had been a mountain storm the previous night. We didn't see a problem as the tarmac roads were dry and the storm was gone. Besides that, we had a limited amount of time for touring.

Two thirds of our way up the mountain and now on dirt roads, the mud became very deep. We were really freaking out as we slid, sometimes sideways, up the slimy steep slope. The drop offs were hundreds of feet and I could only make slow headway in second gear. I barely kept the wheels turning to maintain some kind of traction, but we finally made it to the top. The descent was even more dangerous as we held our breath, some of it I'm sure to detract from the possible filling of our pants.

We made it eventually back to tarmac, but then coming toward us, still quite a way off, was a huge ball of dust traveling at quite a speed. We thought it was a dust cloud being pushed along, but as the dust got to us, a large truck went barreling past us at tremendous speed. We were aghast at the dust he was churning. Then we looked behind us and saw we were doing the same thing.

Fuel was getting low and we came upon a gas station way out in the middle of nowhere. Stopping next to the one pump, I opened the door of the car. Plop. Thud. A foot- wide length of mud a car length long fell to the ground. At this, a bedraggled man came trudging out to greet us with a shovel in hand. As I started to apologize for the mess, he laughed and said, "It happens all the time."

With our tank topped off and a cleaned windshield, we went on our merry way. Later we saw a sign for a great overlook view and pulled over. We were way out in the middle of nowhere but there was a large area of trees across the way. As we walked through the trees, we actually heard a kookaburra. It was an amazing sound for us newbies. Then suddenly, we came to an abrupt stop. It was like the three stooges coming to a halt and banging into each other. A drop-off of several hundred feet was immediately before us. Standing at the edge of a box canyon, we could see for miles down the valley or gorge. Around to our left was a small cataract spilling through a groove in the rock. We made our way around to it, and I stood astride the waterway at the very edge and peered over. It was an exhilarating thing to do, and I got some good photos looking down. We wondered how such a beautiful Garden of Eden could just pop up in the middle of the outback.

We drove on to Tamworth, the country music capitol of Australia, and after two nights pushed on to Warragamba Dam. On the way, we finally saw a wild kangaroo. It flashed across our headlights in the darkness of night. Warragamba Dam was the largest dam in Australia and stretched over one thousand feet across. The place was ginormous and beautifully landscaped.

Some caves were nearby, which turned out to be vast and deep. It was fairly costly to be guided through them, but we decided to pay for one of the shorter, less expensive routes. Money was at a premium at this point in our trip; credit cards were unheard of in this era. The caves were out of this world with the usual caverns and stalactites and stalagmites, but the real wonders were the Aboriginal drawings. They made the money really worth it.

The next morning, early, we headed back to Sydney and the ship. The car having been returned in one piece but filthy dirty, we taxied to the docks and Dido.

In a few days the big event was upon us. Sydney harbor was alive with so many boats it was almost impossible to see any water. The shore line was like a massive ant nest heaving and seething with bodies. Bunting, balloons and flying banners filled every space. Ship sirens and small craft hooters consistently filled the air waves. Flowers and color abounded all around. As the Queen cut the ribbon, pandemonium broke out. The throngs went wild as the long overdue and over budget eighth wonder of the world was finally officially opened. I felt honored to be a part of these festivities and present when this magnificent building was ordained.

Australian sightseeing. Two days later I was on a kind of safari type boat for an excursion I had signed up for to a wildlife park. It was a massive park with every Australian animal possible on view. I got to the koala bear exhibit just as they were being fed their favorite eucalyptus diet. This meant that they were at their most docile and therefore available for the public to hold. My friends and I were in our naval uniforms, the tropical rig of white shorts and white top with the blue piping around the edges. Maybe that's why, when I raised my hand as a volunteer, I was one of the lucky ones chosen. Those babes were heavy for their size! The official photographer took the shot and I bought the resulting picture.

The snake exhibit was quite different. The snake guru was handling a very large python and talking about how they can smell fear. Then they know when to attack their prey. When the short talk was over, he asked for three volunteers to hold the snake for a photo op. This time I didn't volunteer but was eased forward by the group because of my uniform. I couldn't lose face and let the Royal Navy down could I?

I reluctantly stepped forward, and the handler coiled Mr. Python around me while explaining how to hold the head and not move. I was doing just fine until the photographer snapped the shot and the python moved. This put the fear of God into me just as I remembered that they could smell fear and react to it. As the handler removed Mr. Python, I quickly ducked out of the last coil. The whole group burst out laughing at me, but I was good with that. I also laughed at myself.

Later, we had just finished looking at an enormous salt water crocodile and decided to go into a gift shop, which was guarded by some beautiful, very colorful cockatiels. I mentioned to the assistant in the shop that the croc we had just seen must have been at least sixteen feet long and the ugliest most menacing looking beast on the planet. She said, "Isn't he beautiful?"

"I don't know about that," I said. She persisted, and we exchanged various differing views on the croc before I realized she thought I said *cock* for *cockatiel*, not *croc*. We all laughed our heads off.

The next day a couple of us went up river to Manly Island, which is in the middle of the river. We got to ride on a new type of boat which was on huge skis, a Hydrofoil. As the boat picked up speed, it rose out of the water, thusly being able to go faster with more efficiency. That was most exhilarating and it took us to the island where we visited what was the largest aquarium in the world at the time.

Before leaving I did manage to find an authentic aborigine area where I could buy some handmade items. The best souvenir was a handmade working boomerang. They showed me how to throw it correctly, which I tried much later on the South Downs of England. Yes, it actually came back to me but not always.

One more thing, a dozen of us did get to see *Jesus Christ Superstar.*

CHANGE OF PLANS

The Royal Yacht stayed for a day or so before we escorted it out to sea and on its way. Our next stop was going to be Perth on the west coast.

My superiors were now pressing me to take the preliminary professional exam for petty officer. I was a little overdue, mainly, I believe, because of fear of failure. Nobody else seemed to think I would fail, though, especially Jim Austin, my department petty officer. By now I was actually running the workshop routine and the men, not because Jim was lazy but because he was leading me by the nose to be a good petty officer, giving me the experience in advance. How did I keep getting the right people around me all the time? Was there a God in charge of all this?

Fear is something about the future, not the present, and it's good to live in the present. I had been studying the book of typical questions for a while and was as ready as I would ever be for the written test. Remember, the questions were not multiple choices. They were "Sketch, describe, and explain a theory" sort of questions. I also needed to be ready for the oral exam. I had no idea who would be on the board, except for my senior officer. We were in a flotilla of ships, and electrical commanders from these ships would be called upon to preside at my interrogation.

I took the written and prepared for the oral grilling, two weeks later. All the chiefs and petty officers peppered me with questions throughout this time. They would come down to the workshop, stop me in the passageway and call me on the phone.

I think they were getting a kick out of this. It also told me how invested they were in my career and how much they cared.

On the day of the test, I donned my best uniform, brushed my teeth, combed my hair, and went to the senior electrical officers' cabin. I was confident but nervous at the same time. I had the feeling that unless I screwed up big time I was a shoo-in. I knew my history of hard work and persistence with troubleshooting must count for something. Still, I needed to prove my electrical knowledge.

When called upon, I stepped in to see two electrical commanders seated next to my lieutenant commander. "Okay," I thought. "Just like my killick exam—shake their hands and smile with a charm you have never smiled before." Many of their questions were situational, which I knew I answered admirably. Some were on damage control scenarios, another topic I was top notch at. Next was on paralleling generators and transferring of loads. By then I was comfortable and starting to swagger and show off. Normally killicks didn't deal with paralleling generators and play with loads; they were senior rate jobs. I had been attending these actions, though, so I chewed those questions up and spat out the answers. The two commanders threw in a couple of curve balls, which was fair enough, but at the finish I felt good.

I was told to wait outside while they deliberated. It wasn't even two minutes before I was summoned back inside. I stepped into the cabin and faced three beaming faces. They didn't have to tell me I had passed. They all shook my hand and congratulated me on a terrific performance.

Being a petty officer. A day later I was a petty officer electrician in the Royal Navy. I moved into the forward petty officers' mess right away. The mess is in "D" section on two deck, the fourth section from the bow and the most forward mess on the ship.

This meant that during rough weather we went up and down way, way more than when I was used to on three deck. "Now I will see if I'm a real sailor or not," I thought. "It's gonna get rough, kids."

An unexpected thing happened right away. I was asked a question about the mess. "Hey, I'm the new boy in town. That wouldn't be up to me." A couple of the men immediately pointed out that I was a member of the mess and time there didn't count. Everybody was the same rank, and everybody's opinion counted. Because of this, I felt I was one of them right off the bat.

A month later, the president of the mess was leaving the ship and a new president was needed. You guessed it; they voted for me. They wanted new blood and fresh ideas, and I was it. One other reason was probably that they knew I was popular with the chiefs and officers. This would help when I needed a favor or permission to do something off the wall. Also, some didn't want the responsibility. A bad slip-up on the beer and liquor books or mess funds, let alone a serious incident in the mess, and I could be demoted. Yep, I had the weight of the mess on my shoulders. So I went from leader of the junior rates mess to leader of the senior rates mess. Of course, this sat well in my resume for my continued future in the Navy.

Glandular problems. Perth and Freemantle, which are basically the same place, came and went without incident, and back into the briny we sailed. Months later we were sailing in the Indian Ocean when it was discovered that the stern gland was leaking. This was ultra-serious trouble, as this was the gland and bearings where the screw shaft exited the ship. The heat generated was enormous, and special oil was pumped into and out of the bearings at high continuous pressure. The oil was cooled and sent round in a closed loop. The amount of extra oil we carried was relatively small, as it was just needed for topping up.

We were hundreds of miles from land and a replenishment ship. Now what?

A rendezvous was set up by the admiralty, but it was going to be touch and go. The replenishment ship didn't carry very much, either, as it was never really needed. We did get two forty gallon drums from an RN destroyer in the region. We had to get to a port with big enough dry docks to take us, and we had three choices: Perth, South Africa, and Madagascar. The captain suggested a sweepstakes with each sailor having one vote each to guess what would be our destination. Each vote would cost one pound sterling.

In the meantime, Admiralty House in London was negotiating with the governments of each country before letting us know the choice. Nobody was voting for Madagascar, as it had literally just finished a civil war. Naturally, the decision came back that Diego Suarez in Madagascar was the designated port. One person had voted for Madagascar, just to be different, and he grabbed all the money, about two hundred and fifty smackers. Everybody was dumbfounded but cheered for him anyway.

JOURNALISM AT ITS BEST

Prior to going to Madagascar, four of us petty officers had formed a team to put on a radio show. We wanted commissioning stories that told how many of certain store items we had used, and tattle-tale stories about incidents and certain personnel. It took a few weeks of planning, writing and re-writing.

We wrote, for instance, about how many toilet rolls we had used since leaving Chatham, how many tons of potatoes, how many light bulbs, you get the idea. Compiling the list took a lot of research and questioning of all the heads of departments. We also dug up stories that the crew members involved thought nobody knew. We had the scuttlebutt on many of the crew, and much of it wasn't good.

On the evening of the well-publicized show, the four of us went to the SRE (sound reproduction equipment i.e. internal radio) compartment and locked ourselves in. This was a very smart move because some of the personal stories that we told really jabbed some people hard. Several times the door knob was turned, followed by yelling and thumping on the door. That famous naval dictionary must have nearly caught fire from the heat. Threatening notes were slid under the door, along with toilet paper as a message. We certainly created quite a stir throughout the ship. Officers were not excluded and took their whack just like everybody else.

We needed to stay in the SRE compartment long into the night. It was a good thing we had stashed plenty of beer. The passageway finally quieted around 0200 hours and we managed to return to our mess unharmed. The next morning the ship was all abuzz, and the survival of the four of us was tenuous at best.

The senior heads of departments, the first Lieutenant and the captain, all expressed their gratitude and said it was a job well done. The morale of the crew was certainly high, even the ones we exposed. They saw the funny and lighter side of their exposed exploits and stories, once they had got over the initial shock and embarrassment that may have rocked their world.

Steaming into Madagascar. A week later we steamed into the war-torn country of Madagascar and edged our way into the dry dock. Precise measurements of our hull had been forwarded to the dockyard as eight by eight posts were needed, cut to length. These were placed along the hull and wedged in place before the water was drained. A setting was also along the bottom of the dry dock for our keel to rest on. These wooden supports had to be absolutely precise.

Yep, you probably know where I'm going with this already. As they were putting in the timbers, it became apparent that nothing was correct. Also, the timbers were being put in place by swimmers, and the water in the dock was absolutely filthy with oily debris and slime. Many other adjectives could be thrown in for good measure but I'll stop right there.

The next step was to cut the existing long timbers and get new ones for the longer lengths needed. But oh! Wait a minute! Somewhat into this process, some bright spark said, "Maybe the timbers are back to front. They are all correct but placed in reverse order." This turned out to be true, so now we just need new timbers for the ones that we had already re-cut.

One other problem for the whole crew was the toilet situation. Obviously, we couldn't use the ones on board and discharge sewage into the dry dock. This meant that the roughly two hundred and fifty crew members had to use the two, yes two, traps on the dock side. It got worse; one trap had the normal European toilet with a seat. The other trap has those weird French sunken squares with two raised foot placements. There was a hole between the footsteps to aim for while squatting. In this modern age, how barbaric was that?

Naturally, the officers bagged the real toilet for themselves and made it off limits for the lower deck. That went down like a lead balloon in a vacuum. One morning an incident quickly made the rumor rounds of the ship. A hungover chief decided to use the officers' loo as the other was occupied. An officer, himself on the way to the lavatory, saw him enter the Forbidden City. When he got to the door he smote upon it, demanding the chief come out immediately. I believe exceptional wording from the naval dictionary came into play as blue sentences were exchanged.

Later, the illegally pooping chief was charged with insubordination. Apparently everything *came out in the end.* (Sorry, couldn't help it.)

The Madagascan community was very welcoming to us. On our third day in port they put together a free dance for us in the city. I was pegged for shore patrol again that night with a killick and two juniors. Being a petty officer gave me more clout on patrol. More diplomacy was required, as a drunken sailor listened more to somebody from their own level. As small incidents occurred, I let the killick take the lead. If that didn't work, I stepped forward and put a stronger stamp of authority on the situation. It worked out well and nothing major happened.

A new assignment. A week or two earlier I had been informed that seventeen other ship mates and I were being flown home. Our time on the ship was up, and new crew was being flown out. I was to be going back to HMS Collingwood, the electrical training school. On finishing a six month qualifying course, I would be a confirmed petty officer.

One day before my departure, I went on a trip up river. The French had a marine detachment in the area and had a getaway in the jungle. Twenty crew members were invited on a trip for the day with all food and drink supplied. Ten of these people could stay in the jungle overnight in the small barracks room there. Unfortunately, I wasn't lucky enough to pull a long straw.

A patrol boat arrived next morning and we all piled onboard for the trip up river into the jungle. It was a long way, but when we got there it was fabulous. There was a great beach area with tables and umbrellas and all kinds of amenities. The river was tidal and had saltwater even this far up stream. About an hour before returning I was getting really down. I wasn't sure what was coming over me. As we went down river, things got worse and I was sobbing my eyes out. I had been on Dido for four years and three months; the normal ship time was a maximum of two and a half years, but I had requested an extension. I loved it as I was single and enjoyed the adventures.

I was really upset through the night and the next morning at breakfast. I was grateful for one thing, though. The crew who had stayed the night in the jungle were as miserable as sin. They were literally covered in mosquito and horse fly bites, even though mosquito nets had been used. Great big welts were all over their bodies. Sometimes the short straw is good.

The time for me to break the umbilical cord with Dido arrived, and I stood on the jetty with the others awaiting transport to the airfield. I was given a wonderful send-off and been seen by the captain. This was normal for all senior rates, petty officer and above. He thanked me for all my hard work, which included the sports and the running of the ship's newspaper. He told me that I had helped boost ship morale, which made his job much easier and more successful, and he was concerned about the vacuum I would leave on my departure. "There is always somebody ready to step forward," I said. "That's the way it works."

A FLY IN THE OINTMENT

The bus arrived and away we went. Then the bus stopped next to a grass field in the middle of nowhere. Had we run out of gas? Did we have a mechanical problem? The driver got out and asked us to do the same. He opened a gate and pointed over the hill in front of us. We grabbed our luggage and headed out over said hill. Were they going to shoot us? Had I watched too many war films?

On cresting the hill, we saw a large tent across the way with a Madagascan flag flying above it. As we approached the official-looking tent, we could see it was set up as an office with uniformed men and women inside. Okay then; this was the airport. Our passports were stamped, and we were readied for the flight to Tananarive, the then capital of Madagascar. From there we would be boarding an Air France jumbo jet to Orly Airport in Paris and then on to London Heathrow.

Standing in the just bearable heat for what seemed an eternity we waited for the plane. One did eventually arrive but, oh boy, I wondered if this bag of bones could actually take off again. We piled on board from the grass runway and looked down the foreboding field. I made myself as comfortable as I could in the non-padded, metal bucket seat. There were multiple holes in the seat, probably to drain the sweat now running down my body.

It was six hundred miles, give or take, to the capital if we actually made it that far. The chickens in the center aisle didn't seem to mind the ride, so that was comforting. We bounced down the runway and took off almost, it seemed, by accident and certainly a great deal of luck. I foolishly looked out the window to see flaps of metal jostling about, fighting to stay attached to the wing. In what seemed no time at all, we landed, bumping and bouncing, to a gyrating stop. It seemed a very short journey for six hundred miles, I thought.

Oh no! It was just one of six stops on the way to our destination. Five fields and five death-defying landings later, we landed on tarmac. This indicated an arrival at a real airport and transfer to a real plane. I decided that if I ever got a flight like that again, I'd make sure to get a parachute.

We boarded our plane to Paris, but an hour later, we were still at the gate, doors closed awaiting the pull back. Then we heard, "Ladies and gentlemen, we need to deplane and have you wait on the concourse." We wound up staying in a hotel for the night. The next day, back at the airport, they announced we would have to stay another night.

Now this place wasn't like New York or London. The hotel in Tananarive was surrounded by a shanty town, and it was fairly dodgy going outside. The hotel itself was quite luxurious, though, and quite out of place in this area.

We were informed that there was a bowling alley in the hotel and it was free to us stranded patrons. The three meals per day were also no charge and compliments of Air France. Nobody said the bar was free, but Colin and I signed the bar tabs as "Air France" and didn't pay a penny. I wondered if karma would catch up with me later for that.

This sequence of events went on for five days. The British ambassador came down a couple of times to make sure we were all okay. He offered his services and even gave us a number to call at any time if we needed him.

On the fourth night of our stay, I went out again with Colin, my regular run-ashore mate over the time on Dido. I had made friends with a young lady at the regular bar we had been frequenting, and she was very interesting and spoke very good English. No, she was not a lady of the night, and I invited her up to my room.

As we left the hotel room at about midnight, I opened the door to see my roommate snoozing against the wall in the hallway. I woke him up and ushered him into bed, as he may have had a tad too much to drink. The woman and I walked to the elevator and awaited the ride down. When the doors slid open, there were two suited men standing before us—the hotel security detail. A resident on my floor had reported a man sleeping in the hallway and they were investigating. They didn't speak English, but I had a translator right by my side.

They now had a new task. Apparently they frowned upon local women being escorted into the hotel. In the lobby, we were separated and questioned. I couldn't speak French, and they couldn't speak English, but I sensed I was in trouble. I was getting more than concerned about my welfare.

I was really embarrassed about it but made the call for the British Ambassador at 0100 hours. A short while later he arrived on scene dressed like he was going to a ball. I explained my situation and let him take over from there. As I sat silent, he was in full flight, having a forceful-sounding conversation with the security men, who had now brought in a policeman. After what seemed a lifetime, the ambassador told me to go back to my room. Everything had been taken care of.

The next morning, waiting for the bus to the airport that was imminent one more time, I saw the ambassador and apologized profusely. His reaction amazed me. He beamed a huge smile and told me he was actually pleased to have been pulled into action. He said he had been in Madagascar for nearly two years and that was the first time he had helped in any kind of serious situation. I had made his day and made him feel good. Wow. Only I could do something wrong and come up trumps.

A COURSE LESSON

After several weeks of vacation at my parents' house, I reported to HMS Nelson, where I was to serve a short stint as a guide on HMS Victory. A month later, I was back in HMS Collingwood to complete the electrical advanced course for my confirmation as a petty officer electrician. Why they wasted my time packing and unpacking for that period of time in Victory still mystifies me.

In Collingwood, I arrived to almost brand new petty officers' quarters. My personal cabin was very spacious, and the bathroom and toilets were six steps outside my second floor room. Everything was spick and span and still smelled new. Across the road were the dining room, study hall, living room bar and club. Being a petty officer in the more modern Navy was a gift.

I soon got sorted out as to where and when I was meant to be. My class started the next week, so I had time to accustom myself to life on land and life in a new and different blue suit.

Once again, the course started off with electronic theory and higher mathematics. I'm sure this is done to weed out any non-starters before getting into the nitty-gritty of missile systems, gyro compasses and the like. After four weeks and two exams, two classmates were back-classed to do it all over again once the next class started in six weeks. One could only fail two exams and be back-classed twice, or you would be demoted back to the previous rank. One of our two back-classed mates did fail the same exam again and was shipped out. Excuse the pun.

I managed to bumble my way through the whole course without failing any of the twelve segments.

Field gun racing competition. During my time in Collingwood while still on the course I was asked to join another team. I was already playing rugby for them but another annual team competition was on the horizon. It involved racing with a field gun and its *limber*, or cart, on a marked out track on the parade ground. The gun weighed about a ton, and the limber wheels had to be stopped exactly on a designated pair of lines before the crew lifted the whole unit. Others would then swap the wheels before going to the next pair of lines. At these lines the limber was unhooked and the gun spun around 180 degrees. Then a blank shell was breached and fired. The shell casing was removed and thrown back in the limber before reversing all actions including switching the wheels and running to the finish line.

In order to be able to lift and hold these items and race, one had to reach a high level of fitness and training. Before even touching the equipment, we had a four week keep-fit training session every day, twice a day. I would get up at 0530 hours and get down to the gym to join the team. The first morning session consisted of running four miles cross country with a stop every quarter of a mile to do push-ups, jumping jacks, and star jumps until the PTI said "Let's roll." This was a killer for all of us as none of us were anywhere near the level needed yet.

After the first run I got myself to class and sat down. At the first break when I tried to stand, I couldn't. My calf muscles were locked solid. I was unable to straighten my legs and needed help to walk. After class, I reported for my second round of pure torture. Did I really need to be doing this?

When the alarm clock scrambled my brain the following morning, I couldn't even get dressed. My legs wouldn't bend for me to put on my socks. I eventually managed, though, and hobbled down to the gym. How was I going to run four miles and do those exercises?

The rest of the team, thankfully, was in the same state as me. We found that by going very slowly our muscles warmed up and allowed us to run normally after a short while. After a week or so, we were finally getting fit enough not to be affected by the rigorous exercising. This went on for two more weeks.

Our ogre, I mean instructor, now said. "Okay, men, we are now ready for the assault course training. The last four round the course will do it again." Arrgghhh! A dagger in the heart.

After a week of various training techniques, always polished off with the assault course, I heard the torturer say, "We are doing *only* the assault course today." Cheers rang out, but then he said, "We will do it in teams of four and carrying a telegraph pole with us." It was like somebody had cut our throats in mid cheer. Those poles were heavy and cumbersome. Getting them over and through the obstacles was crazy. A week of that with a few other party tricks thrown in, and we are ready for the actual gun and limber running training. This was the fittest I have ever been in my life.

My job entailed running between the two wheels of the limber towing the gun. During the firing, I also placed the shell in the breach and pulled it out, after firing, with a special tool. My opposite number opened the breach and slammed it closed after the shell removal. Timing was of the essence in order to get good numbers. On one occasion, the closer was just a tad too fast and slammed the breach closed while I was getting my hand out of the way. All the skin from the back of my hand and fingers landed on the asphalt. Ouch! We didn't break a stride, though. I finished the run before dealing with the blood.

Another time as we spun the gun around at high speed, we got a surprise. We made too sharp of a turn trying to cut split seconds from our time, and the wheels bit into the ground. Luckily, we had already unhitched the limber as the gun, all one ton of it, flew into the air and turned upside down. Thankfully, it stayed up there for at least a minute, or so it seemed, as bodies flew in all directions as if somebody had thrown a hand grenade in the middle of us. The gun came crashing down like a ton of field gun. Oh, wait a minute. It *was* a ton of field gun. It took the whole team all of its strength to right the situation. That was a close call by any standard.

Another nasty incident happened one day when the fired shell casing was thrown back into the limber it missed. I should explain two things here. When running between the two wheels, we were in full stride with the back leg feeling the wind of the wheel behind us. The wheel would be barely missing the leg as it moved forward for the next step. When my opposite number stooped to scoop up the shell that had been fired that day, the gun wheel ran over both his legs. The whole team heard, *crack, crack* and "Aaaarrrggghhh!" We screeched to a halt and ran to his aid.

Now I cannot explain why, but the entire team burst out laughing almost uncontrollably and could barely stand. Thank goodness passersby sent for help because we were in no condition to do so. Once he was sorted out we were by his bedside apologizing and feeling bad. We couldn't explain our reaction; maybe we were glad it wasn't us.

The day of the races against other shore establishments came and went. There were no prizes for us, but it was a heck of a day and the relief of it all being over was huge. There was a hole in our future days but the torture was over.

A variety show. One night the senior rates club was having a variety show, and my whole class attended and got front row seats. One act was a hypnotist, who was excellent. He asked for some volunteers and naturally I got on stage. After hypnotizing me, though I thought he hadn't, he told me to sit on a chair on the stage. He then said to imagine I was at a picnic and I had sat on an ants nest. I thought, "No way, I'm not hypnotized." That was when I started jumping all over the place and itching my whole body. I put on quite a dance. With everybody laughing at me, I sat back down again with my buddies and supped my beer.

When we were ready to depart the club, my friends got worried as I couldn't respond to any of them. I was evidently still under hypnosis. The main gate was called, and on his return the hypnotist slapped me across the face so hard that my mates yelled and grabbed him. I just kind of blinked and smiled, with no feeling from the slap. I did come out of the trance, though.

More tests of strength. Before finishing the training course, another leadership training session was implemented. As before, I did very well in this, especially the three day hike and incident weekend in the middle. The assault course was to be tackled, but this was different than the one we had done earlier. At the beginning we needed to climb up a single story building onto a flat roof. On the other side we needed to climb down and run down a steep embankment about three feet from the building. A junior rate was on the roof to make sure we knew the edge was upon us.

On the walk around prior to the timed run, I decided that I was going to run straight off the roof and land on the slope, sliding to the bottom. I wanted this course record really badly. So, when the time came, I ran and launched myself into thin air. The junior rate yelled and tried to stop me, but I was gone. I skidded down the hill and was on my way.

The next obstacle was comprised of three ropes close together across a ravine. I again launched my body, onto the ropes this time, and managed to stabilize myself without falling off. Many obstacles later, I leaped over the water jump and rolled over the finish line. I was the new record holder. No extra points are awarded for this, just great satisfaction.

GETTING THE HANG OF THINGS

During my down time after the course, I somehow found out about a commander who was looking for people who wanted to try hang gliding as a sport. I'd seen these gliders soaring overhead on my weekend drives home. Hmmm, I thought. Should I or shouldn't I? I signed up for it just for the challenge.

The following week about five of us headed for the hills. During these early hang gliding days, the Rogallo glider was the go-to craft for beginners, with approximately 400 square feet of sail. John, the commander, showed us the way to build the craft and gave us some rudimentary flying instructions. When I landed on my first short hop on a slight slope, my hands were still wrapped around the bar as it touched down and skidded further downhill. It removed most of the skin off of the backs of both hands and also placed many thistle and dirt particles into my now raw flesh. A few more flights and I'd be no skin and all bone.

Another time on a short run and glide, I ended up halfway into a huge blackberry bush. I needed help extricating myself and spent the following half hour pulling out thorns.

Over the weeks we all made good progress and were actually flying off of escarpments and landing in the valley below. It was a long haul back up those slopes with a glider on your back, but the ride down was incredible. I did manage to stay up for a while and eventually passed my pilot's test to be able to fly alone. This required stalling out at altitude and recovering—recovery a must so as not to receive your credentials posthumously. John did bring a bucket and shovel in case I didn't make it.

Later I did survive another death defying situation. I was trying a larger, 650 square foot hang glider for the first time, fortunately with John. I ran forward to take off, pushing the nose up as required. I wasn't thinking about the extra material and was going to stall out on take-off, thus plunging 600 feet down the steep cliff. John, who was right next to my take-off point, instantly saw my error and grabbed the back point of the glider and yanked me backward. He was strong enough to drag me back far enough to get my feet back onto terra firma. Whew.

Another time I was about to take off when the wind suddenly dropped at the instant I was to leave. This caused my nose to dip, and then the wind picked up and was pushing the nose into the ground as I was running downhill for lift off. I couldn't stop, but at the last second I was saved. There was a two foot cut out drop on the hill just as the nose was going to hit the ground and send me spinning to my death. This caused me to fall backwards sharply and jerk the nose up. Yep, I was in the air and safe. Was it looking more and more like I had a guardian angel?

WHERE IS MY ANGEL NOW?

After six months of Collingwood and being promoted to a confirmed petty officer, I was drafted to HMS Nelson. This was a shore base in Portsmouth with large officers' quarters across the road. I wasn't sure why I was there unless it was a stop off point and rest before the real draft. My sleeping quarters were in the old buildings at the back of the camp. This is significant because there were all kinds of ghost stories about this building.

My job was to be a watch keeper on the main gate. I was in charge of a group of junior rates who, along with me, checked everybody and their vehicles in and out. We checked ID cards and civilian passes.

The night watches were a little scary going to and from my mess. I was on the second floor in a dorm type room with other watch keepers. Out of the window and across the way was a similar building that was condemned. My building was the same age and type, so why wasn't it condemned? It certainly should have been. There was no heating, and no lights worked in the hallway to my dorm or the stairwell and foyer. The back streets outside that led to the parade ground were not lit either.

It was really spooky going back and forth to the main gate. It was literally pitch black once inside the building and I needed to actually feel my way up the stairs and run my hand down the wall until I came to a door into my dorm. Even then I needed to count the steps to my bed before turning on my bunk light. I cringed every time I had to make this journey. A couple of times I saw a faint light moving in the dorm across the way, and that sent shivers coursing through my torso. Maybe it was Lord Nelson himself.

One sunny day on the main gate, an officer yelled at me from across the road outside the officers' quarters. There was a small side gate in a tall wall with one of my men stationed there to check officers IDs. He angrily beckoned me to come over to him. As petty officer in charge, I was not allowed to leave the actual main gate and yelled back this information and asked him to come to me. That went down well, like a submarine in full dive mode. His fury was as deep as the Mariana Trench by the time he was by my side. When I asked his problem, he told me he had forgotten to take his ID outside the quarters with him. He complained profusely about my junior sentry. I explained that my junior was going to get a compliment from me for doing his job and not caving to authority. He told me he had been at this establishment for two years and I should recognize him and let him in. I said that I'd been there all of one week and didn't know him, so he would need identifying. His red, purple and blue face didn't influence me at all as I called the guard shack several yards away from the main gate. I had two of my men escort him to the guard shack while they called the officers' wardroom for confirmation.

Several minutes later the captain of the barracks came across the road and, as I saluted, showed me his ID card on his way in. As the two officers crossed the road and entered the gate, I could see the body language of the captain giving the officer a good old roasting. I did notice during future watches that the captain always made it a point to show his identity on entering the gate. This way no other officer could complain that they had to. I did learn an important lesson there for my future as a senior rate.

Several other small incidents occurred over the next few months, especially as the IRA were trying terrorist tactics in England at the time. People who drove in and out frequently didn't think they should be searched every time. I thought otherwise because they had the very vehicles bad people would watch and, maybe, attach a bomb to.

I was only at this post for three months before getting my next draft orders. The main thing I had learned was that I wasn't a very good petty officer. I was a good petty officer electrician and very capable at my electrical job, but I was not good at being a senior rate and all the other things that came with that.

A big change. On reading my draft chit, I was horrified. I was being drafted to HMS Ganges, the new entry training camp in the middle of nowhere. My horror was amplified when I read on; I was to be an instructor.

Now I had been in long enough to know all kinds of people in the right places, so I knew I could finagle my way out of this by just lifting a phone, or maybe several phones.

Well, that didn't work. Everybody I knew said that this particular draft was non-negotiable. "Besides," they said, "apparently nobody wants to go there, but then nobody wants to leave." I decided I'd better just go change my pants and head out for hell.

My main worry was that this was going to be very military and strict. There would be marching and saluting and immaculately kept uniforms with knife-edge creases. I always had a neat appearance and was well disciplined, but this was going to be at a whole new level. I was an electrician, not a drill instructor and marcher of men.

Actually, I was good at what I *knew*. How well could I swim in uncharted waters? How good was I at handling adversity? How good was I at facing my fears? All this would be tested in the next few months. Fish out of water will certainly die. This fish had to find a way to survive.

INTO THE VALLEY OF DEATH

When I drove to the micro hamlet of Shotley Gate and arrived at HMS Ganges, the gates, appropriately painted black, swung open on my approach as if they were expecting me. They were, and the guards on the gate pointed me to the senior rates mess, which required driving all the way around the parade ground. All the buildings were red brick, which normally meant very old. I had been hoping for better quarters than where I came from.

It was Friday, a strange day to join a new draft. I parked my MGBGT as near as possible to the front doors and entered the mess. The foyer was really nice and had a red phone booth in the middle, which was different. The dining hall was to the right with a closed door to the left. Luckily, a petty officer came down the stairway in front of me. He was a man with substantial confidence, a man who knew who he was and wasn't shy about it. He told me lunch time was half an hour away and showed me to the office.

The chief gave me the same type of greeting, strong, confident and full of energy. His firm handshake almost yanked me over his desk as he smiled and grabbed a key. Later, after putting away my gear, I was about to walk into his office when he leaped up and said, with a smiling face, "Come on let's get a beer and I'll introduce you to some of the lads."

We went through that closed door I'd seen, and before me was a wonderful bar and recreation area. The curved bar was at the far end with a bartender in place. A few of the lads were already ordering a beer; I'm guessing lunch time was upon us.

I enjoyed the gifted beer and some banter before being escorted to the dining room. The chefs greeted me warmly and shook my hand. Two more lads joined my table of four, and everybody welcomed me and made me feel comfortable. Maybe they remembered when they first cringed at getting this drafting.

Having quaffed down a most delicious and tantalizing meal, I headed back to my personal cabin and unpacked my gear. When I returned to the office the chief took me down to the divisional office I would be working out of. I had donned my number two uniform. My regular working clothes were not going to see the light of day for a couple of years.

Having smartly crossed the parade ground, we went down a fairly heavily sloped, wide, tarmacked walkway. At generous intervals there were mess decks on either side with a high peaked roof covering the promenade. I soon found out it was appropriately called "the long covered way." About halfway down we hung a left and went down a cement path to the Faraday Divisional Office.

I was presented and handed over to the divisional chief, George Brand. George seemed to be a stern faced, older type chief without a sense of humor. His dark eyes pierced my cranium as the vice grip of his hand crushed my fingers. Trying to forcibly encourage an infusion of blood back into my hand by vigorously shaking it, I manufactured a false smile. His strong deep voice, which caused me to move back three steps, beckoned me to follow his small but powerful frame. This man was to turn out to be another driving force in my life who taught me so much about dedication to duty. He was a wonderful person with all kinds of magical stories. He was tough but very fair. He was also a genuine riot with his comedy and was as sharp as a tack.

We entered the front and only double doors to the mess. I wondered how this was my mess as it seemed there is a class in there already, and I hadn't been assigned one yet. Oh contraire! The chief, who had been waving his arms hither and thither while showing me the various entities of the mess, started to explain. This class was in its last week of training, and their petty officer had been drafted. With only a two-week class under my belt on how to teach, I was to be in charge of the class.

I believe they used smelling salts to bring me back from my flabbergasted senses. My heart was now racing at triple the pace like after a cross country run. It was struggling to burst out of my body and run for the hills quickly, followed by the rest of my being.

I was to take charge of a class without knowing any of the routines for things like parades in the mornings. On my second day, this class would be out in front of the parade as a "passing out" class. I had no idea what to do.

The chief smiled and said I would be shown the ropes and routine. He told me the class leader would run the class at the parade, and I would just march behind the class and salute while going past the podium. "Listen for the orders of the parade ground instructor for the rest of the routine," he said. My shaking helped the beading sweat of my body run to the bottom of my legs and collect in my socks. I squished to the office and was offered a cup of coffee. A double scotch would have been more appropriate.

The first morning that I went down for breakfast, I was surprised. The tables were well laid out tables with everything one would need. At the food counter, there was very little. On my approach to the counter, the chef asked what I would like and how I would like it cooked. Wow, was this service or what? Yes, I could have whatever I wanted, however much I wanted, and have it prepared to my individual liking. This unbelievable service was available because the powers that be new how hard we worked and how much we needed really good food.

I stumbled and bumbled my way through the weekend and made it unharmed into Monday morning. The class was to pack their case and kit bag and get ready for the busses to send them cheering on their way. I flashed back to how I was feeling when I left my boot camp training—apprehensive, nervous and still wondering what the future would hold.

Normally after a class has finished I would be getting a four or five day leave to rest up for the next six week class. I didn't get that leave as I had only been with a class for two days. I also needed to plan the many lessons I was to teach, get myself into some kind of routine, and reconnoiter the whole camp to get my bearings and meet all the members of the senior rates mess.

The dress code for the instructors, as I mentioned earlier, was the number two uniform. However, we wore combat boots and gaiters instead of shoes. Gaiters are like ankle guards that cover the bottom of the trouser legs and overlap over the boots. These are held tight with two buckles on each outer leg.

The chiefs and petty officers were all under one roof, the only mixed mess in the whole of the Navy. I could tell how everybody got along well and supported each other to the max.

A LEARNING CURVE

The first day of my first class was upon me. "Oh, my lord, here we go," I thought. I crossed from the divisional office to the newest entry group and faced my almost civilians. I wonder if they thought they were sailors yet. I trundled them, in some kind of shambles, kind of marching, to my mess deck. I had no idea of what to say or what to do. I did have one order to give and that was to get their kit stowed in their lockers. That gave me an hour to think before my class in the afternoon down in the instruction area.

We made it to the classroom without anybody tripping over themselves or anybody else. The chief in charge of that area of instruction handed me some overhead projector slides and wished me well. I did not have all my lesson plans done for the five weeks, but I had enough done to keep me ahead of the game. I opened my folder and managed to scratch my way through, although very poorly, I suspect.

After I had a few class lessons under my belt, I was a little better at my presentation. It was but a first small step in a marathon race. The division chief and other petty officers with some free time helped and encouraged me to no end. They knew of their own struggles when they started this gig.

I was advised to collect all the classes' boots and get them down to the camp cobbler. This would include my own. The way recruits were taught to march and walk was to dig in their heels and go forward to the toe. This would ordinarily wear down the heel very quickly. The cobbler, for a small charge, put steel pieces at the heel and toe. The toe was for the sound effect more than wear and tear.

Each morning the first item on the agenda was the daily parade and march past of the podium with the camp commander at the helm. For all of the first week this was very nerve-wracking for the class and me. Although they had marching lessons on the parade ground with the excruciatingly tough drill instructors, they were terrible. I gave extra instruction at night without the bullying manner and scare tactics of the drill team. It must have helped, but not much. This is not a criticism of the drill team; they had an incredibly difficult job. They carried out their task admirably day in and day out. The standards that the drill team achieved in such a short amount of time were quite remarkable.

A class at the pier. One day my first class was to spend the whole morning down at the pier. I had to be shown where it was and then marched the class down there on a blind run. I was relieved that the pier staff would take over and whisk them out on the river in what are known as whalers. They were going to be taught how to come along side with the boat, retrieve a man overboard and stem a buoy. Stemming a buoy meant coming up to the buoy and nudging the bow to it. In real Navy life this would allow a buoy jumper to step onto the buoy and secure a ships anchor chain with shackles.

I formed the class outside the pier office and went in. I said, "Morning, chief. Class 392 is outside ready for the river. I will be down to pick them up at 1130 hours."

He said, "What do you mean you'll pick them up at 1130 hours? You are taking out one of the boats and teaching them." What the heck? I didn't know how to do that myself, let alone teach it. He laughed and said, "Let me show you on the blackboard," as he reached for some chalk.

He went over the maneuvers very expertly and threw me a set of keys. This is when I informed him I didn't even know how to start the engine. "Oh, geez," he said. He smiled again and said to get in the boat and he would send a pier staff junior rate out to show me.

Three boats were going out, so I took a third of the class and hopped aboard, feeling very nervous and skittish. The young sailor of the pier staff jumped the gunnels and said, "Hang on, PO. There is a problem starting this particular boat. Let me do it." How kind and considerate was that? He started the engine as I looked on, and he whispered instructions.

Taking a large deep breath and swallowing hard, I upped the throttle and eased forward while slightly turning the rudder. The whaler slid forward and outward, carrying my class and me to imminent death. The class didn't know my short comings and were oblivious of the danger I was taking them into. Fortunately the river was very calm. It was tidal and could be very rough and have a strong current. I'm guessing that the width of this sea monster was probably at least a mile—no small chunk of water.

I was amazed at my hidden talent as I first showed the boys how to do each task and then had them do it themselves. The ordeal over, we headed back to the jetty having first passed the breakwater to safety.

When I returned to the office, I discovered that the chief had been watching me the whole time through binoculars. He didn't want to tell me that beforehand as I would have been self-conscious. He congratulated me on a job well done. This pier staff chief, Adam, and his team were absolutely marvelous. I was quickly learning how all of the Ganges personnel had each other's backs, especially the new instructors. Maybe this job wouldn't be so bad after all.

Trying but failing. At the end of three weeks, I was to write a report on each of the lads, a report that would follow them throughout their naval service. I spent a lot of time and effort trying to say the right thing. A final report would be written at the end of their sixth week. Twenty-four reports to write each time is quite a task.

I spent a lot of time after hours trying to keep the class up to speed. I put my heart and soul into this snake pit, trying to survive and keep my head above water. The briny was creeping up to my chest as I felt I was struggling. Then, when I was teaching the most difficult subject to teach thus far, the classroom instruction officer came to visit. I was teaching nuclear, biological and chemical defense. I'd had plenty of instruction and training on this, but teaching it was another matter. My performance was pathetic to the trained eye. The lads may not have known any better, but the officer and I did.

The division chief spoke to me the next day and showed me the report from the training officer. The report was unkind, to say the least. It beat me to a pulp with no constructive criticism or any upstroke remarks toward the end. I was devastated and my heart sank. "This job is for the birds and I can't do any better," I said to myself. This is the worst I had felt since walking down those fourteen steps with my dad to the car at the beginning of my service.

A bit of a break. The following weeks were average as I strode through the quagmire and bullied my way to the end. All my classes and training sessions were done by the book without much fun. How could I have fun when I was trying so hard? The passing out parade brought a relief to my system and I drove home for a few days' rest. The lads all passed their tests and went on to their various establishments but I had not done well. Was this the definition of purgatory or what?

The drive back to Ganges wasn't the most looked forward to journey of my life. I was driving back into the gates of hell. The biggest thing on my mind was how I wanted to make a go of this and be successful. I had to get into a positive mode and put on a show. I needed to fool myself and everybody else that I was going to be good at this.

Monday morning rolled around and I cheerfully picked up my second class. I mostly knew the routine now and had a handle on what was expected of me. About halfway through the first week, I got a visitor. A fleet chief from my time on HMS Dido was serving in the admin building. He wasn't an electrical chief but he knew how hard working and dedicated I had been on the ship.

He came up alongside me and asked me to walk with him. "How do you feel about this job?" he asked. I just casually answered that I wanted to make a go of it, and I knew my first class was a disaster. I told him I was going to crack this egg and be a better petty officer and give it my best. My answer was exactly what he wanted and what he expected from somebody like me. He patted me on the shoulder and left me to the class.

I later realized that my divisional officer, who was a helicopter pilot, had set this up. He liked me and my attitude and wanted to know the bottom line on how I was going to respond and was I worth keeping. How could I be so lucky as to have a former ship fleet chief watching my back? His input more than likely saved my bacon. Leaving Ganges with a bad report would certainly seal my fate for further promotion to chief.

GETTING THE HANG OF THINGS

As I got to know more people around camp and became one of them, I got more and more confident. I still had a lot of room for better teaching skills, but things were starting to look up. The rugby team found out I played and invited me into their fray. A couple of more agile mess members challenged me to play squash. I went swimming in the very large indoor heated pool. I used the running track at the bottom of the camp near the river to help keep fit, and the rigorous rugby training sessions built my muscles in the gym. I spent much more time with my class and worked hard at better lesson plans and teaching them to march better on their own time. It was like old times on the ships—sixteen plus hours a day, seven days a week. I was loving it.

Rugby adventures. It was winter with about three inches of snow on the ground when my team played a rugby match with the Norwich Police Department. They were all twice my size, but it was a close game. During a roughhouse portion of the game, the ball popped out to me outside the pile. I snapped it up and ran forward straight into the Jolly Green Giant. There was a splatting noise, and I should have been on my back two inches below the snow. Instead the Jolly Green Giant landed on his back as the whole game came to a stop. I took advantage and stormed off up the field. I didn't score but did gain a lot of territory for the team. Later we all laughed about how physics had gone out the window; I'm guessing he must have been off balance at just the right time.

Another time we were playing away in Felixstow across the river. It had been raining for two days and the mud was awful with one end of the field an inch or two under water. While running back to catch an overhead ball, I didn't notice our full back. He was also running up to get the same ball. We didn't see each other until we ran into each other at full speed. There was a really loud slap and crack sound as our wet bodies met. My thigh took the brunt of the hit, which gave me a tremendous charley horse with great pain. The pain along with the noise made me think I had broken a bone, but ten minutes later I returned to the game. A short while later, I broke two fingers in a tackle, but we taped the broken fingers next to my good fingers. I still wasn't finished being injured, though. Still later an opposition player's finger was accidently poked into my eye along with a spoonful of mud. Now you know why I remember this game. Oh yes; we won.

A scary river adventure. Naturally, there was no smoking on the whalers, so I would take the lads down river out of site of the base and ask if anybody wanted to light up. I always got six or more suckers, and at this, I would turn the boat around into the waves and soak them silly, drenching their cigs. This was followed by me saying, "Rule number one, no smoking in the boat." I always got a laugh and it lightened the lads up. They saw their PO was human and could have a joke.

When I was teaching the man overboard technique, I would ask for a volunteer to jump overboard to be rescued. This was always met with silence and a worried look on all the faces. When I relented and said I was joking, the relief was heard up and down the river for miles. I was having fun and it showed.

A more sinister incident happened when I took the class for a rowing lesson. Another class was also on the river, so we decided to race each other to a buoy upstream. The tide was running very swiftly, and the going was very tough for the lads. We won the race and I turned the boat around to head back to the breakwater.

Things were looking bad right from the onset. The racing tide was carrying us at high speed straight toward a light ship that was anchored in the river. Our time before impact was very short, and if that happened we would be smashed against the hull and, likely, some of us would be knocked unconscious and drown. If anybody survived it would be a miracle.

I was very inexperienced, but needed to stay calm and let the lads know everything was under control. Just before impact, I told the starboard side crew to lift their oars. I then pushed the rudder hard to port, putting the boat broadside to the stern. A few yards from the stern of the light ship, I brought the rudder back and we whipped down the side of the ship with barely a foot between us. The lads were marvelous; they carried out my orders very quickly, which saved the day. As we neared the breakwater, I repeated the rudder maneuver and we made it into the safety of the sheltered marina of the base. As before, the chief had been watching and later said he had his heart in his mouth. I told him I had my butt in mine. My actions were not my own; I wasn't that good. How did I know what to do so quickly and efficiently? Was there a god, a guardian angel, a master of spiritual ceremonies?

Going camping. The camping weekend that was my two day break disappeared. One of the other petty officers from another division on my rotation said he always went camping with his class. He discovered the advantage of seeing the other side of a new recruit. Some who were good in the classroom were out shone by others out in the field. I had a long chat with the color sergeant over a couple of beers about the advantages of going with the lads and decided to skip my break and go along camping with my group.

At one of the venues on the trip, there were four two man and two single man canoes. One third of the boys got to go with the canoes on the first morning so John, the other PO, and I went with them. We each took a single canoe and took off down river, leaving the two man canoes way behind us. John knew where to lay in wait for the recruits and charge out splashing and rocking their boats.

Sure enough, here they came and out we darted. They had no idea we could do such a thing. They soon got into the spirit of things and ganged up on us as we took off again. We had a blast and headed out for the safety of the camp. The lads were drenched but we, as the winners, were relatively dry. The boys had a lot of fun seeing us as human beings.

The second third of the class did community service. This entailed digging up small trees and piling them on piers. Wicken Fen was a farming area but also a national park protected area. The ground was pure peat, jet black soil that was in danger of being overrun with this scrub, fast growing tree. The loose peat made it easy to pull the trees out of the ground to stack them for burning later in the year. The piles would be burnt when the ground was soaking wet. If the peat ever caught fire there likely would be no putting it out.

The final third of the class did camp duties like cleaning and cooking and prepping for the next event. As the days moved on through, the three segments rotated through the different tasks.

The shocker for the lads was, even in the snow of winter, John and I would stand near the tent in the mornings. We would strip down naked and do full body washes. This was when men were still men—foolish men maybe, but it was fun to shock and awe the new recruits.

The trip to these camping expeditions was by a large Navy tarp-covered truck. A Land Rover was also driven separately. One weekend John and I were asked to take the Rover, and I had to drive because John had not passed the Navy driving test. It was the dead of winter which, in this part of England, was freezing cold. On the way back we ran out of gas in the middle of nowhere. There was no radio contact and, on a Sunday afternoon, no passing vehicles. About a mile or so down the road we saw a small duplex farm house.

We bundled up and set out for help. At this time in England the Irish Republican Army was attacking and blowing up certain targets. We were in combat camouflaged clothing and wearing black berets. When we knocked on the second door of the duplex, a very old lady answered. The shotgun resting across her arm was a little disconcerting as she asked what we wanted. We explained our situation and asked to use the phone. We didn't count on her saying no.

After our pleading, she eventually relented and allowed me in the house, closing the door on my compadre and keeping her shotgun still in a position of readiness. I told the camp of our dilemma and roughly where we were before I was escorted at gun point out of the house by the grandma. The camp motor pool civilian said it would probably be a couple of hours before he rescued us.

We had no heating as we sat in the Rover freezing our goolies off. An eternity went by before we spied the cavalry. The motor pool guy didn't stop grumbling the whole time he was with us. This was his weekend we were disturbing. He didn't seem to notice the icicles hanging from our noses and fingertips. I thought he might have brought some hot cocoa with him, but that didn't happen either. Our first stop was a petrol station and some hot soup along with a cup of coffee to go.

The so-called gates of hell were a welcome sight as we slid into the garage and made a bee line for the mess. We were greeted with cheers and ridicule as we made it to the bar and downed a couple of whiskeys. When we told our story of woe with the old lady the laughter increased. The color sergeant had a field day with us and kept the ridicule going.

The Mad Hatter of Sherringham. There was another camp site with which we alternated. This was a small hamlet called Sherringham. There was an old railway station and line that was being restored there, and this is where we camped. I only mention this site because there was an elderly gentleman there called "The Mad Hatter of Sherringham." He looked like Quilp from Dickens' *The Old Curiosity Shop*. A short man with a small stoop, he always dressed in a long, bright red jacket and an old top hat. He also carried a very elaborate cane with a crafted head on the top. His voice was crackly, and he always sounded angry and mean. He was reportedly a wealthy man and owned a really full antique shop.

The color sergeant took me to the man's shop one afternoon, knowing what would happen. As we made our way to the back of the store while calling his name, he suddenly leaped out at us. He was threatening us with his cane and yelling about us wanting to steal from him. Sarge knew the routine but I didn't. He could have warned me, but of course that wouldn't have been as much fun for him. The shop was totally stuffed from floor to ceiling and side to side with two very narrow aisles to step through. The Mad Hatter would lie in wait among the turmoil and scare anybody that came in.

At the pub on Saturday night, the Mad Hatter came in and Sarge bought him a drink, which was normal. We did have a brief chat but he was incredibly difficult to talk to, the grumpy old sot. Sarge was used to him and got along quite well.

ENJOYING THE FUN

The classes I trained got better and better. As of my second class I would get up at 0530 and go swimming with the lads who had failed the swim test. One lad at the pool one day made me laugh. Several of us were standing in the shallow end when he announced he was afraid of the water. I did a double take and asked if he knew he had joined the Navy. I also asked if he knew that warships sailed in the *water*. This got plenty of laughs, including from said recruit. Strangely enough, I had him swimming and passing his test in about a week.

The chefs knew of my trips to the pool and always gave me special treatment. They really liked my dedication and attitude toward the lower deck. Every senior rate at Ganges was top notch. They helped make my life much easier and trained me to be a good petty officer, not just a good electrical petty officer.

One time on the assault course, a trainee fell from a scrambling net head first into a sloppy wet mud pit below. The mud jammed up into his nose and filled his mouth. As he was trying to survive, gagging and wrestling, three of us trainers could not help him at first because we were laughing so hard. We were doubled over and gasping for air as he was choking to death. For some inexplicable reason this made us laugh even more. The poor kid was about to die for real as we were dying with laughter. We did manage to dig, with our fingers, up his nose and into his mouth enough for him to get some air. The close by water hose helped a lot, and we finally got him straightened out. He passed the assault course without having to complete it, which was only fair for the poor kid.

One day while waiting outside of the gym, my class was fallen in three deep and stood at ease. I had my back to them when suddenly there was a lot of snickering. I spun around to find Johnson, in the middle row, pulling up his gym shorts. Mason, the recruit behind him, had pulled his shorts down. I took no notice and when the PTI called us in, I went into the building with them. The PTI said he would be a few minutes so I thought I would teach Mason, the kid behind Johnson, a lesson.

Standing before the class I put on a serious tone and said, "Class, I want to see Mason stripped naked in the middle of the gym on my go...Go." There was a second or two of nothing before Mason bolted from the group. The class gave chase, quickly cornering him and carrying out my order. I stood in front of Mason and told him he was out of *rig of the day* (the correct dress) and to get dressed. The whole class erupted in laughter along with Mason and I left for the PTI's office.

I always stayed and watched the gym period even though it was one of my times to relax. I wanted to see the class in a different setting. A minute or so later I sat down in the bleachers, I flew into a panic. I had left my hat in the staff room. Those PTIs would have my hat at the top of the mast or somewhere else exotic; they were always playing tricks and pulling gags on people. I charged in the room and, thankfully, saw my hat exactly where I had left it. They must have been half asleep, and I was thankful I got away with that mistake.

Later, as I was going across the parade ground for a meeting in the admin office, the camp commander called my rank and name and asked me to come over. "Why is your hat badge upside down?" he asked. AAARRRGGGHHH, they had got me.

That same commander was inspecting my class one Sunday at the weekly passing out parade. He found an error on one of the boys and said to him, "I suppose you're used to your mother looking after you, lad," in a grumbling voice.

Kelly replied, "My mother is dead, sir."

"Well, then I suspect your father looked after you."

Kelly answered, "He's in prison sir. He killed her." The commander quickly shot along to the next recruit. I could barely stop myself from guffawing. You can't make this stuff up.

The commander was always putting some weird advice for us on daily orders. Once, he got on a stint about drinking. "Anybody who has two beers or more a day is an alcoholic," was one of his fabled declarations.

Well, every three months there was a bar games night. It was the senior rates mess against the wardroom. We alternated the venue, and the host supplied all the trimmings. The night it was in our house, the commander asked for a whiskey and water, which we gladly served. As the night went on, we lessened the water and increased the whiskey. Later in the evening, three of us were at the urinal on the left side of the lavatory. We were all pointing percy at the porcelain when the commander walked in and went to the other wall. As we left, we pointed out that the urinal was on the other side and he was peeing on the wall. We never saw him again that night, and the daily orders went back to normal.

The commander had a British bulldog that was a surefire purebred with titles and the whole works. One of our senior rates had a Heinz Fifty-Seven. You guessed it; the commander caught Heinz Fifty-Seven rutting his bulldog. That scandal went through the camp like a wild brush fire. There was only one unamused uniform in the camp.

Getting along on the Ganges. At this stage of my stint in Ganges, I was striding along brimming with confidence at this great drafting assignment. I felt I was so lucky to be a part of this community. At one stage I enrolled in an English writing class that an educational officer had started. Unfortunately, after three classes, I dropped out. My time with my recruits was more important, and the English class was taking up too much time for my liking.

Soon after, I happened upon the education officer, who stopped me for a chat. He was a little unfriendly and wanted to know why I had jumped ship. After my explanation, he threatened me with being thrown out of Ganges. This was most strange, and for some reason I took it to heart.

I didn't know how much this bothered me until I needed to go to the pay office. The camp chaplain was in the pay office, by chance, and while I was waiting for the pay chief he called me over. "Here we go," I thought. "I don't need a lecture about God, thank you very much. Not now, not ever."

He asked me how I was feeling, and I told him, "Okay."

"No, you're not," he said. "Something is bothering you."

" No, there isn't," I insisted. At that, he asked me to step into an empty office.

He told me how that my normally cheerful self wasn't evident. My body language was giving him all kinds of messages.

"What does he know?" I thought. "I'm okay."

He persisted, so I finally told him about my encounter with the officer. He was aghast at this and told me that from what he knew I was doing an excellent job and would never be considered for termination from Ganges. He was going to have a word with the officer. Chaplains wielded a great deal of power. But how did he know so much about me and my progress? I never saw that officer in Ganges again.

A SWAN DIVE

Before the two hour rugby training, I would often run the cross country course, which went well into the country and over a stile, across a stream, over another stile and down a tow path by the river. Immediately over the first stile and partially under the bridge was a large swan nest. I would take it very easily over the stile and talk to the swan before moving on.

During one actual team race, I was running in sixth position, and the person behind me started to make up some ground when there was about a mile and a half to go. I needed to at least keep my position. I slowed for the stile and bridge, smoothed past the swan, and scampered on my way. A short while later I heard a huge squawking from the swan, which had been startled, and a shrill shriek from the runner. He was kept at bay until I got a good lead on him again.

Fun and games. After having supped but two beers one night, a couple of friends and I were returning to mess when I was accosted by two senior rates who wanted to talk with me. They told me that Jim Claxton, a petty officer in my division, was boasting that he could beat Jack Frost anytime, any day, in a one mile race. They wanted me to go to the bar and goad him into a race tonight and pretend I was drunk.

I slightly stumbled up to the bar and confronted Jim. Sure enough, off he went about how good he was. I was one of the fittest men in Ganges, due to my playing rugby and squash and running almost every day, never mind the swimming. A wager was made that the loser would buy two pints of beer for every senior rate registered in the mess, whether they were present or not.

We all drove down to the river to where the running track was. There must have been fifty of us, if not more. All the car's drivers turned on their headlights, and the stage was set. Off we went for four laps of the track.

I figured I'd just stay behind Jim until the final lap and then let fly for the finish. Well, at two and a half laps Jim pulled off the track and said that he was done. "Let's call it a night," he said. I kept running and when nearing Jim again, he yelled, "You've won. You can stop now." I continued running until I finished the full four laps because I knew he would say, tomorrow, that neither of us finished the race so all bets were off. I wasn't going to give him that excuse. Good to his word though, the next day at the lunch time bar conference, Jim paid the bartender enough money for all and sundry to receive two pints a piece. Did we have fun or what?

During the summer, the main sports extravaganza took place. I was asked to run the hundred and two hundred yards races. I said no at first because I'd never run short races before. I'd always been long distance. My team leader told me we had plenty of long distance runners but no short distance, so I caved to his wishes. I had three weeks before the races, so went out and bought a pair of spiked running shoes and went down to the track to practice.

I didn't know it, but one of the senior PTIs had often seen me running while he was with a trainee class. One day after I had timed myself running the two hundred yard race, he came over and said, "That was a much better run Jack. Your style and effort were much better than before." I couldn't believe somebody was taking notice. This really encouraged me to a greater effort.

On the day of the races, the top notch, keep-fit PTI lined up against me for the one hundred yard race. I had been carefully watching and timing how the starter was saying, "Ready, set," and then firing the gun." I was going to take off on a specific count after the *set* word was uttered. I wasn't waiting for the gun. It worked; I took off as the gun was fired. I flew across the finish line first and to top it off broke the track record. As a side note, this record will stand for all eternity. HMS Ganges was closed and the track torn up before another track meet was held!

Next was the two hundred yards race. The same PTI was in it. At the start I wasn't quite aware as the gun fired. I wasn't ready and was ten yards behind everybody at the start of the turn. I dug in and powered my way into second place with sixty yards or so to go. I was gaining on the PTI with each stride and was just about alongside him as I dove over the finish line to beat him. Unfortunately, the track was that red, gritty type. My knee and lower leg were badly chaffed, along with my left elbow and upper arm, and I needed help getting up. The photo finish showed that the PTI was a nose in front across the line. Oh, well; at least I gave it my all.

I did have the three thousand yard steeple chase to run a little later on. I had time to recover and get myself sorted out. I had never run a steeple chase before and didn't realize how difficult it would be getting over those hurdles, especially the water jump. The last two laps were grueling as I barely made it over those nasty jumps. I did finish the race fifth out of nine runners and at least got some points for the team. Our team won the final race of the day, the 4x100 yards relay in which I was the anchor leg.

CLASS SHENANIGANS

The gas chamber test given to my class was always a hoot, for me anyway. I wore some older clothes that I kept just to wear in the chamber. The lads wore their working uniforms and stood there like lambs to the slaughter for me to play with. They were always a tad nervous. I mean, who would willingly step into a cloud of tear gas?

We all donned our gas masks and went into the room of doom. Though muffled by the gas mask, I explained that as I called out their name they would step toward me. They would remove their mask and call out their full name and service number before exiting. Once outside they were to run in a circle to shake out the fumes from their clothing. I always picked the class clown, previously myself in boot camp, or an aloof type of recruit. To this person I would say, "Recite the Lord's Prayer backwards" before exiting. It always got a laugh from everybody except the victim. Of course I would rescind that order and let the kid off.

Let's go back to the parade ground for a moment. One day during a very hot summer spell, we were on the parade ground during another class's Sunday passing out parade. Some of the class had been ashore the night before and a couple of them were not feeling top notch. Thirty minutes into the parade one lad in the center row of three whispered loudly to me, "I'm feeling like I'm going to throw up." I strode around between the front and center rows and faced him. I told him to take it easy and take in a large gulp of air and breathe out slowly. Eventually calmed down, he felt a little better, and I returned to my post.

A minute later the same lad whispered again, only sounding more desperate. I returned to face him and calm him down again. As I was halfway through my spiel, he projected a fusillade of the most disgusting propellant I have ever received. It went all over my number one jacket and trousers, followed by plopping noises on the ground as I danced backwards like a ninja warrior.

Grabbing him by the shoulder, I walked him between the two rows as he continued his barrage of spew. He was splashing it on the rear of the front row's legs and front of the center row's legs. Oh my god, what a catastrophe. I walked him off the parade ground in front of the commander, captain, parents of the passing out classes, and the whole parade ensemble.

Once inside the drill shed, I passed him over to the medics and returned to my class. The larger lumps and greater amount of sick were removed from my uniform at this juncture. The rest of the class was now feeling woozy as they were standing around all of the stomach contents left behind. I took the bold step of marching my class three steps backward and thusly out of line with the rest of the parade. Unfortunately for the class leader, this left him in the middle of the mess. I marched around to him and grabbed his arm, pulling him to one side of the class and out of position also.

The march past mercifully got under way, and we finally moved away from the swamp. Of course, I was sent for by the divisional officer, who totally lost it as my story was unfolded. He relayed my tale of woe to the powers-that-be without me having to go to the commander myself. I'm betting my story was all over the wardroom that lunchtime. It was certainly all over my mess. This was apparent as I stepped into the bar area having changed clothes. The roar of cheering accompanied by ferocious hand clapping and laughter confirmed this.

Another scandal. One morning a scandal hit the mess. One of our petty officers' wives was caught shoplifting a minor item. The story broke because the event was in the local newspaper. Peter was a very proud person who walked very stiffly, his head held higher than is natural. He gave the impression that this job was beneath his role in life. I don't know if that was the case but that was my take on his haughtiness.

Many weeks went by before he and his wife would show their face in the mess. One evening, the mess had more than the usual gathering in the bar and lounge. Multiple people were playing an array of different games. This included carpet bowls, lie dice, bridge, Uckers (a Navy version of Ludo) and various other pastimes. There was a murmur of fun and frivolity filling the room—that is until the mess door abruptly swung open.

There stood Peter and his wife in all their glory. The middle aisle to the bar was a long walk, probably longer on this occasion. A deafening silence cracked across the whole room as all eyes fell upon the couple. They slowly and proudly strutted toward the bar, looking straight ahead with chins aloft. I have to sincerely applaud and admire them; it took a lot of guts and resolve to do that.

As they were about halfway down the aisle, somebody said loudly, "Mind the ashtrays." Well, the mess went crazy with laughter as the breaking tension crashed to pieces on the floor. Peter and his wife joined in the laughter, and everybody went about their games. Throughout the next half hour or so, pretty much the whole mess went up to them and made them feel welcome. From that point on it was like the incident with his wife never happened. The person who broke the silence took a heck of a risk; it could have all gone south from there, but it worked and all was well in paradise.

Now for the biggest story of them all; do you remember Darrin Joyce? He was the huge pain in the lower cushions for me and all the mess members on HMS Dido. Darrin, to this day fifty years later, is the worst person that has ever come into my life. Imagine my surprise when he walked into our divisional office as a replacement for a petty officer that has just left us.

We greeted each other warmly enough, both knowing the history between us. He was probably shocked and concerned, knowing I could tell of his style and attitude. When he left the office I asked the chief to accompany me for a parlay with the divisional officer. I warned them about this individual who continuously went against the grain no matter what. I couldn't help it; he could shatter the camaraderie and status quo for not only our division but the senior rates mess as well.

I shouldn't have worried. George, the chief, was an exceptionally strong man, both physically and mentally. The mess was strong also, with men of great wisdom, strength and character. The canoe was not going to move the aircraft carrier.

Darrin treated the job and his class members with the brashness and uncaring manner that I had expected. On the fifth week of his class, the week they need to be tutored in the evening for the sixth week exams, Darrin was nowhere to be seen. I mean nowhere at all. The classes he was to teach were without a teacher until the rest of us stepped in and did double duty. Where was Darrin?

We discovered that he has gone to London to take a five-day day course on an unknown subject. How this happened without the divisional heads knowing, I will never understand. It turns out they didn't understand either. I'm thinking he must have forged signatures or something like that. He most certainly wouldn't have been given permission while in the middle of a class.

I took it upon myself to go down to Darrin's class mess deck every evening from around 1900 hours until lights out at 2200 hours, to get them ready for the exams. When I went back to the senior rates mess on Friday evening, I was quickly approached by several members in the bar. They told me that Darrin had returned earlier in the evening and was told I was down with his class teaching them. His reply was that that was my problem, and he went to his cabin to sleep. My response to that was zero as I expected nothing more than that from him. My friends were amazed and flabbergasted; I was not.

Saturday morning in the divisional office, he didn't even acknowledge me or thank me. He confronted me later in the day as to why I had ratted him out to the chief. I explained that I had not but suspected that every other senior rate in Ganges more than likely did. I relayed to him how things worked around here, and if he didn't want to do this job, he should leave.

Apparently that particular action was already under way. Later still that same day, Darrin was nowhere to be seen. On inquiring, we discovered he was doing duty as the main gate petty officer. A week later he was on his way to another shore base and good riddance. His departure under a cloud meant his career was pretty much over as far as promotion was concerned. I never saw him again.

LESSONS FOR US ALL

I learned a very valuable lesson from George, the chief, over a period of time. He had a mantra he would often repeat: *When you are duty you are very, very duty. You do not drink a beer before or after bedding the trainees down for the night. You sleep in the small room off of the divisional office, not in your cabin.*

Almost nobody followed these rules, but I did. I wanted to become a great senior, not just a great electrician. When duty, I stayed in the office until dinner time and went to eat. That done, I would return to the office where I had two office runners who made my coffee, went and fetched people I wanted to talk to, and ran other errands for me. I also invited any trainee to come and see me if they needed tutoring. I would often re-teach tying knots for instance. The lads loved and appreciated the help.

One night I was doing a final walk around the division about midnight. I was at the top of the Long Covered Way and heard a slight noise and commotion halfway down on the right. That was not my division, but I thought I'd investigate. I slowly and deliberately walked toward the offending mess, digging my heels firmly into the asphalt so as to make my approach very apparent as the clicks echoed under the roof.

I stomped loudly into the mess across the fifteen feet of concrete and then across the wooden floor. It was pitch black as I stood in the middle of the beds. A couple of lads impersonated a loud snore. Did they really think they were fooling me?

I stood in silence for what must have seemed an age for them. Then I burst forth with a really loud voice, saying, "What's going on here? I want to know now!" There was silence. I asked again. Silence.

"Okay then," I said, "if I don't get an answer in ten seconds, everybody will be forming up outside in their number one uniform ready for inspection."

Then I started the count down, beginning with three. That shook the heck out of them and somebody blurted out the story right away. One of the class members had been letting the class down in a big way daily, and he was unhygienic. They had black boot polished his under carriage and were scrubbing him with stiff yard brooms in the shower. This was not such an unusual internal punishment, and I remembered about my friend when I was in boot camp.

"Right then," I said. "I am going to the office right across from here for the night and I don't want another peep out of this mess." I click-clacked my way outside and heard a low muffled cheer from behind me. The rest of the night was peaceful. I thought about the situation later and realized that if the recruit had complained to the office, I could have been in serious trouble.

Sailing. A seaman branch petty officer named Andrew was a keen sailing enthusiast. He asked me and another petty officer if we and our classes would like to go sailing the following Sunday afternoon. We both said yes and all met down by the pier. There were several large sailing boats that one could sail or row. I believe there were about sixteen of us; it was purely recreational for the lads and on a volunteer basis only.

Andrew took the lead and with the jib sail up sailed us out into the river. The main mast, I am guessing, was roughly 25-30 feet tall and a foot and a half in diameter, with a ton of rigging. The other two sails, the mizzen and the jib, were pretty big in their own right also.

I mentioned earlier that the river was deep and wide, no milk or honey on the other side. We had been sailing and tacking up and down and across the river, and the lads got to work the rigging. It was a glorious day. The sky was blue with those white puffy clouds, and there was a perfect breeze for good sailing. Andrew had also arranged for the chefs to make picnic lunches.

As we once again crossed the river, away from Ganges, there was a horrendous explosion and earsplitting crack. The mast had snapped as we changed tack, and it went crashing into the river. Did I mention the cross channel ferry was bearing down on us? This very large ship could not change course because it was in a deep channel carved out for it. Any large deviation would put it aground and block all other shipping from coming into the very busy port of Felixstow.

Andrew was right on the ball immediately. He instructed the lads to grapple with the rigging and get the mast alongside the boat. We then had to get the oars out, some of which were tangled by the rigging, and get the boys to put them in the rowlocks. We started rowing like crazy, unified. Meanwhile the ferry slowed as quickly as it could. The captain blasted his fog horn in jest once he knew we were going to be safe. As we were being passed, all the passengers around the deck cheered and clapped and waved. Then, of course, we encountered the turbulence from the big screws, which tossed us around like a cork in a hurricane making the rowing very difficult.

With the danger passed and the water settled, we made our way back into the breakwater. The boys still holding the mast against the side were exhausted, as were the rowers. It sounds like the boys did all the work, but we senior rates earned our keep that day.

All in all it was another great day of a life in a blue suit.

Back in the trenches. The next day it was back to business in the trenches. I was preparing the lads for a more serious kit muster. I didn't want them going through what I had in basic training. I explained that the kit inspectors would even turn their underwear inside out. They were looking for and didn't want to see skid marks or tank tracks across the rear end. That always got a laugh, as did many sayings we threw at the classes throughout training.

As we started a third week of one of my classes, a young man was back classed into ours, and I didn't like what I heard about why. He was lazy, unkempt, and generally a poor sample of the human race. Sometimes I think the gene pool needs thinning out.

I am all for giving second and third chances without judgment, but the petty officer who back-classed Overton should have taken the responsibility of dismissing him from the Navy. Instead, he passed the buck, which caused more trouble than one could imagine.

I had a long heart to heart chat with Overton, which seemed to have no effect. His blank face and lack of attentiveness or enthusiasm told me most of what I had already suspected. Nevertheless, I took this as a challenge of my abilities and was going to give him every chance and opportunity possible. Any fall from grace was going to be on his shoulders, not mine.

I gave him a few days to put a kit inspection together just for me, to give him a yardstick to work from. I could have thrown my kit on the bed from ten feet away and made it look better than he had. In addition to this, his class inattention and general lackadaisical attitude toward other class members was proving too much.

Then a bombshell hit the office. One of our petty officers who had been duty the night before had been reported to the officer of the day. Overton had gone to the main gate and accused Alex of sexually touching and coddling him. Alex was a little effeminate in his style of living, but that was all anybody thought. This was ridiculous and an attempt to lash out at a senior rate of the Navy. There could be no truth to this accusation.

Alex may have put his arm around his shoulder to comfort him in some way but nothing more, surely. Overton had gone to the office late at night to complain about his classmates. Did he misinterpret a caring touch from Alex as being sexual? We passed off the accusation as nothing to worry about.

A few days went by, and we were told of the formation of a court martial. Wow! I thought, "Never mind. This will bring out the truth and all will be well." The court case went longer than we anticipated, though, and the secrecy now surrounding the incident became worrying.

Later we were informed that Alex had been court-martialed and dismissed the Navy. What a blow to us and our friend. There must have been a lot more to the story than we ever imagined. Our divisional officer who was in attendance in court the whole time could tell us nothing. However, Overton was still under my tutorship for another three weeks. This was going to be tricky.

Overton didn't seem to be aware of or understand what had taken place. This was rather strange and disconcerting. Anyway, things did not improve for the young man, and I could not bring him around to any kind of team spirit way of thinking. For his own sake and the sake of the Navy, I needed to terminate his service.

The final straw was when all the class had a kit muster to be inspected by the divisional officer. Overton and his kit were just awful. On opening his supposedly empty locker, there was a plastic bag with some dirty socks and smalls inside. How the DO put his hand inside and handled them, I do not know.

I started the ball rolling with a final report and recommendation. The chief took it from there, and so it went up the ladder to the top. I was now thinking I would be the headlines of *The News of the World*, a top flight tabloid newspaper not unlike *The Enquirer*: "Training Officer Fires Molested Recruit" or "Recruit Unfairly Discharged by Friend of Court-martialed Petty Officer." Nothing did actually take place, but the suspense did hang over me for a while.

WHERE IS MY SON?

A funny thing happened on the parade ground after one of my passing out classes had finished their march past. I was walking along chatting with a few of the lads when some parents passed us by, looking for their sons. One boy raised his arm and went to speak to a man walking past us. "Dad, I'm here," he said. His own father hadn't recognized his son. Dad's jaw dropped, and he grabbed his son so tight I thought his innards were going to pop out. He looked at me and asked me what the hell I had done to his son. There was a huge beaming smile on his face, and he was shaking my hand so vigorously my trousers could have fallen down.

After each passing out class completes their parade, the division puts on a tea and crumpet type of get together for the parents. I was chatting with the same dad, who told me he couldn't figure out how in six weeks we had done more for his son than he had in sixteen years. I heard this quite a lot during my tenure in Ganges, and it made me feel proud. The boys were also always very proud of themselves. Some had taken the plunge and gone from being a long-haired punk rock slob to a useful person of society.

Only one of my classes made it to be the honor guard, the special passing out class with the white webbing. I felt two or three of my classes deserved it and grumbled to the parade ground staff, but this always fell on deaf ears.

When I finally got the word my class had been selected, I gathered them in the common room at the end of their mess.

Now, they knew they were good and knew they were in for a shot at being selected. I should also point out that if selected they had to get up an hour earlier and go to the drill shed for special training each morning of their final week. The selected classes never minded this because it was such an honor.

When the class mustered in the room, I slowly walked through the mess toward them, my head down. I stood in silence, looking serious and sad, then said, "Look men, I have some bad news for you." I paused and looked up at them with the saddest face I could create. I knew how much this meant to them. I continued, "The bad news is; you have to get up an hour earlier all this next week." They leaped in the air cheering, and the shouting was heard all around the division.

The Saturday before the parade I went into Ipswich with the class members whose parents were in town. They were all meeting in a hotel at a specific time and wanted to talk to me, of course. The evening was going well when I was cornered by one of the single mothers. I didn't really think anything about it; I was just chatting and making small talk.

Around 2200 hours one of the other POs came by and said they were going back to camp and asked if I wanted to share a taxi. I was about to say yes when the mother said, "No, he's staying with me tonight."

I said, "Oh, I am?"

She said, "Yes, let's go. Time is a wasting. Hey, I was a virile young sailor who lived out in the wilderness, so no judging. She whisked me away and controlled my body for the rest of the night. I did have to make sure I had a taxi call to get me back to camp in time for parade. As it turned out, this damsel was not a mother of one of my class, and I did not see her the next morning. I wondered how often this happened with other trainers, but nobody ever talked about it.

ACT OF HEROISM

Our divisional officer, a helicopter pilot if you remember, saved our bacon one evening. During the Christmas period all the divisional senior rates and officers went on a dinner meal and evening bash at one of those fancy country restaurants.

The previous several days of weather had been really bad. Many inches of snow had fallen and the temperatures had stayed low. This made for fairly dangerous roads. Four cars were taken to the restaurant as we all piled in for a great celebratory evening. It really was a slap up meal and joyous event with many war stories of our classes being shared. Ron, one of the more, let's say rag tag trainers, had a few too many swallows of alcohol. He was also one of the drivers on those winding country roads back to Ganges.

I clambered into the front seat next to Ron and readied for the ride back. Paul, the DO, opened the door and said for me to go back with George, the chief. I said that's okay, but he yanked me out of the car and said no, he would ride with Ron.

We all arrived back at the office about the same time except for Ron's car. Then we were worried. We all hung about waiting for some kind of word and soon heard they had been in a crash. Ron had hit something and sent Paul flying through the windshield. In those days most vehicles didn't have seat belts. We were informed everybody would be okay so we toddled off to bed.

The next day Paul arrived in the office around noon. He just had a couple of scratches from the glass but was otherwise okay. He told us that his helicopter training saved the day for him. When Ron hit something, Paul instantly recognized what was happening, and sort of went into a ball, and basically rolled through the window. Had I been sitting there who knows what would have happened to me. Paul had deliberately taken me away from a dangerous situation and placed himself in danger, recognizing that Ron was not in good shape. My eyes are watering up just writing this story. What a good man.

It wasn't long after this that Toby Meyers, who was married with kids living at the other end of the country, asked me for a favor. He wasn't exactly flush with money like us single blokes and had used up his three free train tickets everybody gets per year. These tickets cannot be used by anybody except the recipient and are non-transferable.

One of his kids was very sick and his wife wanted him home for the weekend, so Toby asked if I was willing to submit for a ticket and give it to him. Even though it was against the rules, I said I would and put in the request at the regulating naval police office. Unfortunately, it was past the deadline for the week. After begging on bended knee, the PO regulator capitulated and agreed to go into Ipswich and get it for me.

That Friday Toby went on his weekend and all was well. Just after Saturday lunch my divisional officer called me into his office and asked what the heck had I done. I wasn't thinking of Toby and said, "Nothing, as far as I know." He told me the senior chief regulator wanted me in his office immediately, and it sounded serious. I trundled up there and went into his office. He told me to close the door. *Did I accidently kill somebody?* I wondered. *What the heck was going on?*

He said, "I am sorry to have to ask you this, but did you get a rail pass?" I said that I did. He then asked me to show him it. I said I didn't have it on me, and he asked, "Where is it?" I figured he knew everything, so I said Toby had it. I was right. He suspected as much. The PO who got me the ticket had got suspicious because I had begged him for the ticket as I really needed it for the weekend. Yet here I was still in camp.

Our senior rates mess was a really tight group that worked exceedingly hard every day and always had each other's back. I could tell the chief was uncomfortable when he said that one of his petty officers had reported it, so he had no choice but to follow through on the charge.

I explained why I did it, and he did say he was going to let Toby enjoy his weekend and take care of it on his return. That was a good thing for him to do as he could have recalled Toby right away. That dirty rat PO was in the dog house with me, though. I told the whole senior rates mess what had transpired, and nobody spoke to him.

The following week Toby and I were on captain's report and stood before him with the divisional officer as our defender. The upshot was that I was fined my other two railway passes for the year, and we were let go. In other words we were let off the charge.

It's funny because idiot chops never showed his face in the bar again, and a day or so later was gone from Ganges. Of course, I had nothing to do with that move, but I was glad he was gone.

MORE SHENANIGANS

Some of the lighter moments on the base involved pranks. One night one of our more gregarious POs was going to be out for the evening. We knew he was going to be drunk when he came back, so we carried all of his furniture and belongings down stairs and out into the playing fields outside of his window. When he came off shore, he unlocked his door and saw a totally empty room. He looked at the door number and then looked in his room again. In his drunken state, he must have thought that he was on the wrong floor. He went down the passageway and up to the third floor to the same doorway. His key, of course wouldn't open that door.

Going back to his original place, his actual cabin, he walked inside. We secretly watched as he came out again, scratching his head. Then he gave up, went back inside, and crashed out on the floor.

The next morning when he awoke he looked out the window and saw his re-created cabin laid out exactly like it was in his cabin originally. He came into the dining room laughing and yelling at the same time. That special naval dictionary sure took a beating for the next several minutes. We all had a good laugh with him and got all his furniture and belongings back to his room.

This type of thing went on all the time. This particular one was a tad bigger than most practical jokes but many smaller ones were always round the corner. One had to have their wits about them at all times.

Moving on again. All good things must come to an end, and the best shore job of my career was nearing completion. Had the camp not been closing down in a few months, I would certainly have volunteered to come back for seconds and thirds. This stint has heightened my awareness of the other side of being a senior rate. It had also boosted my expertise at running the men in my department for future ships and shore establishments. My chances at being promoted to chief had, therefore, been dramatically enhanced.

As always, being a senior rate, I was seen by the DO and the camp commander. Both recognized my shortcomings on arrival in Ganges. They then noted that I had become an exceptional trainee officer and a credit to the Navy. (I know, I know—my arm is in danger of breaking, and maybe I need to bring in builders to widen the doors for my head.)

NEW DIGS, MORE INCIDENTS

It was the middle of May when I rolled into HMS Vernon, named after Admiral Vernon. Vernon was a submarine base on the river in Portsmouth. My job was in the repair and maintenance workshop. We didn't work on the submarines but supported the repair of equipment from them.

When it came to the kind of mess and camaraderie I had enjoyed on the Ganges, I'd been spoiled rotten, but there was still a good atmosphere here. After I'd been there a couple of weeks, I bumped into a chief from Ganges. It was Andrew Pratt, my sailing ordeal buddy. He had taken over as chief when he was promoted.

He was a little lonely and felt out of water, as I did. We decided that every Wednesday we would go on a Guinness and ugly run. This was a run ashore that entailed drinking a pint of Guinness and a shot of Wood's rum. Chug-a-lugging Wood's rum caused one to screw up their faces: hence the word *ugly*.

In the workshop nobody really did anything at all. There was a spare parts store room run by a civilian who was quite elderly and bored. When I came along, I couldn't do what they were doing—or, rather, not doing. I took it upon myself to get some action going.

The shop was wide and long with work benches running down each side. I discovered that there were trailers full of defective electronic trays taken out of subs for Vernon to repair. The shop had all the manuals for each type of tray and all the circuits that could be set up to test, tune, and repair them.

I started to try and build these circuits along the benches and brought in the various types of equipment. Many spare parts needed to be ordered, which made the civilian very happy. He saw somebody actually doing his job and it gave him a purpose.

The building of these tests was very complicated and needed my full concentration. I was leaning over a bench one morning and was totally in another world when suddenly there was an incredible searing pain between my legs. My trousers tightened up, and I crashed to the floor screaming my lungs out.

One of the loafing junior rates had put a large, foot long auger bit into a whole hog electric drill. As a joke, he placed it between my legs and turned it on. Unfortunately for him and more importantly me, the bit caught both my trousers legs and drew them in. The cutting edges of the bit sliced into my flesh in an instant. The excruciating pain made me immediately think that my gonads were no longer attached. This turned out to be not the case, but at the moment I was terrified. I was rushed to the camp hospital, where I was treated for severe flesh wounds on the insides of both thighs.

On recovery, I didn't take any action against my assailant as the chief had already dealt with him. I know the kid was trying to make me jump and no malice was intended, but you don't play with that kind of tooling. Two tools could have been damaged in one incident, the most important one being my wedding tackle. I did survive, though, and moved on.

More sports. At lunch one day I was in the foyer of the mess and overheard a petty officer on the phone explaining that the rugby team of a small ship would still play, only with a man short. I went over and offered my services. The game was in a couple of hours so I called the chief and got permission to play.

This turned out to be the shortest game of rugby I had ever played. Our team kicked off first, and an ogre of a man collected the ball and ran full steam toward me. It was mid-summer, and the clay ground was harder than concrete. I mention this because as I was falling back to planet earth, my head hit the ground first.

As I was stood up, the referee was telling the team to take me to the sickbay across the road. I told everybody I was fine and insisted that the game started again. We argued back and forth until the two people holding either side of me let go. Luckily, they caught me before I hit terra firma again.

The medics got me settled in the sick bay and started asking some simple questions: *How old are you? What year is it? Which ship were you playing for?* These were simple questions with simple answers, and I answered them all with ease. However, I was incorrect in each instance. I got the wrong time, year, ship, and everything else

After a few tests, they sent me to a larger facility a few miles up the road at HMS Nelson. They poked and prodded for a while before sending me to the main naval hospital known as Hassler. Where was my next move, the morgue?

Apparently, I had a major concussion and was kept in Hassler for several days. Mum and Dad were expecting me home that weekend, so I called to let them know I was not coming. Mum answered the phone by saying, "What have you injured now and what hospital are you in?" I had to laugh: she was right.

Yes, I know, this does explain a lot about the rest of my life.

The only other real incident at Vernon was when the chief told eight of us that we were to wear boiler suits to work one morning. He wanted to clean out a large area of defunct equipment that had built up over at least twenty years and needed to be ditched. He expected mice and rat families would be disturbed and all kinds of grungy stuff to be encountered.

When we all set off down the hall, the office writer, who happened to be black, wasn't moving. I said, "Come on. We are all starting the cleanup now." He told me he wasn't going to help, and I said he was. We went back and forth until I gave him an official direct order to get down to the cleanup site. He still refused and started calling me a racist.

At this point, I told him to report to the regulating office, i.e. the Navy police, and I would join him there. He refused to do that as well. I wasn't going to lose this battle and my Ganges training came into play. I called the regulating office and explained the situation. They sent over two leading hand regulators who handcuffed him and lead him away.

I was asked to follow them to write up a report, which I did. I never saw him again but was informed by the regulators that this incident was one of many throughout this man's naval history. Although I wasn't asked to testify, he ended up in the naval prison for three months before being dishonorably discharged. There was obviously more to the story than I ever knew about. Maybe he had been working his ticket. That's when people deliberately get into trouble to eventually be kicked out. It's a tough road to travel but some people do it. I'm glad I could help him on his way.

I was asked where the heck I had been when I finally joined the party. My story did not surprise the chief or the other senior rates. That told me a whole lot right there.

The incident wasn't a pleasant experience for me, so I am glad nothing like that ever happened again. It was another learning experience, though. Was somebody guiding me through these situations?

SHIP AHOY

When my anticipated draft to a ship came through, I was very pleased to get another Leander Class frigate. HMS Bacchante was going to be in Mombasa, Kenya. I was given a plane ticket, and off I trotted for another fabulous adventure.

The landing was at a normal air strip, unlike Madagascar, and I was transported to the docks. There she was. I knew that joining a ship as a petty officer would be different than being promoted and staying with the same crew. I gained the gangway and was welcomed very heartily by the gangway staff. I had a good feeling about this ship the moment I stepped aboard.

The forward petty officers' mess president was paged to the gangway and greeted me with a smiling face. We went down a deck and through the ship to the forward POs mess in 2D section. Several men were there and again I was welcomed with great gusto. I was offered a beer and we shared some history with each other.

I asked if there was a rugby team on board, which changed the conversation to sport. Yes, there was a rugby team, but that afternoon the field hockey team was playing a local Mombasa team. Did I play hockey because the team is a man short? Yes, I played field hockey.

"Okay, we know you are whacked out tired from the trip and time change, but would you be willing to play?" they asked.

"Of course," I agreed.

I had a fairly decent game, which we lost. Then that night the mess was eager to welcome me by inviting me on a run ashore with them. I was beat but I needed to accept their outreached hand. After showering, eating dinner, and resting up a while, a group of us hit the shore and a few bars.

I somehow got into a deep conversation with one of the local women. She spoke excellent English and seemed well-educated. I was losing touch with the main conversation of the mess members and got more and more interested in our separate chat.

Long story short, I ended up at her place, which was a long way from town and at a village in the jungle. It was like the old cowboy towns with the dirt road down the middle and the sidewalks raised a couple of feet above the road.

When I left her abode at around 0200 hours, there was only a bit of moonlight. There were several men on the sidewalks, and I was a pretty little white boy on my own. I felt everybody was looking in my direction, and I didn't know which way to go. At the end of the road was the jungle; the other way went further into potential trouble. Oh dear, what have I got myself into?

I was nearing the jungle, trying to decide if I wanted to risk lions and wildlife or be robbed and killed in the village. As I approached the end of the dirt road, a car pulled into the gap between me and the jungle. A very big Kenyan, who seemed to just keep climbing out of the car, said in an incredibly deep voice, "You wanna ride?" Where had this man come from just in the nick of time?

There was no taxi sign on the car, so now I had three choices, the car, the jungle or the dangerous street. Did this man mean to take me and rob me on his own? I didn't know, but I chose the car and held my breath.

His English was very good, and we had a pleasant conversation as he took me straight to the ship. I gave him what he asked for, which left a few extra notes, so I gave him all I had. He was a gentleman and a scholar.

When I entered the mess, a few of the men got up and made sure I was okay. I'm afraid I had worried several people on my first day of Bacchante. It was so nice that I seemed to have been accepted by everybody in such a short time, less than twenty hours.

The next morning I went to the office and got acquainted with the chiefs of the various departments. I would be head of the communications, navigational aids, and low voltage machinery department. Great, his was right up my alley. Once indoctrinated into the system, I made haste to my workshop. I had one leading hand, one first class electrician, and one young new junior just unpacked out of the box.

We stood and chatted for a while as I got a handle on things. Two defects were going to have to be fixed before sailing and the rest on our daily chores, as I determined. Having given them a thumbnail of my experience and history, I enquired about theirs. Junior had very little to add other than that he liked the Navy. I took Junior with me and sent the other two off to look at the other pressing defect. I explained that if they didn't have a clue after thirty minutes, then come and get me.

The idea of getting them to report back after thirty minutes if they were stuck was to promote their trust in me. I would either let them fix what I found or point them in the right direction to continue on their own. I wanted to have a team I was a part of. I didn't want to stand above them and lord it over them.

INHIBITIONS AWAY

That evening the forward petty officers' mess had been invited to the Mombasa British Patriots Club. The people there were older ex-patriots from the old Colonial Empire days, and some would call them rather eccentric. The evening was going as one would expect with lots of stories and adventures being shared.

When three of us drifted off to the side of the main room, where there was a good sized swimming pool, two elderly, rather portly gals asked if we would join them for a swim. "I would," I said, "but I don't have a bathing suit."

"That's okay," they said. "Neither do we." Then they stripped buck naked and dove into the water.

Okay then, I supposed we could join them. The other two hesitated as I dropped my knickers and, bollocky buff, dove in to join them. We, the ladies and I, were soon joined by two large splashes and two more naked bodies.

This unusual turn at the party wasn't even particularly noticed by other members of the community. It certainly was noticed by the rest of the mess members, though. Our small group had a good time swimming and conversing as the hired help brought us our drinks to the side of the pool. There was nothing sexual about any of this. These people didn't think anything of it; nudity was not taboo but an experience to enjoy.

We had one more day in port so the next day, when the workday was done, I decided to peruse the nearby shops and sights. Just outside the main gate of the dockyard there was a deluge of street vendors selling their wares. It was similar to

Freetown on the west coast of Africa, with bartering and swapping of basically anything. I brought a couple of shirts and a pair of trousers with me in case I wanted to trade for some local trinkets or mementoes.

Mombasa was an exciting place to be. The color and brightness of everything, including the people was captivating. Children ran around chasing and giggling, and there was an air of joy, love and frivolity. I enjoyed about 45 minutes of bartering and haggling to purchase some wood carvings before entering the dockyard area. They cost me one really good shirt, a long firm handshake, and a beaming warm smile which was reciprocated by the merchant.

A bit of competition. Before we sailed, there was a small competition between the greenie electricians and the stokers. I had somehow got into a conversation with an engineering chief over lunch on my second day on board, and we were boasting to each other about how our much better our departments were than the other. The upshot of this was that we would have a tug of war competition between the two departments. I'd been on board only a couple of days and was already stirring things up.

Thirty five members from each department lined up on the jetty either side of the very heavy, thick hemp rope hawser. There were juniors, seniors and officers all pulling together. The ship's side was lined with at least a hundred cheering, baying crew. The pull was on, and both sides had won a pull each. The deciding pull was on.

That was when the hawser tore apart and seventy men went crashing to the ground. Several were hurt a little more than just a bruise and scrape. Oh well, I guess it was a tie. I was sorry for the injuries incurred, but a good time was had by all and it set up a competitive spirit between our divisions.

Setting sail. The next morning we sailed into the wild blue yonder. I was back home and in my element. Although the equipment was different because technology had flown forward, I quickly had a handle on most of the department. I made some immediate changes in attitude and discipline. My team seemed to think it was okay to arrive in the mornings on Caribbean time. I wanted them in the workshop no later than "turn to time," or 0800 hours. Their dress wasn't too sharp either, so I encouraged them to be smarter and better-dressed. There was no need to have unkempt, scruffy working attire as it reflected their attitude to work. I know they grumbled behind my back for a while, but once they got used to it they found it no more trouble than eating a meal.

WORK AND PLAY

I noticed the planned maintenance schedule was not being done properly. A number of cards were handed out each month to routinely check equipment. The cards were to be signed off and returned to myself and then the office. I felt the cards were just being signed off, and the work was not being implemented correctly. I went and inspected some equipment they had supposedly maintained to find that the covers had not been removed. I knew this because the cover plate screws were encrusted in place with sea salt or were painted.

I decided to have a team meeting on how we were going to approach our jobs. I told them very firmly, "This is a warship, not Daddy's yacht." I didn't yell and scream; we just had a quiet heart- to- heart about how things were going to be.

Two or three weeks later we were caught up with most of the small defects and there were no large problems. When they came to the workshop after lunch, I gave them all the afternoon off. They weren't sure what to do or say; this had never happened to them before. I said, "Go on, and scram. I will deal with any problems that come up, and I'll see you in the morning." Things gradually got a lot smoother and we built an understanding that produced a good rapport and relationship between us.

There was no ship's newspaper, so I stepped up to the plate and got that going. The first time I placed copies into the junior rates mess deck, I was greeted with mystified faces. The second week at sea, I was mobbed by everybody wanting to read the paper first.

Our next port of call was Gibraltar on our way back to England and then on to Chatham. I was pleased to see that Chatham dockyard was our home base. I would get to work and collaborate, again, with Gary Dean, my dockyard friend.

Sure enough, when we slipped through the lock gates and came along side, there was Gary. He saw me right away and pumped his fists in the air while grinning from ear to ear. As soon as the gangway was secured, we connected and shook hands knowing we had work to do. He was the go-to man for getting shore power hooked up. Gary and I then got the shore phones connected before disappearing to my mess for a celebratory beer. He had a thousand questions, as did I, as we reconnected our relationship. The next day I made sure he got his quota of pipe tobacco on the chair in his office.

The ship's crew was going to be away on main leave for two weeks. A typical skeleton crew would keep the ship safe with fire party teams and a few people from each skill set. I stayed behind as a skeleton member and went home after they came back. The second leave party always left notes in drawers and various cupboards for the first leave party to find. The note simply said SLIB, second leave is best. I left envelopes for all my team to open. Funny, they never thanked me for them on my return.

One day in the mess Ian, a mechanical engineer, and I were chatting and I mentioned something about hang gliding. He got very interested and told us of a time when he nearly went parachuting. Now, I'm not saying Ian was large, but I was trying to think of how many parachutes he would need to land softly.

It turns out that he had chickened out at the last minute and didn't jump. A bunch of us started chiding him about this, all in good fun. He said, "Okay, the next time it comes around in the Sport DCI, I'll do it if you will." DCI was a pamphlet of the Defense Council Instructions and came around every month about changes to the Navy and protocol and so on. Every now and then a sport one came out, offering free sporting trips. I took him up on his bet and we decided that if one of us chickened out, that chicken had to pay up for a free keg of beer to the mess. Plenty of witnesses verified the deal.

Well, we couldn't believe this, but the very next day a DCI came to the mess about a free parachuting course next month. These sport DCI pamphlets only came around once or twice a year, so we were gobsmacked. Oh no. Now we had to do it.

We applied through our respective offices for the week long school, and we both were granted time from the ship to do it. We arrived in the West Country at the old, almost abandoned WWII airport. There was a Royal Marine parachute instructor, some much younger college students, and some younger Navy jocks in attendance.

The sergeant quickly got us organized as to our bunk assignments and jobs for the weekend. The first thing in the morning we would be going on a two mile run. This would be done every morning before breakfast. I relished this, but the unfit college young bucks and other Navy personnel all groaned. Ian was at an obvious disadvantage because of his age and weight, but the Sergeant had a plan. He designated Ian as the camp cook who would have breakfast ready at the end of our run. Sarge put me in charge of assembling and cajoling the men around the race track each morning. I loved it as I felt like I was just out for a trot before breakfast, compliments of Ian. Mostly the gang dropped to the ground or nearest chair as I sucked down my first cup of coffee.

The first day of training entailed film and explanations of how to jump and land. We also had an intense program of how to fold and pack chutes. This is when we gulped hard as we were informed we would actually be packing our own chutes from the first jump and onward. Later we practiced the landing procedure of tuck, twist and roll by jumping off a raised platform onto a mat.

The next morning we assembled in the packing station and went through the 10-12 step checking list as we put the chutes together. At various stages of packing, a check list had to be signed off as an expert inspected each level of folding.

The next step was the gut-wrenching one: walking out to the airfield and lining up to jump out of a perfectly good plane. Ian was in the group of five before me, so if he jumped I had to jump. Don't forget, he had balked at this point last time. The Cessna 5 was revved and ready to go. Good luck, Ian.

Ian made it to the ground without leaving a crater, so now it was up to me. The loading area sloped heavily from the cockpit to the rear so being the smallest,I had to tuck myself way back there and would be the last to jump of this group. The pilot would fly through the jump zone and one parachutist would be told when to go by the jump master.

The fourth person to climb out holding onto the wing strut was told to go as the engine was cut. He wouldn't let go and wouldn't let go. The engine can only be cut for so long, and time was running out. Because of the "G" forces once on the step and wing strut, it is impossible to climb back in. The sergeant told me to hang on to him as he prepared to literally kick the kid off the plane. When seeing this, the reluctant flyer descended posthaste.

That was all I needed to see before my turn. Great. The pilot went around, and I climbed out. What a rush! At the designated moment I let fly and there I was, in seventh heaven. It was sheer bliss as I floated in a silence that was beyond silence. The view was incredible as I went left and right as instructed by pulling on the left cord for a right turn and right cord for a left turn.

As the mighty earth was starting to rush toward me, I noticed I was a tad off course. I was going to land very close to the perimeter fence. As I got closer, things were getting scary. On one side of the fence was a huge pile of rubble from a demolished building—jagged masonry, chunks of broken glass and rebar sticking out all over the pile. The choice was landing there or trying to clear the twelve foot fence with three lines of barbed wire on top. The other side of the fence had two buildings about thirty feet apart with a third building going across roughly forty feet from the fence. In the middle was a patch of grass. I had just a couple of seconds to assimilate this and make a decision. I decided to try to land between the buildings after, hopefully, clearing the fence.

At the last second I realized I wasn't going to make the fence without tucking up my legs. This meant I might not be able to get into a proper landing pose. Oh boy, too late. The grass it was. I tucked my legs and felt the wind of the passing barbed wire. Shooting my legs down as fast as possible, I was over the grass and aced the landing.

I was outside the perimeter fence, and the main gate was about a mile and a half from my landing. It was early Sunday morning with the sun shining bright as I bundled up my chute and set off down the road. This entailed walking through the small village where multiple people sat out drinking tea and nibbling on their cookies. They all smiled and nodded as I trudged by, some with a wave of their hand. I know they must have seen this a thousand times.

My second jump could have been even worse but for the grace of god—if there was one. Seconds after leaving the plane, I glanced up to make sure that the chute had opened correctly. It had. However, it was on fire. Whhhaaaattttt????!!!. I needed every word from that Navy dictionary. Why didn't I bring a change of underwear?

The fire went out on its own, thank goodness. I didn't know this at the time, but a full panel was gone in the round chute. I was floating down; that was all I cared about at the time. I located the airfield and aimed for it pronto. I pulled on the left cord and went left. Shouldn't I have gone right? I later pulled on the right and went right. Maybe I was confused and forgot my lesson on that. It didn't matter as I could steer myself to the ground.

Approaching my landing, I got myself into wind and against the direction of the windsock, as taught. I landed so hard and fast, the roll was tremendous. I was fine, though, and ran around the chute to lay it on the ground and bundle it up before the wind dragged it. As I was doing this, three jeeps come racing at break-neck speed toward me. Sarge jumped out and hurriedly asked, "Are you okay?"

"Yep, I'm okay, why?"

His reply shocked the heck out of me. All of my controls and procedures needed to be reversed for a safe landing. When my chute opened, it had flipped across itself and changed all I had been taught. When it crossed over, the static had caught the nylon alight which fortunately went out. This explained the reversal of the left and right steering. However, it also meant that I needed to land with the wind to slow the forward progress. They estimated that I landed at over thirty miles an hour. Sarge said he knew what was going to happen and had come to my landing site ready to pick up the shards of fragmented bone. He had thought I was history. Had I not executed a precision land-ing, I would likely be dead. Not bad for a second jump.

That same day, my parents told me the TV news said a first time parachute jumper had fallen to his death. They were wor-ried sick until they heard from me. What a coincidence that was. I know I've been mentioning God and guardian angels quite a bit, but I still wasn't thinking much about spirit and such things. I was a roughy toughy sailor.

The rest of the week of parachuting went off without a hitch and we returned to the Bacchante as heroes.

MARINE TRAINING

I had now been assigned to a two week training session with the Royal Marines in Dover. Whether this was because I could now parachute or not I don't know. A ship always has a landing team, demolition team and a boarding team. I was to be on all three along with several others. This was training in preparations for trouble spots or incidents on our travels.

Things didn't get off to a good start. The marine base was way out in the boonies, not unlike Ganges. The double-decker bus taking us to the base was going through the country lanes and passing under a railway bridge. Actually, it didn't pass under the railway bridge because we got jammed under it. The clearance was not quite high enough. Oops. Two hours later and a long detour around the problem, we arrived as advertised.

The first order of the next day was breakfast before going to an enclosed drill shed. A sergeant major came stomping in and was yelling about lining up to get an SLR. An SLR (self-loading rifle) is the go-to rifle for most British armed forces. We did this, and Sarge told us that we were going to learn how to strip the rifle down, clean it, and put it back together. You know those game shows where the game seems too easy? Well, this was no exception. He added the words "blindfolded." We thought he was messing with us until he handed out large black pieces of cloth.

I have to say, by the end of the morning I was incredibly impressed. In just four hours or less he had accomplished his goal. That makes for a great instructor in my book. For all his bullying and loud thunder he was an expert at his job. He informed us that we were going down to the shore line below the cliffs of Dover for shooting instruction in the afternoon.

We marched down to the beach front along a winding path around a hill and got our instructions on how to correctly hold the rifle. The targets were against the cliff and good ol' me was picked first to fire twenty rounds at one of them. I ended up more like firing in the general direction. This rifle was heavy, and by the time I got to the tenth bullet it was sagging toward the ground. I did manage to fire on the upswing, pulling the trigger when I thought it was lined up close to the target.

My faithful team members were snickering, the sergeant was wincing, and my shoulder was crying from the recoil. The snickering agents were soon silenced as they took my place and didn't fare so well themselves. Once everybody had made a fool of themselves, a marine stepped up to show us how it was done. He fired twenty quick rat-a-tat rounds in less than twenty seconds and demolished the bullseye. I wanted him on my side.

Things got a little froggy on the way back to the barracks. We followed a path that bent right to go around the hill, and Sarge started screaming at us and halted the class. He was yelling about how he hadn't told us to turn and we should have kept marching toward the hill. Well, loud mouth Jimmy popped up with, "Hill and sailor, sailor and hill. Sailors don't do hills," while pointing at said hill. I've never actually seen veins and arteries bulge beyond the framework of a body quite like the sergeants did. The mosaic coloring of his face was also a new experience for my brain to upload. How such a large, normally deep-voiced man could screech at such a high soprano pitch is beyond the imagination, but he managed it.

He seemed to be telling us to run up to the top of the hill and back again, and the last three were to run the same route again. I took off like a rocket; I wasn't going to do it twice. When all was said and done, the last three didn't have to do it again. I'm guessing he was just trying to make us run faster. We marched around the hill at his bidding and headed for lunch.

The following day's morning session was something I really paid attention to. The order of the day was intense and extremely intricate booby trap training, and it went into and through the following afternoon. We were taught how to render the traps harmless and how to set our own. I found setting a new trap was more dangerous than defusing one. When we were tested with these techniques, they used flash bangs as the explosives. If we made an error, they went off. I did not blow one up but a few others did. This training was serious, and my normally relaxed and joking outlook was kept well in check.

More training on the beaches and learning how to defuse and set explosives continued. This was followed by learning how to set explosives to demolish bridges, blow up railway lines, and bring down walls safely. Cordite became our friend as did plastic explosives and fuses. If handled correctly and with respect there was no danger, but let your guard down and watch out. Some of these tactics could be used if we went to aid with disaster relief, say for a hurricane. Unsafe walls and buildings might have to be brought down by us for safety purposes.

Interspersed with all these activities was continued practice firing those darned heavy rifles. Although we did get a lot better with our shooting abilities and marching around hills, we never got anywhere near the skill and accuracy of the model marine. We did get some training with pistols as well. They were much easier to handle, although watch out for that kick hurting your wrist. Wyatt Earp would have made mincemeat outta me.

The day of departure arrived with everybody intact and unscathed. I'm not sure about the sergeant's mind still being in one piece. We did leave on friendly terms as we had come to understand him and he us, somewhat. I'm sure he walked away, as the bus pulled out, shaking his head. Surgery was probably needed to place his veins and arteries back into their rightful positions.

Look out, Bacchante. Here were coming some lean, mean fighting machines.

Not.

GIBRALTAR ANTICS

The ships company had been informed that we would be taking over HMS Scylla, another Leander-class frigate. This was a political move by the government. Spain wanted Britain to give Gibraltar back to the Spanish, but this was not going to happen in a million years. Their response was to close the Spanish/ Gibraltarian border, thus stopping the migration of daily workers going to Spain.

To counteract the lack of work for the Gibraltar citizens, we were refitting ships in the Gib naval dockyard. The Scylla was ready for service and Bacchante was due to be refitted. We were to sail into Gibraltar and switch over to Scylla.

On arrival, we realized how big a job this was. It entailed much more than just crossing over. All the stores were to be moved, maps and food and Uncle Tom Cobbley and all. We spent around three months getting everything up to speed.

It was there that our illustrious leader, the president of the mess, was going to depart the ship for his next assignment. A group of us, including the president, were chatting over a drink. We were mussing about a new president being appointed before the departure of our present one. The pres suddenly dropped a bombshell and said, "Hey Jack, I think you should take the job." I laughed because I was the youngest and least experienced PO. He agreed but pointed out that I was the liveliest and most forthright one. He pursued with his line of logic and the others jumped on the bandwagon. The next day we had a mess meeting, and I was voted in as the new mess president.

It was feeling more and more that my whole Navy career was being pushed along by an invisible hand. Who was doing that? I didn't know. I was still asleep spiritually.

Racing again. During our stay, I learned of an upcoming annual road race to the top of the rock. The road up, which wound its way through many ultra-steep curves, was just over two miles long. I decided to enter the race and started to train in earnest.

Every, well most, mornings I got up at 0600 hours and ran through and out of the dockyard before ascending the beast, the rock. I ran to a restaurant roughly halfway up and ran back again. I figured doing that most mornings would get me in shape enough to at least finish the race. I had the race particulars and found out that if you finished in under half an hour you received a certificate. That was going to be my goal, certificate or bust.

On the day of the race I got to the starting line along with what seemed a thousand people, many more than I anticipated. This would slow everything at the start of the race and soak up some of the time. I managed to worm myself fairly near the front before the gun jolted us on our way.

I did not take off like a rocket; I was going to pace myself and run all the way. On passing the restaurant around the half-way mark, I was in new territory. People around me were slowing and some were walking. Although this is good for me numbers-wise, my actual race was against the clock.

When we reached what I thought was the top of the road, there was still another 150 yards to go. This, fortunately, was on a slightly downhill slope and I could actually pick up the pace to what seemed a sprint. The finish line came rushing up to me, and I could finally relax with a bottle of water that had been thrust into my hand. My time was 29 minutes, 27 seconds. I was ushered to a table where they placed my name on a certificate and awarded it to me. I was so proud of myself and overjoyed.

Winning the lottery? Earlier in my stay in Gibraltar I had met an old acquaintance, Jeff Cook, from my petty officer class in Collingwood. He was a practical joker just like me, and we were cooking up a big one. By now we had fully taken over the Scylla and were alongside a jetty in the large dockyard basin. Jeff and I were going to trick everybody on board into believing that I had won the Gibraltar lottery. It stood at a record three million pounds.

I had let everybody in my mess know that I had bought some tickets. One lunchtime after the drawing, Jeff came aboard down to my mess. He burst in yelling that I had won and was acting very excited. I pretended not to believe him as he was such a joker. We went back and forth with him begging me to believe him. Finally I said, "I'm going to the flight deck shore phone to call the newspaper and check the numbers. I still don't trust you."

I grabbed the phone and dialed a false number. Then I held a fake conversation, repeating numbers that were also false. I was getting more and more excited as the numbers rolled out. I finally slammed the phone down and raced around the flight deck whooping it up.

All around me were privy to what had just happened and I returned to the mess. By the time I got there the buzz had spread over the whole ship. The following morning even the captain and first lieutenant congratulated me. It got worse—or better, depending on how you look at it. In a week or so there was to be a commissioning ceremony on the dockside. It was to be a big affair with a full parade and march-past. The admiral of the fleet would be ceremoniously cutting a commissioning cake on the flight deck as champagne was being readied for a toast. The Royal Marine Band would be playing and, well, you get the idea.

On the flight deck after the parade, cake cutting and toast making, a group of my peers and I were chatting in a group when the admiral of the fleet sidled over. He asked if one of us was the one who won the lottery. We all just about choked on the bubbly. I quickly spoke up and said it was me, to which he gave me a hearty congratulation and pulled me aside to advise me.

He let me know that there was a provision in the military law books that allowed people who came into large amounts of money to request an honorable discharge. I thanked him and told him I would consider it but for right now I enjoyed my life in a blue suit.

One evening Jeff and I were sitting in the senior rates mess of the shore base when somebody recognized me and told everybody I was the lottery winner. By this time my mess mates and a few of the crew knew about the joke. They all cheered and applauded, and I felt obligated to buy everyone a drink. I could afford it and it was worth it to keep up the charade.

Six months later a junior crew member asked what I was going to do with the money when I got back to England. I couldn't believe some people still believed the story.

A new chief. The top chief in the office was soon to be departing. I really liked him as he was on top of his game and very fair. One day as I was leaving some administration offices in the dockyard, an older chief happened to be leaving at the same time. After the obligatory nod, we realized we were headed in the same direction. Then he told me he was going to be the head chief electrical officer on board the Scylla. We started talking about various ways of leading men, and I asked him what he wanted us senior rates to call him. He kind of shocked me as he said, "Chief" instead of his name. I thought he might be joking and hinted at that. He let me know in no uncertain terms that he wasn't.

This railed against the general camaraderie between the senior rates on board. Anyway, that was the way it would be.

He was a tough-talking and rule-following person without any room for fudging. Although many didn't like this, I was okay with it, maybe because of my Ganges training. It did force many other electrical senior rates to get their departments in a better disciplinary standing, as I had. I respected him for holding to his word, and we got on famously. I thought he might loosen up after a while, and he did. It took much longer than I thought it would, but nevertheless it did.

NOSES TO THE GRINDSTONE

We eventually set sail and headed for Chatham. On the way we checked out as many pieces of equipment as possible in readiness for a helping hand from those famed dockies I love so much. We got the ship into an excellent state of readiness and prepped ourselves for the dreaded six week work-up in Portland.

At the initial meeting of key personnel and the work-up team, they asked how many people had done this before. I raised my hand along with about fifteen other people. They then asked how many had done two before. Maybe ten of us raised our hands. How about three? Four of us kept our hands up. "Has anybody actually done four?" they asked? Two of us said yes and they continued. "Surely not five?"

"Yes. Actually six. This is my seventh and hopefully my last," I joked. They had never had anybody with that amount of experience come through before.

The team did their normal exacting investigation of the whole ship. This took a week to complete as we held our breath. Once done, we had two weeks to go back to Chatham and then come back for the six week slog. The electrical report seemed daunting, to say the least. We had a list of 1400 defects. Although not all items needed to be completed, most had to be done by the end of the work-up.

The senior electrical officer called a meeting of all the electrical seniors in the dining room. He sort of bottled out, and I could hardly blame him. I had been there and ridden that bull many times before.

After his rendition of doom and gloom, I asked permission to talk without interruption. I stood before the group and took a copy of the defects and tore them in half. I told them that many defects were going to be dealt with in the first two days by the most junior people in their departments. I then tore the remainder in half and suggested that this number would be erased by their leading hands and first class electricians.

The last quarter would be organized and placed into order of importance by the department leaders and started by the senior rates. Items that required fault finding and not simple fixing would be investigated by the experienced only. Once the problem was found, it was to be passed on to junior rates to repair.

"We are capable of bringing this list down to one hundred items that will be fixed by the end of the first week of work-up," I said, "but we cannot do this by working eight hours a day. The time for putting our noses to the grindstone is here and now. I have faith that we can and will achieve this goal. Are you with us?" I turned to the boss and said, "You can calm down, sir. We've got this situation under control and won't let you down."

The boss replied that he hoped I was right. We all stood to leave the dining room before Brian James, our new chief, stopped the exodus. He applauded my little speech but warned, quite correctly, of complacency and lack of effort and concentration. He gave some more helpful hints and words of encouragement, which certainly boosted my confidence in him and his policies.

I was convinced we were going to win this war. Many of the listed items include things like one nut missing off wire securing clamps when there should be two. We could whittle this list down fast.

As advertised, we sailed into and out of Chatham with nearly all our problems solved.

Arriving in Portland. Portland was soon upon us, and we prepped ourselves for six weeks of intense challenges. With my experience, I looked at this as a game and enjoyed the fun. One early exercise was for the landing team to take over a village controlled by terrorists in the nearby hills. Three of us senior rates had a sub-team each as we planned a three-pronged attack. My team was to come up the center and try to take the high points overlooking the main road.

Knowing the terrain, I chose to scale a hill leading up to a surrounding wall of the south side of the village. Unfortunately, it involved climbing through small gorse bushes, bramble bushes, and rough scrub land. It was slow and tough going, but we ended up at the bottom of the wall we needed to scale to get onto the flat roofs of the buildings.

The ten foot monster was tough, but we scrambled over the parapet and had a good view of the whole road. There was a road block for one of the other teams to negotiate. I guided them through some back alleys and around this obstacle. I noticed a high tower across the way which was in control of an all-around view. I decided to take two of my team and try to sneak up the three flights of steps and surprise them. This was risky, as they had us at their mercy out in the open if they heard us.

We took forever slinking up those metal steps in our clod hopping boots, but did make it onto the landing outside the door. I zipped a flash bang, opened the door, fake-blew them into oblivion, and rushed in with my two henchmen and my pistol drawn. We had the best panoramic high point in the area. With me there and the rest of my team holding the roof tops, we had control of the situation.

At the same time, the team skirting the road block had pulled off a great maneuver themselves. They were now in control of that end of town. The third team had popped off some key sentries, and the village was ours.

The interrogation team which had been ushered in was working over some captured personnel. We needed information for the next stage of the proceedings, and they weren't cooperating. The unfortunate word of torture was coming into play, and the interrogators went to work. It was very cold, especially in the middle of the night. They stripped the captors who were lying on the freezing concrete floor and were dousing them with equally cold water. They folded and complained to the exercise marshals about mistreatment.

The upshot of the night was that we had an incredible report and were heartily congratulated by the work-up squad. It was 0300 hours as we trundled over the gangway where a nice hot meal was waiting for our hungry bodies.

The final day of the war games. On the day of our final war games something went awry. This was the day when the ship went through a final war time battle test. The staff members threw everything at you as if in a full scale fight and gradually built up to a crescendo. I was in charge of the after damage control party and had a well-oiled, terrific team who pulled for me one hundred percent. I had created a great team spirit and even held training classes before Portland to make them the hottest team ever. At least that was the plan.

During the last phase, the staff shut off the huge fans that blow air into the boiler room. Our task was to get emergency wires run to a special box above the boiler room where they could pull a switch and get the fans running again. I drew up the planned route and handed it to my top man, who was beyond capable and a true magician at these tasks. I gave him two men and off he rushed. It took only seven minutes to complete this task. Wow, how good was that? I reported the completion over the phone to damage control headquarters and also sent a written note by messenger.

Thank goodness I doubled my message track. Twenty minutes later I heard the main Tannoy bark out, "Safeguard, safeguard, turn on the boiler room fans." I thought this strange and later found out the fans were not activated, and two crew members had collapsed on the boiler room floor from heat exhaustion.

Fast forward to the after action meeting known as a wash-up, where I got lambasted for my crew's inefficiency and lack of effort. I got really agitated as I explained that my men had completed the task in record time. The heads of operations repudiated this, but I got more heated and stood my ground. After the meeting broke up, Brian James pulled me to one side and started on me again. We both got very heated, and neither of us was giving ground. Eventually the senior electrical officer stepped in and told us to go to the office. The three of us were now alone, and Brian and I started up again. I was not giving in; my men were outstanding and had performed well. I was eventually told that an inquiry would be held.

Thirty minutes later, while I am still seething in my mess deck, the phone rang. It was Brian, asking me in a really calm tone to come down to the office. On arrival, he shook my hand and apologized for what had gone down. I returned the favor as I know I had stepped over the line, insubordination wise, earlier. He told me they had found my time track note in the damage control headquarters. It had been mislaid so no action was taken to turn on the fans. My team was praised for their superb efficiency and speed of performance. We all kissed and made up with no hard feelings.

Whenever we said no hard feelings, we meant it. We had to live together very closely and it wouldn't work if we built up emotions and carried them forward. Anyway, I quickly went to the electricians mess deck and gave them the good news. They cheered and shouted and whooped before offering me a can of beer. All was well.

Scylla blasted through training with flying colors. This period in a captain's career could make or break his future promotional hopes. It could also affect the careers of department heads, which is why our initial meeting in the dining room was so tense. With our heads held high and our egos boosted, we headed for home base, Chatham.

THE SPANISH ARMADA
AND PEARLS

It was almost like the cliffs at the Straits of Dover waved to us as we steamed by. They surely are a sight for sore eyes, especially when heading east and therefore home. This day, however, we were heading west and on to the obligatory stop in Gibraltar.

We were going to be guard ship for three weeks. Those pesky Spanish politicians still had the border closed and were now threatening the Rock with invasion. I'm sure this was a paper tiger type threat but we had to be on our guard.

Gibraltar would always have our protection; after all, the Barbary apes were still roaming this most famous rock. It was said in folklore that Gibraltar would always be British as long as the Barbary apes were present.

A large multi-national fleet exercise was taking place in the Mediterranean Sea. We had joined in the fray and had been away from Gib for five days. This was when we got a panic message from admiralty to fly back to the rock at full speed as five Spanish warships had crossed the three mile limit line and were threatening the locals. This was a miserable scare tactic and totally unnecessary.

On arrival in the area, we witnessed five warships made up of what we call Smokey Joes. These so called warships were probably put together by Fred Flintstone, their crews totally untrained and pathetic. It wasn't their fault; they had just not been prepared for sea or fighting. After we fired some warning shots across their bows, all but one ship retreated back into international waters. The fifth ship, thinking it was the bad boy of the bunch, held its ground.

I was part of the boarding party that assembled on the deck of the enemy, rifles at the ready. Our gunnery officer demanded to speak to the captain of the other ship, which was granted. I don't know what took place, but we re-entered our sea boat and headed back to Scylla. I'm assuming they were warned how badly out-gunned and out-trained they were, who knows? That night we couldn't buy beers anywhere as Gibraltarians celebrated our intervention and bought them for us.

Pearl diving in South Africa. With great fanfare and a cheerful send-off by the locals, we set sail for South Africa and Cape Town. This was better than going to Simon's Town as I could visit my uncle without the dreaded train ride.

Before arriving in Cape Town, I put a notice on the main bulletin board for anyone interested in going pearl diving; names would be pulled out of a hat. Most people knew by now that I had an uncle in the area. I told them he ran a pearl diving boat and took people out for day trips. The payment would be a forty percent share of any findings the divers retrieved. Food and drink would be supplied along with all diving equipment, scuba or deep sea. No experience was necessary as well-grounded crew members would be on hand to assist in any short term training. The offer was so tantalizing that at least forty people put their names down.

Oh my, how foolish could they get? They all knew what a trickster I was, and yet they still fell for my gags. A day later some realized I was spoofing them, and they scratched their names off. Folly, folly, it was too late. Their names all went into the newspaper as being duped by the maestro. Boy, did I get a hard time for that or what? It was great and everybody had a good laugh, even the gullible ones on the list.

More sports in Cape Town. On arrival in Cape Town we got the obligatory warning about the rules of apartheid, thus scaring anybody who hadn't been there before. On the first day in port, we had a rugby game in the highly touted new sports consortium. The game went well despite the loss by only three points. The third half, in one of the conference rooms, was attended by a huge number of people. The band was in full swing and the banter light and cheerful.

That's when the rugby team got together around the piano and started singing "Zulu Warrior," a striptease song. We were soon joined by most of the ship's company who were there, and I'm sure the captain tried to hide somewhere. I was air lifted onto the top of the piano and started the striptease, one item coming off at the beginning of each verse.

The white Africans were a very religious and prudish people mostly, so were not sure what to think. Their rugby team joined in the fray and so did some of the more liquored patrons; it was quite a scene. When I got down to just my knickers, the manager came pushing his way through the throng. "If those come off, I'm calling the poli....That's it I'm calling the police," he said as my last stitch of decency went flying into the air. The customary beer throwing at me proceeded, and I climbed down to get dressed. The whole room was cheering and hooting and hollering and clapping. The returning manager was having a fit and told me the police were on their way.

On the arrival of the boys in blue, they were directed to me. I denied the accusation and was backed up by all the civilians in the vicinity. They told the police that the stripper had left the building and fled the club. Although they knew this was a lie, they didn't want an incident with the ship or to spoil everybody's' fun. They were good eggs and let the incident ride even as the manager protested. He was booed out of the room and we didn't see him again.

I did manage to see my uncle Doug. He threw a small party with his close friends, and we played some contract bridge. I also invited him and his wife Audrey on board for a show and tell. They brought along a nephew of about 10 or 11. After cocktails in the mess, we proceeded to a special lunch my chef buddy had prepared and they got to tour the ship. My relatives, of course, felt very special as they got to see a lot more than the average citizen could.

We were only in town for three days so when they departed the ship, that was the last I saw of them. They were a wonderful break for me and treated me like a king.

AN EXPLOSIVE SITUATION

The following day I was required to go ashore as part of the shore landing team. We weren't aware what our task would be, but we did get a list of the stores to take with us, which included explosives and all the required paraphernalia. After a long drive, the lieutenant in charge told us what we were going to be destroying, and I began setting up. Once the plastic explosive was in place with the blasting caps, we ran wires back to the plunger from the blasting caps.

The officer in charge and I stood in front of a tin shack with the plunger before us. The rest of the team tucked themselves in the shack for better safety. When everything was ready to blow, I asked, as is protocol, for permission to proceed. I forced down the raised plunger that generated the voltage to explode the caps and was shocked. There was only about a foot between myself and the officer. Before we even heard the boom of the explosion, a stone flew between us at lightening speed. We didn't even see it but heard it hit the shack. On hitting the deck, we realized that it was already too late to save our lives if anything was going to hit us. I've heard of dodging a bullet but nothing about dodging a stone. We looked at each other with bugged out eyes. I can tell you it was a successful day and a job well done.

Off to Bahrain. We left Africa in our wake, with the next stop the Persian Gulf and Bahrain. Bahrain was as hot as expected, blistering hot to be precise. There was a detachment of the Army stationed there, and they challenged us to a game of rugby. The field, if that is what you want to call it, was a loosely marked out patch of sand.

We asked where the blades of grass were stored because there were none on the ground. They just laughed.

A massive roller with a huge pulling handle had been rolled up and down the field to pack down the sand to make it hard. Have you ever run for eighty minutes on sand while playing any sport, let alone rugby? It was brutal. These desert rats were much fitter and used to it, but us sea-legged sailors were at a loss. I swear that after only five minutes of tearing up the sand, it was like playing in glue. The energy was sapped from our bodies like a sponge soaking up water. We did put up a good fight and only lost by fifteen points. Not so bad considering the pain wracking our bodies.

EXPERIENCE IS EVERYTHING

Our next stop was Gan in the Maldives before heading for what was by now my second home, Singapore. After docking alongside the jetty and hooking up shore power and phones, I retired to the mess. Here came the dry cleaners and podiatrists and manicurists. Tony Dry Cleaners and Peanut were the first in the mess. They saw me and said, "Hey, Jack Frost, congratulations on your promotion." Wow, they remembered me and realized I had been promoted.

I had all my nails cut, scraped, and cleaned by the manicurist. They worked so fast and furious that you dared not move an inch for fear of losing a digit. It felt really great even though I knew ship work would wreck my hands within only a couple of days.

We stayed a while and had the usual dockyard assistance to fix and maintain overdue work. I took a few trips down to Sembawang Village. The traders there also recognized me and we had some good chats. There was something special about having these long distance friendships that united our countries.

One evening my friend Charles Mateland and I went to Sembawang Hills Market. It was a taxi ride away, about halfway to Singapore City and in the middle of nowhere in particular. I had been there on each occasion to Singapore at least once. There were vendors of all shapes and sizes selling everything under the sun. The stalls all had open bulb lighting on them and they stretched out along a side road seemingly forever. There was music and dancing and crowds that didn't quit—a hubbub of human flesh rising and falling with sound and frivolity. I always found something unique to buy and enjoyed the roiling, swaying scene.

I happened to know that at the far end of the market was an out of the way country restaurant with the best sizzling hot plate of steak, baked potato, mushrooms and onions in the whole wide world. The desserts were to die for and I always got two because I didn't want to miss out on the one I wouldn't get. Slowly savoring this fine meal along with a couple of glasses of wine was worth the rather large bill it demanded. The walk back through the throng of humanity to the roundabout and main road to Sembawang removed most of the weight gain from the fine feast, though.

Hong Kong or bust. Hong Kong was our next go-to place, and on the way I was to lose an excellent first class electrician from my shop. He was to be replaced by Jeff Burton whose report card was the worst I had ever seen. It ran something like this: lazy, untidy, unkempt, work habits and ethics much to be desired. It went downhill from there with a more detailed unflattering essay.

The first morning he arrived at my workshop I pointed out my two rules hanging over the work bench:

Rule #1: The Petty Officer is always right.

Rule #2: If the petty officer is wrong, Rule #1 applies.

He smiled at this, which actually told me something, at least. Oh, and he was late for the first and last time. We ironed that rule out right off the bat.

His shirt and trousers were un-ironed, and his shirt had a button missing. His shoes were dirty; according to him they were only work shoes, so what was the big deal? I explained that the clean work shoes showed a mind-set and attitude, but I'm not sure if that sailed over his head or not. I told him to go back to his mess and make good all the items I didn't approve of.

When he got back, all spruced up and acceptable to my standards, we had a long private conversation. I read his report from the previous three workshops and/or departments. He wasn't looking at me but had his head down as he spoke. He said, "I suppose I'm done for, even before I start. I don't care anymore."

Then he jerked his head up to stare at me when he saw me ripping the report into shreds. I dumped the shreds in the waste bin and told him we were starting afresh. I explained that if he was willing, we (and I emphasized *we)* would make him a worthy member of the electrical branch. If things progressed well, I was willing to help him study for promotion to leading hand. He laughed at this and shook his head. I doubled down on my offer and asked if he was up to the challenge. His eyes watered as he turned and got up to leave, saying, "Yes."

After that, he seemed to be cooperating and trying to make a mark, and we even had some evenings studying in the workshop. He was still trying to protect his bad boy image with his mess mates, but that was okay.

A major turning point for us was on the first day in port after a long stretch at sea. Jeff was not duty watch so could go ashore, but I asked him to assist me that evening and he said yes. We had a major job to fix on the low voltage switchboard. Most of the board needed to be shut down for safety reasons, which shut down a tremendous amount of electronic equipment. We were going to work well into the night and remove a huge multi-contact switch. There were about sixty connections that had to be removed and marked. The switch then needed to be removed and replaced and rewired. The cover plates we removed had approximately 120 small screws holding them on. I say this because on completion of the job at 0300 hours, I told Jeff to go get his head down for some sleep, and I would button up the cover plates.

He told me no, that he would take care of that.

"I'm used to not sleeping, and you're not," I said. "Go to bed and I'll finish up."

His reply was, "I'm the junior rate, and you're the senior rate. It's my job not yours."

Sure enough, he completed the task and was front and center at 0800 hours, ready to roll. I was really feeling good about what was happening with him and made sure the powers that be knew about his transformation.

Several months later, after multiple evenings studying together, he passed his written and oral examinations for leading hand. I believe he just needed somebody to care about him and prod him in the right direction. Once he realized he didn't need his previously stoked bad boy image, he let it go.

SHORE PATROL AND SPUDS

Hong Kong was its usual fantastic self. I took the pleasures of the Island and Kowloon in my stride and enjoyed the relaxing stay. I did get to take in the Botanical Gardens again and as always, enjoyed the back streets and alleys.

On the way to Singas, the automatic potato peeling machine in the galley failed. The spare parts were not available to fix it and wouldn't be until reaching our second home. The first lieutenant had a plan for the men under punishment to hand peel the spuds. They would be joined by one member of the duty watch from each department and one cook. The PO cook would supervise, and the task would be started at 2200 hours, with the men working until completion. Murphies were eaten at all three main meals, so that made for a lot of peeling to feed 250 sailors.

I went to work to help the situation and ran speaker wires from the nearest mess deck speaker to the galley so the trogs could at least have music while they peeled away. I then had a weird sense of duty or responsibility that I cannot explain. I decided to help peel the monster pile of spuds every night.

Now I was a senior rate and did not have to do this at all. I can tell you this, though; the lads' morale definitely improved. I was the only volunteer, and they knew it. Their thinking must have been, "If he's willing to do this, I have no gripe for myself." The chore did turn into more fun than you would think because we formed a sense of teamwork and camaraderie. We even had little competitions as to who could peel the next spud the fastest or even make a figure of some kind out of the potato.

DRAMA IN KARACHI

Sadly, on leaving Singapore for the last time of this trip, we made our way to Karachi in Pakistan. This was somewhere new and exciting for me. Most of my mess mates and I decided to ask permission to run a SODS opera. SODS stands for Ships Own Dramatic Society. With permission granted, we went into overdrive to put on a good show for the crew.

Next to the audience, we wanted to run a bar on the flight deck called the Shy Talk Inn. In the Navy, seagulls are called *shitehawks*. We asked for the bar to have almost no limit, beer only, and the captain said yes but we were responsible for not letting anybody get too over the top. We then set up two barbeque pits by cutting a forty gallon drum in half and making two trestles. Dinner of steak, baked spuds, and salad would be served before the show started. The stage, against the hangar doors with side curtains, was built out of cases of beer.

This, of course, took a few days to put together, but we had time before arriving in port. The acts were put together from many of the talented crew. We had a singer, some Chelsea pensioners in wheel chairs from the senior chiefs' mess, and of course a comedian.

I did a magic show using the flight deck audio loop. I wore a turban which covered the flight deck headset I was wearing. I had an accomplice tell an audience member to pick a playing card and I would say what the card was. My man was wearing a cloak and scarf, which hid his throat mike that told me the said card.

One young sailor had been teaching himself to play the flute and came up in front of everybody. He was absolutely awful, playing single notes with long gaps in-between. It went on forever and ever before he finished. I tell you this because he got the loudest and longest applause of the evening. The crew really appreciated his gutsy willingness to try this in front of all his peers. It was a testament to everybody onboard.

The whole evening was a major hit and lifted everybody from the captain to the lowest junior seaman. The forward petty officers' mess got massive kudos from the skipper, especially me, as I was the president of the mess. I did make sure he knew it was all of us who chipped in.

Now for the sucker punch. At anchor not far from us was another Leander class frigate called Naiad. They had seen our frivolity and barbeque happenings and quickly put in place their own plot against us. They rowed across to Scylla, climbed the anchor chain, and stole the two ceremonial chrome-plated tampions covering the gun barrels. Tampions are covers that go over the opening of the gun barrel to stop water or other objects from going down the barrel. At sea they are just heavy canvas covers. In harbor they are polished chrome with the ship's crest on each one. This was quite a scoop for them.

We didn't know about the theft until the next morning when the skipper received a message from the Naiad's skipper demanding two bottles of whiskey, one for each tampion to be returned. I will return to the conclusion of this story much later.

Getting scammed. Two days later, I went ashore with Tom into the city which was quite a way from the ship. On the jetty were a slew of normal taxis and a bunch of taxi type transports made up of a Lambretta motor scooter with a two seater contraption attached with a hitch. We wheeled and dealed and bartered for the trip to the city center on the Lambretta just for fun.

When we got to our destination, I noticed the meter read less than what we had agreed upon and wanted to pay just that. After fifteen minutes of arguing, I called over a passing policeman. On explaining the situation he told me that in Pakistan a deal is a deal. We had agreed on a price for the ride and that should stand. He could not tell the driver to adhere to the meter amount. We begrudgingly coughed up the bartered amount and went to the main kasbah. This was more thrilling than the alleys of Hong Kong. It was an enormous maze of thousands of vendors and a mass of seething humanity.

In an instant, a very young, lively boy just bouncing all over wanted to show us where to go and be our guide. After a dozen no thank-you attempts, we moved on but with the boy still tagging along. We did listen to him and he did still guide us into and out of the labyrinth of stores for an hour and a half or more.

When we got back to our original starting position, the excitable young pup wanted to be paid quite a large sum. Since he had forced his way with us and we didn't really want him, we didn't feel obligated to give him anything. We ended up relenting and offered him some rupees in the amount we thought fair. He refused the offer and would only take the amount he asked for. When we said, "It's that or nothing," he walked off and said, "Then it is nothing." Then we felt bad and his guilt trip game won him the day. He was obviously well practiced at this art.

Before returning to the ship, I found a wooden necklace to buy for seven rupees. I only had a one hundred rupee note, and the stall owner couldn't change it. He called a small lad over and told me the boy would run to the money changer for me. I was very skeptical about this and hesitated. The stall owner was very insistent and wanted his sale, so I caved and crossed my fingers.

Forever went by and I was definitely not comfortable as there was no way I could do anything about it in this market. I remember Indiana Jones as I am writing this. Finally, the bright faced, fleet-footed boy arrived with my money. I paid the vendor, who gave me an "I told you so" smile, and gave my young banker a tip.

The ship beckoned and the open road was ours to survey. All along the roadsides were super-size cardboard boxes and tattered cloth squares hanging over wooden frames. It was sad, because these were people's homes. The appreciation for my life and my level of living was heightened once again.

At the dockside, I came so close to a camel it was hard to breathe. Those things stink to high heaven. I also knew to be careful it didn't spit at me, as they are prone to do. I do like to indulge in different experiences as I sailed around the world, but some I could do without. I jumped aboard the ship's sea boat and headed back to safety. The only camel there was a cigarette.

More practical jokes. One early evening I was walking around the flight deck relaxing and watching four or five people fish. Many other crew members were taking in the fresh, albeit warm, air. I stood by one of the fishermen while he reeled in his line to prepare for replenishing the bait and re-casting. As the hook came up, we noticed he had hooked another hook that had drifted under the ship. This was from somebody's line on the other side of the flight deck.

We couldn't let this go by could we? Carefully pulling it up, we tied it around a nearby bollard on the ship and tugged on it. The group on the other side got all excited and the fisherman tried to reel in his catch. We pulled the line even more as he was advised to let the catch pull a while and then try reeling it in again. They were figuring they had caught a shark or at least something big. This went on many times until we couldn't contain ourselves any longer. We were laughing so much the other team looked around and realized what was going on. I always seemed to be in the right place at the right time, for fun.

THE STAKES ARE HIGH

Back at sea, I got a notice that the wind speed and direction equipment was out of alignment. This requires going up the mast and along to the end of the yardarm. I would not tell anybody else to do this as it was very dangerous. As I prepared to go up, one of my junior rates said he wanted to try it. I gave very clear instructions, telling him to rest his shins against a lower bar that hung about a foot below the yardarm and sloped slightly away from it.

Up the mast he went inside the main trunking, which had a vertical ladder leading to the top platform between the port and starboard yardarms. I was watching seventy or so feet below as he climbed out and maneuvered onto the arm. Oh my god! He was climbing out hanging upside down, the wrong way. He was literally hanging on by only his arm strength. I was inwardly freaking out while staying calm and saying nothing.

As soon as he got to the end and strapped himself on, I bolted up the ladder. At the top I told him to stay out there as I made my way out to show him how to come back. He told me that he thought it was more difficult than I had described and was scared. No kidding, Popeye, I thought.

Something else happened while up there. In order to go up the mast at sea, there was a key board that had to be given to the officer of the watch. These special keys were taken out of all the radar sets and two from the boilers. The boiler ones stopped the boiler room staff from blowing soot, which was extremely toxic and could kill you.

But well into the repair, the funnel blew soot. How was this possible? The keys were with the officer on the bridge. We immediately dove into the hollow mast and descended the ladder. I left all the tools and spare equipment up there.

I have to admit that I did lose my cool as I burst onto the bridge and lambasted the officer of the watch. He backed up, seeing my anger and told me to cool it and slow down.

"Slow down? Slow down?" I said. "Who gave the keys back to the boiler room? I could have been killed up there! What the hell is going on?"

He apologized profusely but didn't give an explanation.

Later, I told the chief about it, and he was furious. I'm guessing the problem went up the ladder from there, and I let it go. I still had to return to finish the job. I took junior with me and let him continue the original task. I wanted his confidence restored and his ability to go *out on a limb* in the future. (Yeh, I know, the puns are just awful.)

Getting back at the Naiad. About six months or so after the Naiad had stolen our tampions, we were on our way back to England, stopping for a few obligatory days in Gib. Who should be there on the other side of the basin to us? Why, the infamous, Naiad. This was her last foreign port before returning to the U.K. and being de-commissioned in readiness for the razor blade factory.

This meant that when it sailed, one day before us, they would be leaving with great fanfare. They were going to be sailing with all the bunting flags flying from the bow to the top of the mast and down again to the stern. The ship's side would be lined by all spare personnel in their number one uniforms. Bands would be playing, and the admiral of the fleet would be saluting from his podium. This podium sat atop a high cliff and at the bottom of a long winding path that led to Admiralty house. It overlooked the passage of water ships took to exit Gibraltar. It was going to be a grand old affair for sure. How proud they will be, snicker, snicker.

The night before the big day, some of us rowed across the basin with a paint roller and a can of battleship grey paint and a paint pan. The ship's number, painted on the side of the ship, was F71. It took no time at all to run the paint filled roller up and down the "1" and leave "F7" showing.

We instigators collected on the bridge wing the following morning with binoculars aplenty. As Naiad proudly slipped away from the jetty, nobody would think to look over the starboard side. Why would they? The fog horn blasted as the ship left its final port and eased forward for the flag-waving sail past. What a moment it was for them, and us, for very different reasons.

As Naiad came up to the sweet spot, the admiral bent down and spoke to a junior rate. He ran back to Admiralty House as we swung our binoculars back to Naiad. A moment later a rating came onto the bridge wing and ascended the short vertical ladder to the bridge top and the captain.

Another officer bellowed something to a seaman petty officer on one deck, and he ran along and looked over the side. I would have loved to be able to soul travel and be by his side. Horror was surely filing through his veins as he apparently confirmed the F7 on their side. How do those two bottles of whiskey taste now, Captain Tampion?

An hour or so later I heard my name being paged. It seemed my presence was required at the captain's cabin. I wondered if he had a communication defect for me to fix.

It turned out there was no defect. "Frost," he said quietly. "Do you know what happened to the '1' on the Naiad's pennant number?"

I knew I was safe because he called me "Frost," not "Petty Officer Frost." Rank and name meant trouble; just the name meant friendly conversation. "No Sir," I said while patting myself down and checking all my pockets. "I don't have it; I wonder where it could be." The captain smiled, thanked me, and opened the cabin door. That was my cue to leave. As I stepped into the cabin flat, I said, "I think we're even now, don't you?" There was no reply, and I didn't look round. I can tell you this without a doubt: he was thrilled to bits. The story of that incident raced around the fleet faster than the wind could carry it. Nobody messes with the Scylla, nobody.

AN EVENT-FILLED JOURNEY

Our duties away from Chatham came to a close, and homeward bound we went. It was good to see the white cliffs of Dover wave to us again, welcoming us back to Blighty. A quick turn up the North Sea, a hard left in and through the locks to safety again. The fabled dockyard mateys, along with Gary Dean and his team, had us all ship-shape and ready to roll in no time.

Soon we headed north to some exercises off the Scottish coast and take in a visit to Aberdeen. The exercises went well, although, as usual, the submarines sunk us several times. The surface battles went well, as did our live firing of sea-to-air missile tests. One scare comes to mind, though. We had Sea Cat missiles on each side of the ship just forward of the flight deck. During one live firing of a real explosive-filled weapon, the rocket got stuck on the launcher. The rocket burned at full thrust while jammed on the launcher, which was directly above the control room. There was only one thickness of deck plate between both areas. This was an incredibly dangerous situation as the rocket could explode. Fortunately, the rocket ran out of fuel before doing any real damage except to the minds of the control room men below.

Before going to Aberdeen we got an emergency call from the admiralty. A Scottish nationalist terror group had warned that a bomb had been placed on a North Sea oil rig. We were to head there and, on the way, take on a marine bomb squad with the latest bomb detecting equipment via helicopter. Could they find us in the pea soup fog that had descended upon us? We did turn on our signal radar but locating a ship spot on and then landing a chopper was going to be a crap shoot.

The warning gave us twenty-four hours before the either timed or remote detonation would take place. The chopper did find us by noticing a strong wake mark in the sea. They later said they didn't know if it was us or not but took the risk.

We located the oil platform and evacuated everybody onto our ship with the sea boat. Were they happy campers, or what? After the marines set up all their detection equipment, we proceeded to sail around and around the rig in a tight a circle and as close as we could. This was risky but necessary for a greater chance of success. The detection equipment being used from the ship had a better chance of detecting electronic bomb receivers the closer we went.

Many hours later it was determined that nothing dangerous was at hand; it had just been a threat. The marines did, however, get onto the platform and do a closer, more thorough sweep with finer tools in hand. The threat over, we headed for Aberdeen at last.

Aberdeen visit. Our visit to Aberdeen was purely to show the flag. For two days we were going to have the ship open to visitors and on the third day take some school children out to sea.

Our mess deck decided to have a social event for the local women. During the event, I somehow got very close to two women who were very interesting. The evening went really well, and we arranged a meeting the next day. Paul and I got the following afternoon off, and away we went to meet our new-found friends.

It turned out that Joan, my half of the duo, was a nurse. My brain went into overdrive, and I said I would try and get her aboard for the children's day at sea. I figured we needed some kind of medical assist in the form of a female. After much chortling at my "persuasive" arguments, the powers that be allowed Joan to come with us.

It was a good day on the water as the seas were calm and inviting. Before our departure Joan, Valerie, Paul, and I had a couple of nights together and phone numbers were exchanged. I really liked Joan and hoped to get together with her at a later date.

Next stop. Our next stop was to Faslane and HMS Neptune, the nuclear and Polaris submarine base on the Clyde River. A couple of mess members suggested we have an official mess dinner while here. I thought that a good idea and went about setting it up. Myself and Richard, a good old boy, went ashore looking for a location that fit the bill. We eventually found a really classy restaurant in a Scottish castle. It was a little pricey, but we arranged a meal for twenty people.

Because of an official mess dinner on HMS Dido while I was president of the mess, I knew my duties and obligations. I would sit at the head of the table and, at an appropriate moment, give a speech about how well we were doing together.

On the day of the dinner during the latter part of the afternoon, people were getting ready when I entered the mess. They were getting into civilian clothes, which I thought odd. I told them this was a number one uniform official mess dinner. A few of the older members agreed and were all for it, but some resisted, James in particular. After some back and forth, I put my foot down and informed them that I was going for a shower. When I returned, they needed to decide if they were going to go in uniform or find a new mess President. On my return all the members were dressed in uniform except one.

James had also put his foot down and stated that nobody was going to tell him how to dress to go ashore. I said, "Maybe not, but you will not be attending the mess dinner unless in uniform."

He said, "Fair enough, but I want my money back."

I told him he could have the beer money back but the meal was already paid for. He was okay with that, but this wasn't how I wanted to start a wonderful night out.

I have to say, everybody else was on my side, and off we went via the arranged coach to celebrate. The restaurant lived up to its billing with an incredible three course meal served by a multitude of waiters in Scottish attire. It was all very formal and exactly what I wanted.

About two thirds through the meal, an elderly Scottish gentleman came over to the table and told how he was enjoying our get-together from across the room. He was old Navy and was almost in tears watching our camaraderie and frivolity. He told a waiter to bring two bottles of their best rum to the table and add it to his tab. This was most unusual and extremely generous of him. When the bubbly arrived I asked the waiter to pour everybody rum plus one more. At this I took the extra glass over to the kind gentleman, handed him a glass, and toasted him with us all raising our glasses to him. He was quite overwhelmed.

The next day at the lunchtime tot ceremony James stood and apologized to the whole mess for his actions the previous night. He then turned to me and told me he supported me as president and regretted his actions. We all raised our glasses and slugged back the rum. Later, I quietly thanked James for what he did and told him it was pretty classy and gutsy to do that. All was well in the mess.

Drunken trouble. A kind of funny incident happened before leaving Faslane. Between us and the dockyard gate was a stretch of top Secret land surrounded by a fortified fence with three barbed wire runs along the top. This made the walk back to the ship at least five times as long. The open land was only about one hundred yards wide.

Two of our drunken shipmates figured they could make it over the fence and across the field before being caught. They didn't figure on the instant alarms and searchlights being activated. If that wasn't bad enough, the German shepherd dogs stopped them in their tracks.

Handcuffed and looking sheepish, they were returned to the ship a little worse for wear. The security team deemed them to be harmless and just plain stupid and didn't press charges. And no, I was not one of the reprobates. Not this time anyway.

It seemed an eternity before we were headed back to Chatham following multiple exercises with NATO, but all good things must come to an end. We were going to be in port for a two-month maintenance period with dockyard assistance once more.

Falling in love. I managed to return to Aberdeen for some weekends with Joan, and I felt things were going smoothly except for one thing. For the first time in my life, I was with a woman I cared about. This was weird for me, as any sex in my life thus far had certainly not been borne of love. I didn't know how to handle this scenario, for sure.

On the weekend forays I had too much respect to, as they say, go all the way. Each time I went to see Joan I said to myself, "This time we shall make love." Eventually we did, but I'm sure it wasn't to her great liking. I wasn't so good at this when I cared so much. I didn't have the tenderness nor the finesse. I was like a bull in a china shop or a fish out of water. I was starting to fall in love for the first time and I don't know how to handle it. She was the best woman that had ever been in my life so far. I felt different, and I liked it.

LIFE'S MYSTERIOUS TURNS

Eventually, our time in dock came to an end, and we were going to sail for the Caribbean and the Americas after doing a stint of fishery protection. This was going to take place up and down the Atlantic off the approaches to the English Channel and the coasts of Ireland, Spain, Portugal and France. Our first stop, however, was going to be Portsmouth for ten days or so. I did get the final weekend off and drove the approximately five hundred miles to Aberdeen and Joan.

I was asked to meet at her friend Valerie's' house and then we would go from there. When I arrived, Joan wanted to go out for a meal at a local club with just the two of us. I thought that was nice, as I was going to be gone for three months. We sat down in the bar/restaurant, and Joan told me that we were not going to continue as a couple. I don't remember much about the discussion as I was a little numbed, including my brain.

I didn't fight this decision as I strongly believed that you cannot make or influence somebody to love you or like you. I also revered Joan so much and my love was such that I respected what she had to say. We went back to Valerie's house, and Joan left without coming in. They knew what was taking place and received me in a very loving and thoughtful way. I had been holding everything together to this point but immediately broke down in tears. Valerie's father went to bed and Valerie and her mother stayed up to console me.

The next morning I climbed into my car and set off for home. I cried all the five hundred miles to Lewes. On the way, I went over several mountain passes with hairpin bends and severe drop offs. On three occasions I drove hard at the bends and wanted to end my life. Fortunately, I braked before the bend each time and made it into England safely.

I had asked Joan why she had let me drive one thousand miles just to tell me it was all over. She told me she respected me and didn't want to end something like what we had together on the phone. I have to say, I agreed with her.

I arrived home to the comfort of mum and dad, something I hadn't needed since leaving home for the Navy. I was still in tears when telling them of our breakup. Two days later, the Scylla quietly slipped into the English Channel as we bid Portsmouth adieu, and we were in my comfort zone. I was back in the saddle and as always, at sea, too busy to dwell on the matter. Don't get me wrong, I was heartbroken for quite a while. My first true love was gone, but I would like to thank Joan for pushing me along the path of love and teaching me something about love's ways.

Danger in the middle of the night. The first night in the English Channel brought a dangerous situation into view. I was nicely nestled into my bed asleep, as deep as I dare to go at sea. At 0200 hours I was suddenly awakened by the sound of silence. That's right, the sound of silence. The many sounds of the normal ship equipment running were non-existent. I did hear some large fans running down to a stop and the weird eerie nothingness of a quiet vacuum. My dopey brain snapped open like a cracked walnut. I shifted into overdrive and leaped from my bunk straight into a prepared pair of shorts next to my shoes on the deck. Underwear was not an option; I was in too much of a rush.

We were having a major steam failure. This was one of the most dangerous situations at sea. It meant we had lost all electrical power to everything, had no movement or control of anything about the ship, and could not steer. We were dead in the water and in the pitch black darkness of the busiest shipping lane in the world. Wonderful.

I burst out of the mess and flew along the main drag to G section, down a regular ladder, and then slid straight down a vertical ladder. I went in the diesel generator room through the small door to the side and was getting the auxiliary switchboard ready to put the generator on load, onto the switchboards.

The stoker, a mechanical technician, was hot on my heels and flashed up the generators. We had worked together many times under less strenuous times. This was a blessing as I didn't need to ask him when he was ready, nor him I. We had a tremendous synergy between us and both knew the other knew his job well. This was poetry in motion.

Remember, we were in total darkness except for the small emergency light at each doorway and ladder. We were basically working by feel and familiarity with 440 volts and 50,000 watts. This is why we had trained constantly and with sincerity. It worked. I could hear that the generator was ready for load—another lesson learned from experience and practice—and started the procedure for bringing the ship back on line.

At this point the senior chief, Brian James, clattered into the switchboard room. Wisely, he didn't say a word until I had got power onto the main buss bars of the board and the main breakers activated. He knew I had a handle on everything and let me do my job, a sure sign of a great leader. The ship now had electrical power and the radars could be in action, though we still couldn't move without steam and were still dead in the water. Brian was beaming from ear to ear as he slapped me on the back and congratulated me for a job well done. Stokes came into the switchboard compartment and also got a slap on the back from Brian as Stokes and I shook hands. We knew how important all this was.

It was now 0230 hours, and we were still not safe. It got worse. Unbeknownst to me at the time, there was thick fog in the

Channel with virtually zero visibility. We couldn't use the fog horn as there was no steam. We had a sailor on the focsle right at the bow ringing a large bell, but that's the best we could do. Can you imagine a super tanker with all its noise hearing that bell? It takes a few miles for a super tanker to stop in emergency and at best they would have a few yards. Even though we now had navigation lights, they also wouldn't be seen until it was too late. The captain closed the ship down to *damage control state one condition Zulu*. This was the war time highest state of readiness.

It would be many hours and morning before the boilers came back into action. The problem had to be found and repaired, which took a while. The morning sun did burn off the fog, which made it a little safer, and eventually we got under way and the nightmare was over. Many people did a fantastic job that night. The captain could take a great deal of credit for having his crew so ready and able to handle a serious situation so seamlessly. I often wonder how many crew members were even aware of the situation. This brings me to one of my favorite sayings: "If you are cool calm and collected while all about you are in a panic, you are not fully aware of the situation." I've always got a kick out of that phrase.

Bad weather ahead. As we prepare for our fishery protection patrol we were warned of impending bad weather. We were heading into gale force seven and eight, which is coming up on hurricane strength. On leaving the somewhat protected Channel, we start tossing and heaving at a level you don't really want.

Our fishery protection patrol was going as planned, though. What we did was stop fishing boats in the protected fishing grounds and check the size of their nets. There were international laws in this regard, so smaller fish were not to be caught so they could reproduce. The pirate fishing smacks didn't care and took all sizes.

When we stopped these boats, the good guys were always pleased to see us and appreciated our inspections. It helped them by keeping the pirates from poaching their catches and keeping the fishing grounds and schools healthy. Also, they always gave us fresh fish to have in our galley. It doesn't get any fresher than that! The bad guys, however, gave us a hard time, and my boarding training came into effect.

One evening with everybody settling down for the night, we were all suddenly springing back into action. The seas were very high and the waves enormous with the wind whipping across the deck and the crests of the deep blue. This is when a lookout spotted a red flare shooting skyward. It was quite a way off, so in those kind of seas, the trip over to investigate was going to take a while. As we closed into the approximate position, at least sixty of us were straining our freezing eyeballs trying to spot anything that could have sent the flare up.

Suddenly, there it was, a fairly large yacht just heaving and flailing around haphazardly. As we slowly closed in for a closer look, we could see nobody on deck. With these high waves it was very dangerous for the smaller vessel as we could rise up and slide into it, crushing and sinking it.

Surprisingly, our very experienced captain nudged us alongside the yacht as it bobbed up and down next to the flight deck. One brave and daring young officer timed the jump and did manage to get aboard. He found the brave or dumb yachtsman passed out inside the cabin, barely alive. An hour later we had managed to get him onto Scylla and into the sickbay.

Then what? We tried to lash the yacht to our side, but that wasn't working. Next we got a rope around a cleat on the focsle and tried to tow it behind us. This resulted in ripping out the deck of the now defunct boat. A seaman finally got aboard again with the intent of putting a hole through the hull with an axe. He almost broke his arm as the axe bounced off the deck that turned out to be metal. We could not, by maritime law, leave an unmanned vessel at sea, so the captain decided to back off and sink the yacht by gunfire.

The following morning when our maritime mastermind came out of his long sleep, he inquired as to how his yacht was. Nobody wanted to tell him Davy Jones had it. When he finally learned of its fate, he informed us he wasn't insured. The reason for this was that he was delivering the yacht to his daughter in the Caribbean as a surprise twenty-first birthday gift. The insurance companies wouldn't insure him because the trip was far too dangerous at this time of year and they didn't like the odds. He was a quite elderly lone yachtsman making a very precarious journey. At this point the owner let us know that the boat was worth 1.5 million pounds sterling. Still, we had saved his life. The man had been totally exhausted and had used his last flare trying to get help.

The seas worsen. Well into our sixth and last week on patrol, the seas continued to be amazingly brutal. During a particularly brutal attack sequence on our ship and bodies, several huge waves crashed over us. They were so ferocious they not only bent one of the ribs under the plating but cracked a part of the deck where the front superstructure met the deck behind the 4.5'gun. Under the split on two deck was the sonar electronic warfare room. This was a major problem as water was spilling all over the equipment. Fast moving and thinking crew soon got the situation under control but we were in trouble.

There were two days left on patrol before returning to Portsmouth, so the captain sent a message to Admiralty House. He requested we come in off patrol early and said why. The reply was to stay on patrol until relieved, as planned, which was absolutely ridiculous. The captain thought so, too, and sent another message to the dockyard personnel. "Expect us in on an ETA of

2000 hours tonight." It was short and to the point. Our captain, who had been passed over for promotion many times, was going to be in big doo doo.

On arrival there was a big black official car waiting to chaperone our skipper to meet the admiral of the fleet. I imagined that tea and sticky buns were not on the menu. Nobody will ever know the conversation but I sure would have liked to be a fly on the wall. The repairs weren't as time-consuming as we thought and soon we were on the way to our relatively calmer and much awaited trip to the west. Our beloved captain probably had a slapped wrist and continued his commission with us.

WESTWARD HO WHILE CROSSING THE LINE

After our refuel visit with the Barbary apes in Gibraltar, we set off across the pond to sunshine and sandy beaches. On the way we would be having a crossing the line ceremony as we straddled the equator. I had attended a few of these and had a small part to play in one of them. This time I would be a main participant, instigator, antagonist and agitator as I was going to be King Neptune's wife.

The team got together on many occasions and everybody knew what to do. I spent many, many hours secretly making my costume as King Neptune's wife. The greatest amount of time was spent making the hair. I got hold of a twelve foot long piece of white nylon rope. I then unraveled all of the strands down to the finest thread there was. It took forever, and keeping it under wraps was difficult to say the least. I got together some material from flags and bunting to make a dress. I also put two square boxes over each of my nipples just to be different. The sea will do that to you. I planned to cover any exposed bare skin with a concoction of coconut oil mixed into a combination of brown, yellow, green and red crushed grease crayons.

As the ship approached the equator after sunset, the captain announced that he had received a message from the deep to stop the ship for Neptune's queen, who wanted to deliver a message. Right in the peak of the bow on the focsle is a little known small, round hatchway. Under the hatch is a straight ladder going down to two deck. My plan was to shine a strong light up the hatch and have two crew members blast C02 fire extinguishers up the hole. As they did this, I would emerge through the mist, making it look like I came over the bow.

When most of the ship's crew had assembled on the focsle, I made my way to stand high on a breakwater where I had placed a main broadcast microphone. I yelled my message of warning into the belly of the ship and the attending crew on deck. The ship was to go to a specific longitude and latitude at a dead reckoning to receive Neptune. They would dive into the depths, forever lost, if they failed to carry out this order.

After my scary message, I leapt from the breakwater and disappeared down the hatch as they again blasted a cloud of C02 into the ethers. I later found out that a lot of crew members wondered how I came over the bow and disappeared back over the bow. They figured it must have been very dangerous and risky. So the ruse worked!

That night the flight deck was set up with two huge canvas squares with supports to be filled with seawater the next morning. A stage was also built right next to the two potential pools. A bar stool that could be tilted backward was clipped down next to the edge of the stage.

When the ship was stopped, things started to wind up. The majority of the crew was on the flight deck to watch the proceedings. Unbeknownst to some, they were to be a victim as well. As Neptune and his entourage appeared, I ordered everybody to their knees in tribute to the king, and everybody obeyed. They didn't want to be picked out for a dunking later.

That is, everybody obeyed except the captain, who thought he was above the law of the deep. I strode over to him and, placing myself nose to nose with the skipper, bellowed, "That includes you, you peon of the seas." At this, I smote my camel whip upon his shoulder and pressed down. The crew went wild, and the skipper sank to his knees to even more cheers. He was laughing and yucking it up with the rest of us. On the stage was King Neptune himself, the prosecutor, the judge, the barber, the chemist, and two bears. Other bears were at the ready to hunt down any officer or sailor who thought he could run from the court.

The first to be summoned, of course, was the captain. He ascended the steps onto the stage to raucous cheering from the lynch mob of a crew. His charge was, "You have dared to remove all the ship's company from their wives, girlfriends and families for an extended period of time. How do you plead?"

"Guilty as charged," he replied. More cheers.

"Your punishment is three curry balls washed down with one pint of limeade and thrown to the dunking bears after being shaved by the barber."

I should explain that the curry balls were made of almost pure curry powder, and they had to be swallowed. Afterward, the head was tilted and the limeade was offered. The limeade was so strong it would cause you to gasp. Gobs of shaving cream were then smothered all over the head, and huge plastic shaving knives scraped it off. After this, the stool on which victims were sitting was tilted back by two bears, and the convicted were then dunked, the amount of times prescribed by the court. They were then thrown into the second pool which, after more dunking by even more bears, washed off the rest of the goop. They then stepped out into the safety of the mob.

"Next," yelled the prosecutor "is the senior engineer. His crime was to allow the engines to take the crew from their loved ones." The senior catering officer was next, followed by any person deemed to be a leader of any kind. Some prominent senior rates and regular sailors who were well-known are also chosen.

The whole event was a massive success. At the end of the show, several of the crew made a grab for some of us court members as we made a dash for the senior chiefs' mess. We all made it, but we had to rescue two of our team and drag them through the door. We were all exhausted from the two day spectacle, along with the rehearsals and preparations for the event. We weren't too exhausted to down several pints of beer, though, and cackle about all that happened during the show. Many of them thought I took a chance at yelling and striking the skipper like I did but also thought it was great. Our captain was a true leader who could roll with the crew as well as being a captain to them.

BORN AND BREAD

The crossing the line ceremony behind us, we made tracks for our destination, Barbados. On the way I asked our PO chef if I could help make the bread for the ship's company one night. I had helped and tried various kinds of major tasks from all of the departments except the cooks'. This fresh bread making was quite the task. He was glad for the assistance and said yes. At the allotted time I met him in the galley and we got to work.

I could hardly believe the amount of each ingredient that was used and the large batches of dough that were made at a time. Once the dough was ready, it was really hard work cutting the amount needed for each loaf and molding it into shape for baking. The whole process was something to be learned over a period of time, for sure. I'd always had a respect for the kind of work the chefs did, and at all kinds of hours, but not to the degree I now had. It was around 0800 hours when we finished the following morning, and the chef asked if I wanted to take a fresh loaf to the mess.

As I entered the mess, unknown to me, the cookery officer was behind me on his way to the pay office opposite our mess door. He asked me why I was taking a loaf of bread from the galley and suggested I take it back. When I told him I had helped all night to make it, he said, "Oh, really? I've never heard of that happening before. Good for you. I guess you are entitled to share a loaf with your mess mates. Carry on."

I thanked him and we parted ways. Later, to my advantage, the captain learned what I had done. How did I keep getting the right people in the right place at the right time? I still was not a person who thought spiritually at this juncture in my life.

A problem with the broadcast system. For three months I had been trying to find an intermittent problem on the main broadcast system. The day the problem started I said to my friend, a radio branch PO technician, "That sounds like a teleprinter bleeding over onto the broadcast system." A teleprinter was an electronic typewriter that, when typed upon, converted each key hit into a radio signal and transmitted it across the airwaves. Likewise, it received signals from other teleprinters in the fleet and converted the signal to print on paper.

There was a very strong rat-a-tat-tat noise when these machines were operating, and I was often hearing it when the main broadcast was in use. I was assured this couldn't be the case. The Chatham dockyard had tested the Faraday type cages around the sixteen or so machines and said they couldn't possibly leak any radio waves.

I had spent many, oh so many, hours on this problem. Whenever I had any down time, I worked on the problem but wasn't even close to solving it. Then one day I needed to go into the RCO (radio communications office) just as a message was coming over the broadcast system, and it was as clear as a bell. A few moments later another message was broadcast , and it started out clear. Just then a teleprinter started up. Guess what? The message started breaking up again. Well, that got my heart racing.

There was a main broadcast microphone in the RCO, and I started checking the system while using the printer and not using the printer. Sure enough, this printer was the problem. This was exactly what I had said three months ago. "Oh yes," they said, "That particular printer is not classified secret so is not in a Faraday cage." This meant that it wasn't tested in Chatham. It turned out that it had a capacitor that was defective and that was the problem, as the wires from the printer ran right alongside some main broadcast wires.

Here's where things got a little hairy. I leaped outside the RCO and placed my hands on the ladder to go down the hatch just outside the RCO to my workshop. I was so pumped and wanted to let the lads on my team know and the section chief know what I had discovered. I grabbed the top of each rail and swung my legs through and onto the same railings. I shot down the rails, thusly missing all the steps, at high speed.

The problem there loomed quick and large. The senior electrical officer was on the second step from the bottom, coming up the ladder. As we made the crushing bodily contact, I grabbed him around the upper torso. My momentum shot us backwards across the deck five paces and we slammed into the bulkhead across the way. The two small valves with hand wheels on them jammed into his back, but not too much damage was done. As we were flying across the deck, I was screaming, "I've found it, I've found it!" into the startled face just one inch from mine.

The chief came running out of his office, maybe thinking I was attacking our leader, I don't know. Once all the fracas had died down, I eventually slowed my heart to a pounding gallop and explained all the details of my revelation. What a relief this was to me, and to think I'd had it right from day one. I learned a valuable lesson here: *Follow your own truth even when nobody else believes in it.* I had brought up the printers on multiple occasions and was talked out of my theory. What I should have insisted on was to turn each printer off, one at a time, and test the broadcast. Oh well, onward and upward.

A PROLONGED DIP

The seas were remaining calm and we made good headway, easily slicing through the clear mirror-like briny. The flying fish were ever prancing above the waves with the fabled dolphins and porpoise plunging and leaping around the breaking waters of the bow. Life was great and the cool Atlantic, engineered breeze, mopped our brow. What could be better? Stopping the ship for a dip in the deep of Neptune's swimming pool. This was done on rare occasions if the ship was ahead of schedule and the seas were calm. There were always a few, myself included, who wanted to be the first ones in the water. Once the accommodation ladder and flight deck side netting was lowered, we were ready. After the safety sea boat with a rifle on board was launched, in case a marauding shark came by, we needed to wait for the bridge officer to say, "Hands to bathe." In I dove and up I popped.

When I had done this in the past, the ship's side and therefore the accommodation ladder were but a few feet away. But this time I looked toward the stern from a distance not to my liking. What happened? Was I caught in a current? I didn't know.

I did know that I couldn't be seen from the ship. I stuck my head down and struck out for the ladder. After several strokes I popped my head up and saw I was even further from the ship. Too much knowledge can be detrimental to one's sanity sometimes. From the deck of a ship a person in the water is virtually invisible. Just the head is showing in the vastness of the surrounding sea. If you shout for help, nobody can hear you because of the huge extraction fans and other running machinery noises at the stern.

Two other crew members were close by, and we all wondered what the heck happened. Hands-to-bathe sessions are usually very short. I didn't think we could make it back in time before the ship moved off. I decided it would be best if the three of us conserved our energy, having faith we would be missed and picked up soon, but this was a heart thumping decision met with skepticism from my floating partners. It was up to them. This needed to be a unanimous decision. Striking out for the ship would be strength sapping and, if we didn't make it, disastrous.

We stayed and took our chances; it was now on me if translation to another world were upon us. I wondered how Mr. Jones was doing these days.

The ship was getting smaller. At first we tried to stay together because if the ship found one of us, then all would be found. But the small eddy currents kept pulling us, and we started to drift apart. We could still see each other as the ship finally turned to port. Thump, thump, thump, thump, my heart was pounding out a message in Morse code. I mean, I was always being paged to the bridge or ops room or somewhere. If I didn't turn up they would wonder where I was, wouldn't they? Suddenly *they* was an important word in my world.

It's funny how extraneous thoughts enter your head in a situation like this. The depth of the Atlantic did not allow me to see even six inches below the surface. I had heard of giant squid, manta ray, octopus, snakes, and jelly fish, not to mention sharks and electric eels and snapping turtles and all the other wonders of the deep. Even a piece of seaweed or an undulation of a ripple of water that touched me was scary.

Finally, the Scylla started getting larger and larger, and I now hoped it wouldn't hit me. Three short blasts on the fog horn told me we were safe. The sea boat was lowered and all three of us were picked up no worse for wear. A good hot cup of cocoa followed by a long hot shower put me right back on my feet. I did take the rest of the day off, though.

It turned out that the ship had not come to a full, proper stop when the page "Hands to bathe" was announced. Hence, us fly boys who wanted to be in first caught the short end of the straw. All's well that ends well, but I'll bet the officer of the watch got a good drubbing from the captain.

HOT UNDER THE COLLAR

Onward we pressed, passing the hole in the wall and slipping deftly into the Caribbean Sea. Peace and tranquility reigned, and this was truly the life in a blue suit. No sooner was I thinking this glorious thought when I get a call to the electrical office. "Look Jack," the chief said. "We need somebody to go into the funnel. The fog horn isn't working."

For the word "somebody," insert the word "Jack." Although I could have asked one of my men to do this job, it didn't seem right. That just wasn't me.

From the outside, the funnel seemed to be a place where the smoke from the boilers poured into the atmosphere. Well, it was, but inside the outer plates were two large tubes, one from each boiler, which poked out the top. Where the funnel met the deck there was a small watertight doorway for access inside.

I got changed into my boiler suit, found a pair of asbestos gloves, donned a safety hat, and opened up the door. My safety man was to stand at the bottom of the ladder that ascended to the top of the funnel where the fog horn was. The temperature was about 180 degrees or more, and the railings of the ladder extremely hot; hence the asbestos gloves. With my trusty tool bag, I made it to the top. Even before reaching the first step of the ladder, I was running water out of my body like a shower sprayer on high. I knew I needed to work fast because of the possibility of passing out from dehydration. The greatest difficulty was trying to work with small tools while wearing those big gloves. There was only a small two foot platform on which to perch; that wasn't too helpful either.

Once I had everything taken apart, I descended the ladder and refilled my body with liquid. There was a small team of observers outside on the deck. That was reassuring as one was the chief and one the sickbay attendant. Davy Jones was not going to have another crack at me so quickly was he?

Re-hydrated, I climbed back into the fray and finished the task at hand with no incident. At least the second time in I knew what to expect. If anybody was interested, I had a sure-fire method of instant weight loss.

On to Trinidad. A few days later Trinidad poked its head up, and we headed for Port of Spain, the capital. This island, at the time, was quite unremarkable. In modern times it has had one of the best economies in the world. When I visited, it was more like one of the worst. Traveling into town, I passed many a person living in a large Kellogg's cornflakes box—not the kind we tip our flakes from but the large boxes that hold all the small boxes. The amazing lesson I received from this type of poverty was that the people still, generally, held their heads high and were still very proud.

One night, a bunch of us ended up in a night club type place and at one point in the night were well-oiled. There was a stage in the club where young women would dance and eventually remove their clothing slowly and provocatively. I had a seat, as it so happened, right next to the stage on one side. One particular girl seemed to take a liking to me and teased in my direction a lot. Eventually, had somebody given her twelve inches of dental floss to wear, she would probably would have felt overdressed. Grinding toward me, she got way too close for decency and things went south from there. The cheers of the ship's company rang around the club like a crowd at a football game.

Next up was an Indian rubber man who could contort himself like a pretzel and limbo dance under a wire just a foot from the ground. The music was loud and the crew was having a great time. Jim, a regular user of the mess bar was feeling gregarious, to say the least, when a well-endowed and skimpily dressed lady juggled her wares very close to him. She said, "Hey, baby, I'm pretty hot stuff," with a big smile. Jim thought if she was hot she needed to be cooled down, so he poured his half glass of beer onto her voluptuous valley of flesh. She screamed and slapped his face as we grabbed Jim and separated the two as quickly as possible. A bouncer was on scene then, but we managed to appease him as we profusely apologized to the indignant young lady. We gave her a handful of tip money and everybody calmed down.

We were about to leave the club a little later when the manager announced that everyone was to remain in the club. Later we were told a Trinidadian was in the stairwell with a knife and was threatening some patrons as they were leaving the club. The wonderful Trinidad police quickly took care of the situation.

I am not sure what happened after leaving the club. My next conscious moment was somebody shaking and telling me to wake up. I stirred into life somewhat and realized I was in a bar asleep over a table. Two ship mates were acting very concerned and said we had to get out of there and back on board ship. Apparently it was about 0300 hours, and I was in a bar way into the jungle down a dirt track. How I got there I do not know, and why I had not been accosted and robbed I do not know. I am probably lucky to be alive. The bar tender called for a taxi and we made it back to safety in one piece.

A question for me was, "How did these two friends get to this particular bar and why?"

The next morning I got up on time for work but no breakfast. I had a sticky, sparkly stuff on my face from the night before, and everybody was making fun of me.

IN A FIX WITH M16

That deliciously magnificent island of Grand Cayman was our next adventure, and what an adventure it was. I didn't know what was going to be at stake, but it sure turned out weird. The first night in harbor there was to be a governor's cocktail party. There were so many officers invited, then a lesser number of senior rates followed by a few junior rates. As I owned a mess undress uniform, I was selected from the volunteer list. The mess undress is a uniform with a dinner jacket and special dress shirt and cummerbund accented with a bow tie.

An hour into the festivities, I was well engaged with two wonderful women when the Island's lawyer and wife walked in to cheering and applause. It seems the heralded lawyer had just returned from the United Nations annual meeting. The U.N. was trying to make Cayman go independent, as was their goal for all countries and territories. Mr. Lawyer had managed to filibuster the time allotted for the island, and it wouldn't be brought up again for at least fifteen years.

My two women friends didn't like the lawyer's wife, so they wanted me to play a trick on her by pretending I knew her. They told me all kinds of information that only a close friend would know, like where she went to school, the bowling alley they went to after school, when she came to the island, when she got married, and on and on.

So I walked past her and stopped while calling out her maiden name. We engaged in a lengthy conversation in which I finally convinced her we had gone to school together. She wasn't too happy when I mentioned she had worked at Woolworths as her hoity-toity friends were all around listening. We finally disengaged and I went back to my two doubled over lady friends, who were having a blast. The evening went well for the rest of our party, and I returned on board.

Five days later after we were safely back at sea, I was summoned to the captain's cabin. As usual, I figured he had a communication problem. This wasn't the case. He firmly asked what the heck I had done in Grand Cayman. My runs of shore were quiet and normal, so I couldn't think of anything untoward that I had done.

That's when he inquired about an incident at the cocktail party. He then told me how I had pretty much terrified the poor lawyer's wife as she really didn't believe she knew me. So how did I have all that information? As she was a dignitary, the Secret Intelligence Service, or MI6, had been dispatched immediately and had been following me the whole time we were there. Oh boy! What had I done? The captain, I presume, relayed the story to the office dudes of MI6 and cleared up the matter. He asked me to be more careful in the future and left it at that. There was never a dull moment when serving life in a blue suit.

WHERE AM I GOING?

The gorgeous beaches and wonderful hospitality of a dream-land adventure slipped away as we set sail to my next calling. Christmas was closing in, and our next stop in St. Petersburg was on the horizon. Florida was a good place to rest and relax for the holidays, we spent six days in harbor and I had a gentle run ashore.

The people of St. Pete lined up every day to take us out for the afternoon and evening. There were so many that the captain just had an emergency fire crew stay onboard, and the rest of the duty watch could go ashore so long as it was with a local resident.

I remember a young sailor not returning off shore for three days. The civilian who was treating him finally called the ship and said we would get him back when she was finished with him. It became the joke of the ship, and when the poor guy got delivered back he was not punished. He looked very much worn out, though.

My treat, along with my parachuting buddy Ian Solter, was to be entertained by Joanne Withers. It turns out she was a sports writer for The St. Petersburg Times. We were treated to a wonderful day of sightseeing, entertainment and food. We wound up back at her place where a small party of friends had gathered and had a pleasant evening. On the sideboard in her living room I noticed a photo of a good friend of mine. He was two years ahead of me in a school my sister attended and was also a patrol leader, before myself, in our local scout troupe. I enquired about him and sure enough they had hooked up several years before. The Disney attraction, "It's a small world after all." came to mind later on, but I did not get to go to Disney World on this occasion, unfortunately.

The following day was the last in port, and I needed to investigate a small matter involving the gyro compass repeater in the ops room. It was probably an easy diagnosis and fix but nevertheless had to be investigated. This meant I couldn't go ashore on the final evening as we were sailing on the high tide at 0730 hours.

I'm telling you this because around 2000 hours Gary Barnes came off shore and was looking for a second person to hook up with for a foursome date. I had to decline, and he went off around the ship to find anybody willing to help. Gary was a little effeminate to some and he wasn't the easiest person to be with. He wasn't a well-known PO and not exactly a socialite, so you get the picture. Thirty minutes later he hunted me down again and pleaded with me to go ashore with him.

I had made good headway on my troubleshooting and had narrowed down the area of the problem. I caved and got ready for a quiet last night in harbor. We taxied for a long while and ended up at a house with two men in their twenties. They took us to a house on the water. Gary met with his lady friend, who was alongside the second woman. She was very attractive. The six of us then went to another house where a big party, with many ship mates in attendance, was spilling out onto the street.

I chatted with multiple people and was having a good time. One of the older women, not old but older, came over and said, "If you're not careful you are going to lose the girl you came with." I wasn't that bothered but did pay more attention as a politeness to her. I didn't figure sex was part of our evening plans and was just enjoying myself. She did have two children, about nine and eleven years old.

The party went late into the night, and I knew I still had to fix the gyro repeater. I can't remember exactly when we were dropped back at the ship, but I'm thinking around 0400 hours. My young lady said she would come back down before sailing, with the kids, and see us off. I said, "Sure," but couldn't imagine that happening at this late hour. We kissed our goodbyes, and I thought that was the end of that.

I went straight to work and got the defect analyzed and fixed in good time, but needed to do pre-sailing communication checks on finishing. With the checks done and reported it was close to sailing time. I was on deck as it was to be a ceremonial sailing with the crew lining the top deck. Next thing I know, there was a toot, toot, on the jetty as said young lady with two beautiful children hopped out of a car and waved. I scampered down the gangway and we had a fond, long lasting farewell. I was the last body off the jetty before the gangway was swung away and the stern eased away from the dock. We waved until we couldn't see each other anymore.

Off to Nassau. Nassau was in our sights as we headed there for the New Year's celebrations. This trip was taking its toll on my wallet and my body. It's a good job I automatically sent half of my pay checks to my bank in England.

Nassau was a happy, vibrant, good clean run ashore. On the way into town the open dockyard was filled with colorful vendors of all shapes and sizes. The buildings were colorful and the streets clean and full of life. I had a great day visiting the local shops and eateries and chatting with the local people.

The following day a bunch of us made it to the beach. As ever in these islands, the beach was pristine and glorious. The glistening sand was being washed and rinsed by the gentle roll of the minute waves scurrying up the slight incline. After sliding to a stop, they whimpered on back to their source only to be thrown back for a return visit. Swimming in the lukewarm water was a reprise from the burning sun's rays as we wallowed in our dream world for as long as we could.

My life changes. The evening that followed changed my life forever, even though I didn't know it at the time. It was New Year's Eve, and we went ashore fairly late. I didn't want to get wasted or even mildly drunk that night. I just wanted to celebrate the New Year and go back to the ship. I went ashore with some of the married men in the mess, which assured me of meeting my goal. They were always very mindful and loyal to their wives and children and didn't generally live the life that I did. For one thing, most of their money was, more than mine, automatically sent home.

About half an hour before mid-night, I had a bright spark go off in my head. I knew the young lady in St. Pete was having a party at her house and as I had her number, I thought it would be cute to call them at the witching hour. We were ahead of them by one hour so had plenty of time to find a telegraph office open 24/7. Before going back to the ship, I arranged a timed call for their mid-night celebration. I could hear all the cheering and excitement in the background. This phone call, ultimately, was the beginning of the next phase of my life. It led to me writing a letter that led to future meetings with Janet.

On leaving Nassau, we had some pretty intense and long exercises with the U.S. Navy on our own, followed by a NATO fleet that then joined us both. During this mammoth exercise I received a letter from St. Pete saying how much she enjoyed our visit and chat on the jetty. This was significant as we were soon to be docking in Norfolk, Virginia, for a couple of weeks. The captain had already posted the possibility of the crew taking a stretch of four or five days' vacation if they wanted to. Maybe I could go to St. Pete and see Janet and the kids.

On arrival, I called Janet and made arrangements to visit along with Gary Barnes, who could see his girlfriend. It turns out George, another mess member, would like to visit the young lady he was with also and had already called for that to happen. So the three of us rented a car to drive down together. I was the only one with a license so the onus was on me.

The drive down was a long haul. I didn't realize there was a speed limit as there wasn't one in England at the time. I pulled over as a car with flashing lights seemed to require my stopping for it. As I got out of the car the uniformed policeman told me to stay in the car. That was funny because that, again, was not what we did in England. He informed me I was doing 110 mph, which I acknowledged, but I didn't see the problem. Apparently the limit was 65 mph. My Camaro didn't seem to mind but the officer did.

After explaining who we were and what we were doing and showing him my British license and Royal Navy ID card, he gave us a warning and we were on our way. He said that by the time I got a fine letter and court date, I would be on the high seas, so it wasn't worth his paper work. He was a nice enough gentleman given the circumstances. I felt like I was crawling the rest of the way but at least we had something to look forward to.

On arrival the three women were waiting at Janet's house and after a snack and drink the other two couples departed. The kids were not around so Janet and I got more acquainted at a more intimate level as we disappeared into the bedroom.

The next morning I discovered the kids were away for the weekend at a friend's house. What this meant for me was a weekend of fun and games. We did hook up with the others and drove to Disney World for a wonderful and extremely long day. That place is amazing, especially when going for the first time. Another day was spent together at Busch Gardens in Tampa. All in all, I had one of the most enjoyable short vacations I had ever had. The kids arrived for time together for the last day and a half, which was a great deal of fun also.

Alas, all good things must come to an end, and my mates and I set off again for Norfolk. We left way too late for my liking, which meant driving all night to get back on time. Driving on unfamiliar roads at night and being totally exhausted to boot was scary. Then the torrential monsoon type rain came pouring down with visibility almost zero. Unfortunately, it was at this point that I was looking for the turn onto an interstate highway. I saw the sign and turned onto the on ramp which happened to be the off ramp. Luckily, nothing was coming my way as I looked up and saw a sign saying "Wrong Way."' I managed to turn around without any other cars exiting where I was.

I needed to stop for a rest as I couldn't keep my eyes open. However, time was running out and we couldn't afford the luxury of that. The other two weren't being very helpful as they both fell asleep and left me to it. Fortunately the sun was coming up and that helped as I pulled into Norfolk. The signs to the dockyard were big and plenty as I picked my way through traffic and the huge base to the safety of the ship. We had thirty minutes to spare as we almost crawled up the gangway and home, shattered.

Now it was catch-up time. There was plenty to do, especially as this was designated a micro refit period with dockyard assistance. I worked very long hours for the next couple of weeks with little time for shore leave and relaxation. Was this the life or what? One day you're basking in the sun the next you're basking in work. I loved it all.

WHAT AM I DOING?

The rear view mirror showed us Norfolk getting smaller and smaller as we headed down to the fabled country of Belize again. This was a strategic visit as we wanted to remind Guatemala that we still had a presence in the area. The jump jets were still there with the Air Force, along with the Marines.

On arrival I got two pieces of mail, one from the Navy and one from Florida. The Navy letter was my new draft chit. When I filled out my preferences, the top choice for my shore base, because of my love in Scotland, was HMS Cochrane, which was the closest base to Aberdeen. You guessed it; that is where I was headed, the farthest shore base from my home and friends. Cochran was in Rosyth just outside of Edinburgh on the river Forth.

The second letter from Florida was a very nice letter from Janet about what a wonderful time we'd had. I responded, asking if I could come and visit for a while. The reason for this was that I was leaving the ship in Barbados, our next stop, and had eleven weeks leave to take before joining my next assignment in Rosyth.

Janet's next letter gave me the green light, and I started to make arrangements with the chief regulator on board. He told me he couldn't change my flight plan but could delay the flight from Dulles airport with the Air Force flight for a month. All I had to do was be on time for the Air Force.

I did need a visa to enter America as I was traveling as a civilian. Two days before the end of our Belize stay, I walked into the embassy to try and get that visa. I was told it would take at least two weeks to pass. I convinced them to let me speak to the ambassador the next day, my last day in port. I spent over an hour with him and he got the paper work and signed it. Whew! That was a close one. About that spiritual force, was it for real?

Belize brought a bit of a rest as we mainly just had routine maintenance work and regular working days. We visited our favorite bar and exchanged pleasantries with our local friends. The boat ride was two miles in and out to the ship with the last night time liberty boat leaving at 0100 hours. Unfortunately, one night, Gavin and I got back to the jetty to see the last boat plowing through the brown yukky briny. The next boat was 0700 hours, darn it.

The jetty had a two to three inch high curb running along the water front, so we lay down and tried to sleep with our heads on the hard pillow. The beer consumption helped in this matter no doubt. It wasn't long before something awoke me. Oh! A small crab-like creature had just run over my face. And, oh! There were all kinds of creepy little things like cockroaches running all over the place. Arrrggghhhh! We jumped up and hurriedly brushed ourselves down all over, maybe several times, maybe more.

We wandered along the wharf looking for some kind of resting place. A low-slung barge seemed okay; the deck had that kind of top that was like a tent. There was a peak and two sides that sloped down to the deck. We walked up on that and fell asleep. An age later but while it was still dark, I needed to relieve myself and scooted down the slope. There was enough moonlight for me to see we were sleeping on a glass panel. I had scraped the thick dust off while sliding down. I carefully woke Gavin and ushered him down to me. How in the world didn't we crash through the glass? I now knew I was being ushered through life in a ball of cotton wool.

Back on the jetty we were giggling like two school girls. Again, the booze probably played a part in that. Further down the wharf and onto a small beach we saw some large coils of rope and settled down inside one in relative comfort for the rest of the night. The rising sun brought us to our more conscious, more cognitive selves. All was well for about three seconds. That's when the large snake snoozing with us moved and rubbed my leg.

I am here to inform the human race that man can fly. We just need the proper amount of motivation. Gavin and I propelled ourselves out of that coil of rope like a Saturn rocket. With our hearts pulsating against our chests and our lungs pumping like a steam engine we ran across the beach to the wharf. Again with the laughter, once we had reached relative safety and sanity of rough tarmac.

We saw the sea boat chugging its way from the ship and idled our way to the pickup point. Our legs were still a little shaky, but we were in one piece. Needless to say, we didn't miss a last liberty boat again.

My time on Scylla was coming to a close. During the trip across the Caribbean and the last few days in Barbados, I worked my tail off. I wanted to hand over the department to my relief with zero defects, even minor itchy ones. I did achieve this goal but only with the tremendous help of my trusty team. I told them what I would like and they buckled down to help me get there.

The goodbye to a ship which has been a home for so long is always sad. I'm not sure why the word "goodbye" is used because for me there was nothing good about it. I shook as many hands as I could on the flight deck and jetty until my transport came to whisk me off to, well, I didn't really know where.

Visiting Florida. Once at the airport I made haste arranging, with the airlines, for my diversion to Tampa with a month layover. It was easier than I thought and cost me nothing. In today's world it would have been impossible; I wouldn't even have got a visa so readily. The trip to Tampa was going to involve a change of planes in Puerto Rico but that was all right. Janet knew my flight plans and flight number so would pick me up on landing.

I landed in Puerto Rico and, this being a port of entry into the USA, went to the immigration desk. I should explain that because our Belize trips were of a war type nature, our ship movements were a security concern. They were even under normal circumstances but even more so now. I was instructed before leaving the ship that I was to give no information to anybody. My passport would cover me in that regard as the occupation line read "Government Service." This gave me a diplomatic level pass for travel.

Unfortunately, this didn't rub too well with the obstreperous immigration commandant. It jumped to his attention that my visa was issued in Belize but I travelled from Barbados. The problem was I had no stamp in my passport saying I went from one to the other. He naturally assumed I must have gone between the two illegally, probably transporting drugs. I did assertively point out my diplomatic immunity, but he was in charge, not me. He would decide if I came into the country or not, and he firmly told me I would not. I asked to see his superior as all the other passengers looked on; they all disappeared to the customs area.

Mr. Supervisor eventually came along, took one look at my passport and waved me through. Okay, now the customs people had got the nod from immigration guy, so they went through everything with a fine-toothed comb. They removed everything from my luggage onto the benches.

My next problem was that I had brought along some English custard powder from the ship. It must have had the color, texture and consistency of some drug groups. I was so totally in the dark about such things and had no idea what their problem was. The two gargantuan gorillas that were summoned to my side asked if I would come with them. I looked at my watch and said, "Sure, I've got a few minutes to spare, cream, no sugar I'm sweet enough." I found that this wasn't the time to joke around. The stitching on the inside of my jacket was fairly painful as it was thrust into my armpit. The gorillas had me very tightly in their grasp under each side as they half carried me away. I did protest that I was a government official, but they seemed to be deaf. Maybe hearing wasn't a requirement for the job.

In a small interrogation room I explained the custard powder. I'm sure they knew it wasn't drugs anyway but were getting their own shots back for the egotistical immigration thug. The goons were not amused when I offered to make them some of my famed custard.

They did release me eventually and, as was probably their intent, I had now missed my connection to Tampa. The next flight was in the morning, if I could get on board as a stand-by. I got some food and drink before lying down on a bench in the almost empty airport and snoozing as best I could.

Forever and a year later, morning eventually acknowledged my drooping eyelids, and I sank a coffee and sandwich before getting down to the departure gate. I felt like I looked like a bag lady or man. My mother would say I looked like the wreck of the Empress.

Of course, after slinking off the plane in Tampa, Janet was not there as she had no idea where the heck I was. I grabbed a taxi and pulled up outside her house within about half an hour. She hugged and kissed me and hugged me some more, and I felt overwhelmed with the emotion coming from her. She knew I had made it to Puerto Rico and then there was no sign of me. Her thoughts were of me being found in a back alley or something and she was sooooo glad to see me in one piece.

WHAT HAVE I DONE?

It may seem to have been a little reckless to risk staying for a month. Staying with somebody for a few days is a lot different than staying a month. Luckily, everything worked out just fine. The kids were fun and interesting, and we spent a lot of time together playing and swimming. I did see the ugly side of parenting as well, but it wasn't too bad, nothing out of this world. I helped in the yard and around the house and we did a lot of fun things together. I received a lot of fun and joy from Janet, her kids, and a whole multitude of her friends.

The month went by rather swiftly, and it was time to say goodbye again. Dulles airport soon accepted me, and I found my way to the special Royal Air Force area. I was in plenty of time and lay back waiting for my final leg of the journey home. I was thinking back to that initial phrase when joining the Navy. What was I doing? Where was I going? What had I done?

Gatwick airport was the surprising arrival point as I expected to be landing in Brize Norton, which was the typical destination of returning Royal Air Force personnel. Luckily, Lewes, my home town, was not even an hour down the track. Mum and Dad welcomed me in their usual nonchalant fashion. They were used to me coming and going and breezing through. I did try to do anything and everything for my parents as Dad was very sick now and suffering greatly from emphysema. Mum had her hands full with my younger brother, born twenty-three years after me. This time I had plenty of time on my hands as I still had seven weeks of leave left before going to Rosyth and HMS Cochrane.

I was wondering what the heck was in store for me in Scotland.

Life in Scotland. Then my life went into an even larger spin than it ever had before. The long drive to Rosyth made me aware of how isolated I was going to be from family and friends. I did have an aunt and uncle living in Middlesbrough, which was about 130 miles to the southeast. They were my favorite relatives, and maybe I could visit them on an occasional weekend.

The gates of Cochrane slipped past my windshield, and I got organized in my very spacious cabin/room. I shared it with Paul but there was so much room we almost needed a phone to communicate. I met with some of the members of my work team that same night over a couple of beers and got my head down for another adventure to begin the next day.

I had breakfast with a soon-to-be close friend before walking down to the workshop and offices in the dockyard. This dockyard catered mainly to a fleet of minesweepers that we supported. The lone electrician on board a sweeper was mostly a leading hand and often needed technical help and aid in completing a larger job. To my surprise, I knew one of the petty officers in the workshop. We had been together on the Dido. He lived ashore with his girlfriend. I also knew a senior chief, Brian James, from the Scylla. He worked in the office that arranged all the work loads and had become a paper pusher. I have to say, though, that he was excellent at figuring out all the logistics and personnel best suited to each task. He lit up when I first went to the office, as did I. He was a good man.

Once more in my career, I felt like a fish out of water. The attitude of the workshop didn't gel with mine. I didn't actually know what it was at the time but now I do. Because of my ethics and working mentality, I didn't do things the same as them. I also had a very different view of the world in general. I never did feel like I fit in, and they didn't let me join their club. Trevor, my new-found friend, seemed to be in the same boat, which is probably why we teamed up. On my few sorties ashore we would go together and even got tickets to the Royal Military Tattoo in Edinburg Castle. That was a fabulous night out and worth every penny.

The duty night entailed sleeping in the dockyard on call for any eventuality on a sweeper. I was joined by a leading hand and two grunts. One night around 0200 hours I got a call that a mine sweeper was slowly sinking. This was something new but brought back memories of the boiler room in Bangkok. We dashed down to the jetty posthaste and found the vessel to be listing away from the jetty slightly. Sweepers are made of wood with chinking of tar between them. Some separation had occurred and thus the leak. It wasn't too bad, so I dispatched bodies to get some submersible pumps and hoses. I also got a crane driver and got some strops around the hull just for good measure. There was no super emergency and we saved the day until a full dockyard matey presence was in charge in the morning.

A major change. The major change in my life thus far was upon me. I still didn't know it yet, though. I got a letter from Janet in Florida saying she was going to an Eckankar seminar in Baltimore. I knew that Eckankar involved some kind of spiritual path she was following which, at the time, I thought a little odd. It was a weekend deal from Friday through Sunday 1200 noon. Now don't ask me why this harebrained idea slammed into my head, but I thought I might join her there. But how the heck was I going to get there, since it was only about a week away?

Freddy Laker Airlines flew one plane from London to New York and back once a day. It was a very cheap fare. One got in line and bought a ticket just like getting on a bus. This was simple enough, but I wasn't guaranteed a ticket even after driving hundreds of miles to London. Then in New York, how was I going to get to Baltimore? Oh! And how was I getting back in time for 0800 hours on Monday morning? Add to that the fact that one isn't allowed to leave the country unless approved ahead of time and then only when on a main leave, not a weekend leave.

I told the chief of my intentions and asked what he thought. He said, "Go for it," and he allowed me to leave on Thursday night after work. The drive down was very tiring, but I was in line for a ticket before most other people Friday morning. The flight over went well and New York was upon me. I asked around for information on how to get to Baltimore, and they pointed my way to a commuter airline running a non-stop flight to Philadelphia. There was a huge line of people waiting to buy a ticket, which was very disconcerting—that is, until I saw what was happening. As people edged up and bought a ticket, they went through a tunnel and boarded a plane straight off the tarmac. When it was full, it pulled forward and another plane rolled up. This was so amazing to me.

Thirty minutes later I was up, up and away in my wonderful machine to Philly. After arriving, a nice man pointed me to a Greyhound bus that would take me the rest of the way— another line, another ticket. What the heck was I doing on this wild goose chase?

I arrived in the downtown Greyhound bus station at exactly midnight. The place was basically shut down with minimal lighting and the only personnel around were drug addicts, drunks and homeless people. Did I mention I was dressed to the nines with a bunch of cash in my wallet? Everybody was staring at me as if I was crazy for being there. I, of course, was crazy for being there.

I made it to what I thought was safety, outside the door, where I would get a taxi. Only a crazy taxi driver would be there at this time of night, though. Outside the door I was met by a sidewalk, then a narrow road, then a 25 foot plus vertical brick wall. I was on my own, trapped, with no clue which way to go.

Next thing I know, a cab did pull up with his taxi light out. An extremely large black man wearing a fedora and a heavy black overcoat kept getting out. More and more of him just kept getting out. "Do you want a ride?" he drawled. Remember Mombasa, was this the same guy? I decided I could stay and get beaten and robbed or go with the large man. His multiple gold teeth glittered in the head lamps of the polished Mercedes as I climbed into the front seat. I expected him to drive me around for a while before landing me at the hotel, given me by Janet, and charge me the earth. How wrong can one man be? It wasn't even five minutes before he pulled up outside my destination and told me the small fare. I gave him a very nice tip, he was so helpful and cool.

At the reception desk I gave them Janet's name, but they didn't have anybody by that name staying here. I thought she might have used my name, so gave them that, to no avail. I did get a look that said, "Oh, yes, your mistress is not under either name." Just then the phone rang, and it was Janet. She had found a hotel closer to the seminar hotel. I got another taxi and landed like a floppy fish at my final dock.

The seminar. During this spiritual Eckankar seminar, a number of answers were starting to unfold as to my fortunes over the past fourteen years, enough to pique my interest anyway. After the Saturday evening session, Janet bumped into another Eckist from St. Petersburg and we had a long chat. Out of the blue, he asked if I was now going to join Eckankar. Wow. I hadn't even given it a moment's thought, but I blurted out, "Yes," surprising myself.

It was a strange weekend of sex, religion, and sex, but as it came to a close, I was conversing with some strangers about my travel arrangements. They said they were driving back to New York Sunday afternoon and would drop me off at the airport. Although not having a huge understanding of the beliefs of Eckankar I did know that they believe everybody has a spiritual guide. It seemed this was taking place right now. There was obviously much more to this spiritual path.

I bought a ticket home and mentioned to the receptionist how lucky I was to be so close to take off time. This was when she told me that this ticket was for the next night, and today's plane was full.

I needed to be back by 0800 hours in the morning, and that was in Rosyth, not London. She refunded my whole fare, and I took off for a tour of the other airlines. At the British Airways curb there was a sandwich board sign that said, "Cheap tickets to London NOW." There was a flight leaving in forty minutes for a bargain price of $125.00. I had $128.00 to my name, say what? My luck was holding and I was riding a wave.

I arrived in London around 0500 hours needing to travel 400 miles to Rosyth in just three hours, including getting out of the airport.

I didn't make it on time. I arrived a little after 1300 hours and quickly made it to the dockyard. The others in the workshop would wonder where I was that morning. The chief saved the day and immediately asked, in front of everybody, if I had finished that job in the dockyard yet. He was making out like I had been busy working in the dockyard while he knew I was just getting back from America. Later we talked and I thanked him profusely. I was beginning to understand how well looked after I was. Because of that seminar, I started to delve into why.

A SUMMONS AND A
COOL RECEPTION

A few days later I was summoned to the upper office by Chief Brian James, my former Scylla chief. This sounded ominous, I thought. Had others found out about my late arrival from America?

No they hadn't. Brian was smiling like a Cheshire cat and beaming from ear to ear. He grabbed my hand and just about shook it away from my forearm. "Congratulations," he said. "You have been nominated for promotion to chief electrician."

"Whhhaaaatttttt? You have got to be kidding me. I haven't been a petty officer long enough have I?"

He told me I was now the youngest person to be granted CPO electrician.

When I got back to the workshop my news was greeted very coolly by others. Two petty officers even grumbled about how long they had been waiting and wondered what I had that they didn't. "Charisma is one thing," I thought to myself.

Because of my newness to minesweepers, they did know more than me at this job so far. They didn't know my history, and I knew from their typical daily attitude that they didn't have the dedication I had. Even the chief of the workshop had a look of disbelief on his face.

Trevor was over the moon for me and congratulated me heartily. That evening I did put a barrel of beer on tap in the bar, and I was invited to the chief's bar for a celebratory beer or two. The mood wasn't overly ecstatic in my own bar.

Another transfer. In November I received a draft chit and was transferred to FMG in Chatham dockyard. This was great news for me (and probably for my Cochran team, too. Who knows?) The date was set for January 21, and it couldn't come soon enough. I knew the types of ships and more than likely knew many of the men. FMG stands for Fleet Maintenance Group and is used to assist any ship in the fleet to either catch up on planned maintenance or help with a sticky defect they cannot fix.

In the latter case diplomacy was important. Sometimes defects were fixable in just a few hours or so, embarrassing for the petty officer or chief and maybe even for the weapons electrical officer. I would tell them I was lucky, or some such thing, as I had come across this particular problem before. "Hey, what's the matter with you dummies that you couldn't figure that out?" didn't seem appropriate.

Two huge decisions. During the last year I had been back to Florida on several occasions. Each of these visits drew us closer and closer to a more permanent future together. Every time I flew home it seemed to get harder and harder to leave her. We wrote letters practically every day; even the guys in the mess joked about it. I got along famously with her kids and they had been without a dad for six years. Everything seemed to be falling into place.

I finally popped the question on another visit to Florida, and my whole life was now in transition. We were to be married in the April of 1979.

I had reached my goal of being a chief so was satisfied with my naval career. I decided to leave the Navy, a very heart-wrenching move, but I often did tread where angels feared. I had stepped out through what I considered my safe boundaries on many occasions. Why not try another?

It was a massive game changer for me. As I said, the kids' father had died six years earlier, and I didn't think it fair to give them a dad who was going to be gone for large chunks of time. Mum and Dad who had initially resisted me joining the Navy were now resisting me leaving.

After the wedding we lived in married quarters just down the road from Chatham dockyard until my discharge in September. Even then, I was being looked after. Married quarters can be a bit of a rabbit warren existence although I have never experienced it myself. I got called to the married quarter's office for my assigned address and they said that because I was a chief, I was lucky. A section of the officers' quarters was being used as an overflow for the lower deck, and I had been given one of these abodes. It never ends does it?

THE FINAL CURTAIN

Later, during my exiting plan I was assigned to help on one of the Leander class frigates and met an old stores buddy of mine from back on the Dido. In conversation over a lunchtime beer he told me they were soon going to the Caribbean and USA and stopping in Miami. He offered to store my moving crates and have them on the jetty in Miami on a given date. You see, it just didn't stop. There had to be something about the balance of life, just like this Eckankar taught. I felt I was being rewarded for much of the hard work and dedication I had loaded into my naval life. I even had a chief who drove lorries (trucks) for the Navy, come to the house and pick them up. He was from a previous ship, notably, the Scylla, and somehow I bumped into him, by chance, in the dockyard one day.

It got better. One needed to hand in an eighteen months' notice to the Navy. I had filled out the forms in January and needed to get them signed by the commander of the dockyard. I personally took them to the admiralty offices, where I expected him to just take them and tell me to come back in a week or so. Instead, the secretary walked me straight into the commander's office. Sitting behind the desk was the previously known sub-lieutenant electrical officer from the Dido. What are the odds of that? He pumped my arm vigorously while congratulating me on being a chief. I returned the compliments on his rise to commander.

Two cups of coffee and an hour later he told me of a way to exit the Navy in three months. Say whaaaaattttttt? Anyway we decided on the sixth of September as this would get the kids back to Florida in time to start the new school year.

On the day of the races, we were to report to the de-mobbing office in Portsmouth and get all the paperwork done. This was surprisingly simple, and I walked out of the office feeling incredibly empty and alone. Janet was with me but I was in a state of shock and awe. Where was I going? What was I doing? What had I done? Does that sound familiar?

The next morning day I was on a plane ready to start my third life in this lifetime, daring to step over the horizon and hoping the world wasn't flat.

ABOUT THE AUTHOR

 Barry "Jack" Frost grew up in Lewes, England, traveled the world with the Royal Navy for 15 years, then married an American and moved to the United States. Before retirement, he worked as an electrical specialist, using skills he learned in his years with the Navy for many organizations, including a company that built communication systems for the Space Shuttle.

Made in the USA
San Bernardino, CA
09 June 2020

72795824R00268